ON ATTACHMENT

ON ATTACHMENT
The View from
Developmental Psychology

Ian Rory Owen

KARNAC

First published in 2017 by
Karnac Books Ltd
118 Finchley Road
London NW3 5HT

Copyright © 2017 by Ian Rory Owen

The right of Ian Rory Owen to be identified as the author of this work has been asserted in accordance with §§ 77 and 78 of the Copyright Design and Patents Act 1988.

All rights reserved. No part of this publication may be reproduced, stored in a retrieval system, or transmitted, in any form or by any means, electronic, mechanical, photocopying, recording, or otherwise, without the prior written permission of the publisher.

British Library Cataloguing in Publication Data

A C.I.P. for this book is available from the British Library

ISBN-13: 978-1-78220-452-7

Typeset by V Publishing Solutions Pvt Ltd., Chennai, India

Printed and bound in Great Britain by TJ International Ltd. Padstow

www.karnacbooks.com

CONTENTS

LIST OF FIGURES   vii

ABOUT THE AUTHOR   ix

PREFACE   xi

PART I: THE RECEIVED WISDOM ABOUT ATTACHMENT

Introduction to Part I   3

CHAPTER ONE
Attachment phenomena and their background   5

CHAPTER TWO
The standard interpretation and its processes   35

CHAPTER THREE
Psychodynamics, motivation, and defence   67

vi   CONTENTS

PART II: THE ROLE OF ATTACHMENT IN REDUCING DISTRESS

Introduction to Part II   91

CHAPTER FOUR
Meta-representation and motivation   93

CHAPTER FIVE
The good life is correcting imbalance   111

CHAPTER SIX
Achieving rebalance   131

PART III: INCREASING SECURITY AS A CONDITION OF SUCCESSFUL THERAPY

Introduction to Part III   153

CHAPTER SEVEN
Psychodynamics of attaching   157

CHAPTER EIGHT
Attachment processes in assessment   183

CHAPTER NINE
Some complex cases   209

CHAPTER TEN
Conclusion: therapy as secure process   231

REFERENCES   241

INDEX   257

LIST OF FIGURES

FIGURE 1.1
Control systems theory   22

FIGURE 1.2
Control systems theory as it applies to seeking care and
   its receipt in any form of attachment   24

FIGURE 2.1
Secure attachment   39

FIGURE 2.2
Anxious attachment   41

FIGURE 2.3
Avoidant attachment   43

FIGURE 2.4
Disorganised attachment   44

FIGURE 3.1
Good mental health sustained   78

FIGURE 3.2
Psychological problems modified by defensive exclusion
   maintain imbalance   78

viii   LIST OF FIGURES

FIGURE 4.1
The intentional relationship between distal causes of attachment
   problems and contemporary triggers and processes   105

FIGURE 5.1
Specific instance of emotional dysregulation in borderline
   personality disorder   126

FIGURE 5.2
A twenty-four-hour formulation of distress and ineffective
   defences   126

FIGURE 6.1
The type of emotionally regulated response in secure
   attachment and coping   132

ABOUT THE AUTHOR

Ian Rory Owen was born in New Zealand in 1960 and holds a first degree in engineering and a masters and PhD in counselling and psychotherapy. He has qualifications in cognitive behavioural therapy and medical anthropology. Previously, he was a senior lecturer in counselling psychology at Wolverhampton University. Since 2001, he has been a principal psychotherapist in the British National Health Service in Leeds. He practises brief individual therapy with people with complex psychological needs. *On Attachment* is his fifth book.

PREFACE

Currently, attachment is like a talisman for the practice of the many brands of psychotherapy and forms of mental health care. However, there are many ideas about it that are accepted in uncritical ways. To prevent the acceptance of false ideas about attachment, this work makes clear trustworthy research about attachment in children and adults. It appraises the way that attachment is interpreted by commenting on empirical research to clarify the theory that supports therapy practice, and furthers research, and mental health care. The difficulties of getting help to those who deserve it involve problems in the therapy relationship that interfere with creating acceptance and change. The therapy relationship is always the medium of delivering any care or service. Therefore, the problems of poor delivery of care concern mismatched expectations about how the care is provided—and the felt quality of the care—and these problems vary according to the complexity of the problems experienced by the public. When there is complexity in the relationship, and in the felt experiences on both sides of it, then there are problems in determining what belongs to each individual alone. The living face-to-face interactions occur between the person who occupies the caring role and the one who receives the care. Attachment theory is a map of the dynamic aspects of the felt experiences of harmony and disharmony that can be followed to help both persons be in balance.

Attachment processes are observable in the parenting provided by all mammals. When it comes to considering attachment between human beings there are observable phenomena where infants and children seek their carers, because they are more able, and carers can show their children how to respond well to difficulties. On receipt of care, children are soothed and return to other activities. Attachment has lifelong influences concerning access to sources of succour and support. Consciousness retains past learning, and the earliest presence of those who cared first leaves the strongest marks. If the quality of care received in childhood is deficient then the earliest qualities of separation anxiety and avoidance on reunion are also long-lived. Parallels occur in relationships between adults despite their behaviour being so much more complex. People who provide comfort and guidance, and support the needs of others, come to realise that some of their clientele cannot access help in a straightforward manner. Infancy and adolescence are highly influential, and in recent years there is the growing acknowledgment that attachment concerns the quality of intimate relationships across anyone's personal history. This means that a current form of relating can be continually updated by experience that is more recent.

This work is a no-nonsense technical report to explain the substantive issues within the developmental psychology of attachment. The empirical testing of hypotheses called falsificationism is the ultimate test of the difference between true and false ideas (Popper, 1959). In falsificationism, a hypothesis needs to be stated and tested, so that it can be open to the possibility of it being disproved experimentally. For falsificationism, a hypothesis can never be proven beyond all doubt. This means that empirical findings are only held as provisionally acceptable explanations, until they are disproven. It is not the purpose of this work to go into detailed critical appraisals of different methodological approaches, yet there are the difficulties of replication of findings in psychology. Below, the empirical claims of John Bowlby, Mary Ainsworth, Mary Main, Everett Waters, and colleagues, are accepted as the benchmark of trustworthy experimental design and findings. There follows an emphasis on what can be observed of the repeating processes of attaching. The aim is to promote accurate descriptions about what exists psychologically so it can be discussed and shared between communities of colleagues. Attachment across the lifespan concerns how security can be found with others, or not. Attachment can express the anticipation to invest emotionally, or the fear and inhibition of investing emotionally. Attachment expresses a major aspect of creatures whose existence is relational. When security cannot be found, particularly during the earliest years, and violence is perpetrated on young people or adults, then this has consequences in how able they are when care-seeking and engaging in emotional intimacy to redress their here-and-now problems.

Ideas are tools to do specific jobs. However, if the empirical findings used are inaccurate, then the justifications produced for organising therapeutic interventions will be ineffective. The point is that a view attuned to the nature of attachment demands an ability to understand processes and sequences of repeating behaviour between adults. Attachment in therapy has been studied by watching video of interactions between clients and therapists and this type of material has been interpreted to draw conclusions on what adults respond to. Therapy interventions require accurate understanding of the phenomena in order to succeed.

The study is in three parts. Part I: The received wisdom about attachment, sketches the major contributions from the empirical literature. Part II: The role of attachment in reducing distress, is an interlude for considering attachment phenomena as meaningful experiences between people in a way that understands how emotional regulation and dysregulation have their origin in the important relationships with persons in childhood and adulthood. Part III: Increasing security as a condition of successful therapy, applies the clarified understanding of the psychological processes in attachment to inform a psychodynamic view of therapy and mental health work. The case of individual therapy with adults is used to provide some teaching examples. There is discussion of the original ideas of Freud in relation to resistance, a reluctance to self-disclose and get help. Arguments are made to focus on shared attachment processes. One point of this text is making clear, formulating, or interpreting what attachment is in a way that supersedes the traditional interpretation of the inner working model (IWM), or script, as the inferred model of the attachment relating of one person (Delius, Bovenschen, & Spangler, 2008). On the contrary, the process between two people in an attachment relationship is argued to be important and be the proper understanding of attachment, because it concerns the quality of inter-relationship between self and other.

xiv   PREFACE

A decontextualisation occurs when considering individuals as solo beings. When considering individual differences, attachment only ever appears as repetitive processes between people in various versions of what is preferred and easily repeated. When theorising human relationships, if there is too much of a focus on one person in a two-person, or in a multi-person relationship in a family, that will detract from proper attention to the contributions of all the persons in it. However, the message for practice is that the work supports a return to the basics of good practice. Back to basics sees the connections between ethics, the therapeutic alliance, the secure frame for therapy, sometimes called holding or containing, and the aim of psychotherapy stated as the ability to engage the public, more often than not, in a secure process, or to help people be supported in receiving the care that they need. Regardless of the brand name of therapy, the job is a practical one. If therapists do not help the public in giving informed consent to the details of their treatment, including the ground rules of the worker or clinic in which the meetings occur, then the need for briefing new clients and assessment is revealed in the problems that follow from not providing clarity about the treatment.

Attachment theory occupies an integrative position between psycho-analysis, psychodynamic therapies, cognitive science, and developmental theory. I use the word "psycho-analysis" throughout in the way that Freud wrote it and I am only referring to his approach when I do so. I do not use the general term "psychoanalysis", which is an umbrella terms for a number of approaches following him. Inherent to the psychology of attachment is the homeostasis of a control system, sometimes called cybernetics or systems theory. John Bowlby took control systems theory as a central explanation of attachment and was influenced by a number of thinkers in the twentieth century about evolution, the body, consciousness, and unconscious processes. Mary Ainsworth showed that the meaningful transmission of attachment is best understood as forms of interconnection between the participants. These forms of interconnection can be understood according to several different theoretical perspectives, each of which emphasises some aspect, but in different ways. For instance, the behavioural genetic evidence shows only a small extent of genetic heritability of attachment (Verhage et al., 2016).

An attempt has been made at standardising the terminology used in the field. In this work, the term "therapy" refers to individual talking and action therapies of all brand names. Attachment "pattern" only refers to attachment classifications or scripts in infants and children. "Process", "state of mind", and "attachment dynamic" refer to moment-to-moment relating between adult attachment figures, co-creators of intimacy and distance. Because there is a variation in the naming of the same mental processes in the literature, the following terminology is used to emphasise the same processes. "Secure" refers to children and secure-autonomous adults. "Anxious" refers to resistant, enmeshed, anxious, ambivalent children, and insecure–preoccupied adults. "Avoidance" is used for fearful, withdrawn children, and insecure–dismissing adults. "Disorganised" similarly includes all disoriented, unresolved, and unclassifiable forms (excluding the attachment disorders in children). The gold standard of experimental formats are the Strange Situation Procedure (SSP) (Ainsworth & Wittig, 1969) and the Adult Attachment Interview (AAI), which analyse the narrative styles and content of speech of participants who describe their relationships with their parents, particularly their mothers (George, Kaplan, & Main, 1996; Main, Goldwyn, & Hesse, 2003). To be precise, there is a fifth attachment form for children and adults, the unclassifiable form that is comprised of two types of reunion behaviour in SSP and equal scores for adults in the AAI, or where there have been multiple refusals to answer the standardised questions (Hesse, 2008). Just to be clear, the following listing compares the names used.

SSP	AAI	This work
Secure	Autonomous–secure	Secure
Insecure–resistant/ambivalent	Preoccupied–insecure	Anxious
Insecure–Avoidant	Dismissing–insecure	Avoidant
Disorganised/disoriented	Unresolved/disorganised	Disorganised

The Standard Edition of the Complete Psychological Works of Sigmund Freud is used for comments from Freud. The following disclaimer is also necessary: although this book is in part based on my experiences in clinical practice, no real individuals are intended by the brief case vignettes mentioned. Any resemblance between persons mentioned here and real persons is entirely coincidental.

Finally, thanks to Everett Waters, professor of social and developmental psychology at the State University of New York at Stony Brook, for email discussions about the nature of attachment in children and adults and for authoritative comments on methodology. Thanks to everyone at Karnac in London for editorial help and grammatical corrections. Thanks also to Susan Darlington for editorial comments on a previous version of the manuscript.

PART I

THE RECEIVED WISDOM ABOUT ATTACHMENT

Introduction to Part I

A ttachment theory spans a wide range of phenomena concerning seeking care and providing it. On the positive side, there are experiences of love, connection, and belonging, plus the basic ability to trust and personally feel worthy of, and eager for, contact with others. On the negative side, there are the experiences of worry about being dependent on others, compulsive self-reliance, and a confused, uncertain approach to and fear of intimacy. Among mental health professionals, there is the expectation that attachment theory can deliver clear answers and provide direction. However, attachment theory is the interpretation of empirical data and replicated findings. If the perspective for interpreting the data is inaccurate with respect to what the phenomena actually are, there will be disarray in the research base. Consequently, inaccurate understanding would be taken to research and practice. If this were the case, practice and research would be rendered incoherent. In order to prevent such dis-coordination in the research base and its applications, this work aims to unite researchers and practitioners around a meaningful formulation of the key aspects of attachment as readily observable occurrences.

The history of psychotherapy has at its centre the postulating of mental processes in relation to their objects of psychological sense,

4   ON ATTACHMENT

which makes it important to maintain a focus on formulation as the contemporary version of interpretation in Freud's sense (Alexander, 1963; Breuer & Freud, 1895d; French, 1933; Freud, 1894a, 1911b, 1915e, 1923b, 1926d). This first part defines attachment processes in such a way that psychological explanations can be made about attachment phenomena. Although the phenomena of attachment in children and adults are different, the hypothesis proposed is that definitive forms of mental processes are shared across the lifespan. A theme that ties these parts together considers the conditions of possibility for understanding and deciding between various aspects of attachment before working with persons in distress. Several brands of therapy believe that attachment theory has explanatory worth for understanding events in love, relationships with intimates, friendship, and for understanding the influence of parenting and health behaviour.

This first part makes definitions about attachment in relation to the qualitative and theoretical necessity of understanding attachment processes between people across the lifespan, regardless of the specific types of relationship between the persons involved. Chapters One to Three below set the scene for making a basic understanding of attachment in such a way that variability in strength, stability across time, and flexibility between their sorts is included. Because the first three chapters extend the standard interpretation of the Bowlby-Ainsworth model of attachment to focus on interactions between self and other, the first distinction to argue for is an emphasis on understanding attachment as psychological, to mentalise it and make it clear what it stands for, and not to get side tracked into details of the naturalistic approaches, even though these are popular perspectives. There are approaches to attachment that emphasise neuroscientific, evolutionary, and other aspects of what it is to be a person in a social world, but the first case to be made is for approaching attachment as a psychological process, because the study of mental processes between people requires its own type of explanation.

CHAPTER ONE

Attachment phenomena and their background

This chapter explains the issues that surround attachment theory. Attachment theory contemporarily comprises various schools of thought. Attachment theory is a map of relating in everyday life and caring relationships of all kinds. This chapter provides an overview of attachment in the context of child and adult development for understanding how the patterns begun in childhood continue into adult circumstances, where they might be limiting or inappropriate for a variety of reasons. Attachment is one part of human development, so below sections sketch the background of child development. The purpose of the chapter is to prepare the ground for the definitions of the patterns and processes of the following chapter. Below, there is a deepening of attention to the detail of how consciousness defends itself against the consequences of suboptimal care provision and creates its own solutions to psychological meanings of distress. It contributes to keeping clients in mind, in empathising, and understanding the pushes and pulls in any relationship between two or more people. According to the different roles of care-givers and receivers involved, there are specifically different sorts of provision and receipt. Through understanding the secure base phenomenon of the secure process, the key aspects for understanding attachment theory are explained.

Introduction to the psychology of attachment

The psychology of attachment is a complex area with many different perspectives vying for expression. Attachment is a complex set of interlocking awarenesses between self and other comprised of a number of contributing factors (Cassidy & Shaver, 1999, 2008). Attachment is ripe for a process interpretation because it is primarily psychosocial and refers to a number of psychological objects that are recognisable by common sense. Not just in infancy and childhood but throughout adulthood too, attachment phenomena are evident. Attachment as a felt experience begins with the first context of early childcare (DeWolff & van IJzendoorn, 1997; Goldsmith & Alansky, 1987). Attachment research shows that the quality and quantity of care creates long-lasting semi-permanent influences for adults in terms of how they relate with others and how, as individuals, they manage their emotions. Attachment patterns in childhood and adulthood processes are identified against the background of each other, comparatively. Attachment is socially learned and plays a bridging role in development across the lifespan. Not only does the receipt of sufficient care for infants promote their potential for later full bloom, the effects of such care have an ongoing semi-permanent effect on the mental and physical well-being of adults. At any later point in the lifespan, the type of care first received creates tendencies about how to relate to others in times of distress and relaxation. When under stress, there is variation in the responses that individuals make, not according to their intelligence or chronological age but according to the influences acquired much earlier. This learning varies according to the cumulative effect of the semi-permanent attachment processes that operate when adults are stressed.

Before explaining what attachment theory shows, a note on empirical methodology is required. This study does not make an in-depth appraisal of empirical methods and psychometrics to support confidence in some methodologies and expose the weaknesses of others. However, the original focus on attachment, between 1944 and 1987 approximately, was achieved by developmental psychologists who used observational experimental formats and rated phenomena between children and their adult carers. Since the 1980s, social psychologists began to explore attachment phenomena in adults with methodologies such as Experiences in Close Relationships (ECR) a self-report questionnaire that asks general questions rather than about specific attachment relationships of the participants (Brennan, Clark, & Shaver, 1998, pp. 69–70; Hazan & Shaver, 1987). However, ECR does not correlate with findings from either the SSP or the AAI (De Haas, Bakermans-Kranenburg, & van IJzendoorn, 1994).

Developmental psychologists also produced the AAI and versions of it such as the Current Relationship Inventory (CRI), a modified version of the AAI that enquires about a current relationship with a long-term partner, and these do correlate with SSP (Crowell & Owens, 1996). A newer version of Experiences in Close Relationships, Experiences in Close Relationships Revised (ECR-R), does not investigate specific attachment relationship either—only relationships in general (Fraley, Waller, & Brennan, 2000). So, the self-report measures of the social psychology of attachment do not correlate with AAI and SSP cannot be considered because ECR measures different phenomena altogether, namely generalised beliefs and expectations; not partner-specific ones. What this means is that the findings from the two different sorts of measures cannot be mixed. To be strict, it means that ECR and social psychology findings that do not correlate with SSP, and home observation, and are not about specific attachments should not be called attachment.

A word of caution needs to be stated about the forms of research design. The general readership does not realise that ECR and ECR-R do not tally with SSP and AAI and assess different phenomena. The empirical approach by social and personality psychologists may use priming experiments and self-rating questionnaires, but if the enquiry is not about specific attachment relationships between adults then the conclusions made are not about attachment. Everett Waters explains that when it comes to understanding adult attachment the "limitations are that there is relatively little research on whether a person establishes similar attachment with different people over time. The alternative is that the type that sets up in close adult relationships is greatly influenced by the characteristics of the partner. Thus one does not necessarily have a series of very similarly organised relationships when going from one primary partner to the next: no doubt, the inherent longitudinal nature of this question explains the lack of data" (personal communication, 2016).

The secure base phenomena are well-proven in children and developmental psychology has shown that the AAI correlates with

SSP findings. However, there are then epistemological difficulties in showing how attachment appears for adults. Accordingly, quality assurance of the methods and manners of interpreting is demanded in order to ensure that all involved are facing in the same direction and involved in the same project. The remedy, described below, is to be clear about attachment phenomena for children and adults in different contexts. Attachment theory proceeds with caution and draws conclusions from cross-referenced and validated sources before applying empirical findings (Waters & Beauchaine, 2003).

Because attachment theory is a discourse drawn from developmental psychology, more of the context needs to be considered before passively accepting conclusions from different procedures. Like has to be compared with like, and experiments need to be replicated. This means that the same experiment that was carried out by one research team, when carried out by another, should show the same results within an acceptable band of error for the conclusions to have credibility. What dominates the understanding of adult attachment is the well-proven format of the AAI, a standardised interview procedure to investigate attachment memories and verbal accounts in adults (although other formats are available). Moreover, it is interesting to consider what is motivational for the four different attachment teleologies. A meta-analysis of American mothers who were given the AAI found that fifty-six per cent had the secure process, nine per cent the anxious process, sixteen per cent the avoidant, and eighteen per cent were disorganised (Bakermans-Kranenburg & van IJzendoorn, 2009). Each process works to deal with the emotional-relational territory in which it lives and in which it experiences any new occurrence. Yet because what are being discussed are semi-permanent processes, observable across varied relational contexts, each IWM control setting of the attachment thermostat produces a self-maintaining set of habits, beliefs, and conditioning, influenced by past and current interactions. In relation to the IWMs that a person has, and the quality of the connection that arises, Bowlby defined what could be called the automatic primary process of making sense and the emotions involved, as follows:

> Both the nature of the representational models a person builds of his attachment figures and also the form in which his attachment behaviour becomes organized are regarded in this work as being the results of learning experiences that start during the first

ATTACHMENT PHENOMENA AND THEIR BACKGROUND   9

year of life and are repeated almost daily throughout childhood and adolescence. On the analogy of a physical skill that has been acquired in the same kind of way, both the cognitive and the action components of attachment are thought to become so engrained (in technical terms overlearned) that they come to operate automatically and outside awareness.

... the disadvantage [is] that, once cognition and action have been automated, they are not readily accessible to conscious processing and so are difficult to change. (Bowlby, 1980, p. 55)

Attachment is due to unconscious processes of the connections between the many forms of mental process. Attachment is engrained in that it consists of lived experiences of the habits that are made and yet there is scope for change. Attachment is semi-permanent across the lifespan and shows change yet has inertia to change (Ammaniti, van IJzendoorn, Speranza, & Tambelli, 2000; Crowell, Treboux, & Waters, 2002; Crowell & Waters, 2005; Thompson, 2000; van IJzendoorn & Bakermans-Kranenburg, 2014). The view that Bowlby held was that there could be ways of detecting the accuracy between a map and life's territory, so to update the map by influential relationships and experiences (Bowlby, 1969, pp. 82–83; 1988, p. 130). Yet the type of conditioning is open to enquiry: it is not the sort modelled by behavioural theory's classical and operant conditioning because the strength of the bond can both increase and decrease according to the meaning of the events happening and the attachment tendencies of others (Waters, Weinfield, & Hamilton, 2000). Attachment is meaningfully motivated and operates according to the understanding that is achieved by the participants. Consequently, observable behaviours are considered meaningful motivational sequences and wholes of sense that have a form that can be interpreted according to how the processes compare with each other.

Even the smallest meaningful units have a beginning, middle, and end, and exist within greater temporal contexts of motivated and meaningful behaviour. Such processes around the self operate in different ways and have their distinctive forms and functions. The four processes are continua in their strength and frequency of occurrence, yet exhibit persistent motivations to act in ways that are born in infancy and have similar psychodynamic motivations that run throughout adulthood. Yet what happens in any relationship, minute to minute, is variable across the lifespan and differs between relationships and contexts. In

10 ON ATTACHMENT

babies the "instinctual responses" (Bowlby, 1958, p. 362) of sucking, clinging, visual following, crying, and smiling are observable patterns of interactions with carers that have the ultimate function of "safe-guarding the individual and mediating reproduction" (Bowlby, 1958, p. 362). There is an evolutionary aspect of attachment in infancy that is linked to how attachment shapes the relationships in adults. Care-seekers can experience a secure base when anxious or needing comfort and the type of response provided forms the attachment pattern of the recipient. The influence is so powerful that the child pattern can remain stable for the first twenty years of life and may produce similar attachment processes throughout later life—for better or worse (Waters, Hamilton, & Weinfield, 2000; Waters, Merrick, Treboux, Crowell, & Albersheim, 2000).

Attachment conclusions refer to the set of phenomena that are common to intimate relationships. However, rather than there being one consensus on attachment theory, there are a number of perspectives. Some emphasise attachment as biological, a part of personality, or as social psychology, related to culturally acquired childcare practices, or emphasise the neuroscientific and physically developmental aspects (Insel & Young, 2001). Sroufe and Waters (1977) argued that attachment is an intervening variable or organisational construct in human development that is supportive of the normative aspects of social learning, and the cognitive-affective aspects of intimacy. It is also possible within the same conversation, or within the same relationship over a series of meetings, to experience different forces of attraction and repulsion leading to the inter-relation of the secure, anxious and avoidant processes (Kobak, Cole, Ferenz-Gillies, Fleming, & Gamble, 1993). For others, and particularly those who overuse the anxious process, there are transient phenomena that change according to the impressions gained of the intentions of others with respect to self.

The phenomenon called the secure base exists between adults too. There are attachment phenomena of the two insecure suboptimal types where the secure base is absent. The fourth categorisation of disorganised attachment is a mixture of the two insecure sorts. The problem to be solved is that if attachment phenomena are unrecognisable in the clinical situation, then theory concerning them cannot be used to understand the public nor facilitate their abilities to use the therapeutic relationship, the medium through which any health care is supplied. What is of crucial importance in attachment theorising is citing conscious evidence and stating how it has been interpreted.

A very brief history of attachment

The birth of attachment theory was John Bowlby's work at the London Child Guidance Clinic where he began studying the after-effects of disruption and distress on children during the Second World War. He noted a number of recurring relational patterns that differ comparatively (Bowlby, 1944). Since then, the research literature has burgeoned. What attachment really means is the study of love and caring, and its vicissitudes across the lifespan. "Many of the most intense emotions arise during the formation, the maintenance, the disruption and the renewal of attachment relationships. The formation of a bond is described as falling in love, maintaining a bond as loving someone, and losing a partner as grieving over someone. Similarly, threat of loss arouses anxiety and actual loss gives rise to sorrow; while each of these situations is likely to arouse anger" (Bowlby, 1980, p. 40). Note the motivated responsiveness in this phrasing to both actuality and possibility, for merely the threat of loss, as well as actual loss, promotes distress. When consciousness acts in the intimate world its ways are meaningful, motivated, and temporally structured. Understanding from the past guides future restorative action. Bowlby defined attachment as mapping the intimate life: "Attachment behaviour is any form of behaviour that results in a person attaining or maintaining proximity to some other clearly identified individual who is conceived as better able to cope with the world" (Bowlby, 1988, pp. 26–27). For instance, small children call out at night for those who will help them when they are upset. To "say of a child (or older person) that he is attached to, or has an attachment in, someone means that he is strongly disposed to seek proximity to and contact with that individual and to do so especially in certain specified conditions ... [Thus attachment] refers to any of the various forms of behaviour that the person engages in from time to time to obtain and/or maintain a desired proximity" to attachment figures (Bowlby, 1988, p. 28).

The means of testing mere intuitive observations is called falsificationism. Empirically though, attachment is shown as four discrete patterns of relating that can be identified from infancy right through to processes between adults in later life. They share meaningful and motivating causes of emotions, the empathies of others, and the interpretation of the sense of self in the here-and-now type of relationship that self has with others. Thus, attachment is influential across many aspects of relationships between self and others, and how selves self-reflexively see themselves (Fonagy, Moran, Steele, & Higgitt, 1991; Fonagy & Target, 1994; Waters & Cummings, 2000). The empirical way forwards is to cross-reference findings from the SSP with home observation and be careful in drawing conclusions about attachment in its myriad adult settings. However, there should be an awareness of the psychometrics and the metapsychology of how measures tally with the observable experiences of attachment itself (Crowell & Treboux, 1995; Waters, Crowell, Elliott, Corcoran, & Treboux, 2002). What is required for justification is an attention to experimental detail, the psychometric properties, and the pros and cons of the methodological designs used. For instance, there are a number of ways that stress can be experimentally induced in adults to ascertain how people behave during it in comparison to its absence. This mimics the attachment situation (Meredith, Strong, & Feeney, 2006). For instance, stress can be induced by asking participants in an experiment to do mental arithmetic and asking them to repeat the task from the beginning if they make a mistake.

After Bowlby, developmental psychology expanded and contributed to the experimental data. An attention to the detail of the influences on adult relationships and contexts is required to support a wholistic view of human beings as biopsychosocial wholes. Accordingly, the view taken could pan out and focus on the larger context of the particular social environment around a family with young children, where the specific quality of care-provision is the focus against a background of other developmental processes. The psychology of attachment shows that there are discrete processes of connecting with others, each of which has its own way of defending against problems whilst being potentially capable of increasing emotional intimacy with others. However, one insecure attachment process can be overused and remain as a suboptimal way of managing intimacy, as shown in detail in the next chapter.

John Bowlby was the first to indicate the secure base but it was Mary Ainsworth who innovated and proved that it is a genuine phenomenon (Ainsworth & Bowlby, 1991). Small children seek out the care and comforting presence of their parents, or an available family member in times of need (Bowlby, 1969, pp. 371–372; 1988, p. 11). In the secure process, caring adults soothe children's distress as the children rightly expect. Children acquire learning in relation to seeking help when frustrated or feeling threatened: the secure base phenomenon of returning to the attachment figure for calming and reassurance, being soothed in the context around them enables a return to other activities such as playing with toys and exploring (Crittenden, 1994; Thompson, 2009). In this way, children learn a caring connection that is ongoingly established at times of distress. This phenomenon of a clearly identifiable pattern between parents and children (or between adults for that matter) shows the way that toddlers learn to understand the people around them.

The attachment perspective was developed by Mary Ainsworth and colleagues (Ainsworth, Blehar, Waters, & Wall, 1978) who made observational studies of infants, twelve to twenty months old, with their parents. The lab procedure is well known. Two separations occur for three minutes each in a standardised procedure used to display the differences that occur. The SSP experiment shows regular patterns of relating between mothers and children, when the behaviour of adults remains the same within basic parameters (Waters, 1978). The SSP experiment is a fixed format where only the child and mother pairing is different and all other aspects remain the same. The SSP is a play in eight acts:

1. The first act is that mother and child are introduced to the laboratory setting with a hidden video camera for one minute and the mother interests her in the toys in the room.
2. During the next three minutes, mother remains seated and is responsive to the child's bids to interact. The infant is allowed to explore the toys and the room.
3. A stranger, an experimenter belonging to the research centre, enters the room for the next three minutes and sits quietly for the first minute, then initiates the infant in an interaction for the second minute, and interacts or plays with a toy for the last minute. Then,
4. Mother leaves the room and the infant remains with the stranger for three minutes. If the little one cries, the stranger is allowed to offer comfort. If the child refuses or resists what is offered, the stranger does not persist. If the distress of the child is high, this act is cut short.
5. For the next three minutes, the mother returns and there is a first reunion while the stranger is absent.

14   ON ATTACHMENT

6. The mother leaves again for another three minutes leaving the infant alone. But if the child is very distressed, this episode can be cut short.
7. The stranger returns for three minutes and offers contact if the child is crying. If the child cannot be comforted or the mother requests it, then the episode can be cut short. The stranger leaves.
   And for the last three minutes,
8. The finale is that mother returns for the second time, offers contact and comfort if necessary, and, when ready, permits the child to play with the toys or explore the room, ending the experiment.

What the SSP shows is that instead of there being an infinite array of responses, despite variability in the behaviour of infants, what happens falls into four discrete forms of response with some variation of responses around two dimensions, separation anxiety and avoidance on reunion, a topic that will be explored again.

The idea of "the script" expresses the repeating attachment dynamic where interactions between carers and children are like a repeating performance: the relational understanding played by both parties often remains the same or is enacted in a regular manner, although the participants cannot explain their reasoning because it occurs automatically at a pre-reflexive level of awareness of how to be in any relationship or social context. The idea of a script is equivalent to the IWM but has a more participatory way of capturing the causal turn-taking involved in a dynamic way, and it abstracts from the full experience, to formulate the repeating processes between people (British Psychological Society, 2011). Following Everett and Harriett Waters (Waters, H. S. & Waters, E., 2006, p. 188), there are eight facets to the secure base script, which represent the constitution of a drama and its restitution into balance once more. The secure base script of the secure process and the return to a secure base is a positively toned motivational sequence of a drama that receives restitution:

1. The starting point is the felt sense of positive connection between adult attachment figure and child, such that the two feel in balance with each other in a positive collaboration whilst the child explores or plays in the adult's presence.
2. When there is a threat or overwhelm caused by an event or the activities, the child becomes distressed or even overwhelmed and this primes the attachment need.

ATTACHMENT PHENOMENA AND THEIR BACKGROUND   15

3. Then the child ceases exploration and play, and asks for problem-solving help and care for her distress or the problematic meaning of the event.
4. The child is aware of the quality and timing of the help that is offered.
5. The child accepts the help.
6. The help is timely, sensitive to the child's needs, and accurately tailored so it works for the child.
7. The help is accompanied by emotional soothing and comforting that reduces tension and distress.
8. The end of the interchange is a return to balance in a positive collaborative connection between child and carer, with the child returning once more to exploration and play.

The secure base phenomenon in children and a first definition

Beginning with childhood, attachment behaviours are observable. For instance, the behaviours of the children in the SSP takes calls, looks, gestures, and verbal communication and interprets them as the "activation of an inferred and not directly observable *attachment behavior system, distinct from and not dependent on other motivational systems, such as hunger or sex"* (Stevenson-Hinde, 1994, p. 62, original italics). This is an important point because specific observable phenomena occur between any two persons, and some of these are categorised as indicating attachment whilst others merely form its background. But if the provision of care is one of the insecure forms, or includes neglect and abuse, then completely different repetitions occur in the SSP and in home observation. These insecure processes of relating are repeated when children are under stress. Insecure processes occur when the behaviour of others, and the distress experienced, provide subliminal and explicit cues in varying degrees and qualities. Yet individual differences in attachment are repeated and are capable of being modified and influenced. The following six observable phenomena form the most definitive aspects of the contemporary research on attachment in children (Colin, 1996; Mercer, 2006, 2011; Prior & Glaser, 2006).

Phenomenon one: At any age attachment is the potential to bond and emotionally invest in specific persons positively, to want to be physically close and connected with them, and so experience a secure base in connection with attachment figures, who for children are usually their biological parents. Attachment starts in infancy with the care received

16   ON ATTACHMENT

from parents, other family members, and paid carers who tend to the needs of children. The effect of the secure base, if there has been the responsive type of parenting, promotes lifelong positive influences even despite extra-familial influences to the contrary (Main & Cassidy, 1988). Attachment is a biological predisposition with weak genetic causes that produces personal and social effects in being relaxed and confident in exploration and play as infants, and in their equivalents in adulthood. Secure attachment is motivationally caused by current psychological and social motivations to create individual differences that are observable as general tendencies to invest positive emotions in others and maintain contact with them. If separation occurs, then according to the place in the lifespan, different forms of distress are communicated in wanting to regain intimacy or be frustrated and disappointed due to its absence.

Phenomenon two: Attachment patterns are discreet and are a function of the care received in infancy in the parental relationship, for the most part (Ainsworth, Blehar, Waters, & Wall, 1978). However, once initiated, the pattern of attaching is long-lasting and slow to change—the "prototype view" (Rutter, 2006). The most fundamental causal forces are the degree of avoidance of an attachment figure on reunion and the degree of anxiety experienced in relation to separation from one. This creates a learned IWM that creates a motivational field for individuals where they are motivated into four discrete processes to seek attachment satisfaction, defend themselves, and avoid distress.

Phenomenon three: Attachment produces explicit behaviours, communications, and implicit expectations about how attachment figures will behave and how the self needs to behave in relationship to them. When care-giving is involved, it is likely the care-givers will become attachment figures. Yet there can be *potential* attachment figures where the attachment bond is not yet fully formed. And there can be *latent* attachment figures when attachment is not formed (Prior & Glaser, 2006, pp. 59–60). The balance of care-giving and care-seeking is different in parenting, friendship, and between adults. When secure children feel distress they seek care and contact, and their expectations are satisfied. The bond usually forms between six and eight months and is most evident between two and four years of age in children and has its adult parallels between friends, lovers, and in providing childcare. Once formed, bonds become distinctive ways of relating with others in intimate relationships throughout the remainder of the lifespan. In cases where insecure qualities form when attachment needs are rejected or are met with inconsistent care-giving, then entirely different tendencies to relate and feel about self exist that also form life-long tendencies and show inertia to change.

Phenomenon four: When there is separation from attachment figures after the bond has formed, then there is protest, pining, and searching for the absent persons. If the separation is long-lasting, there is a mourning of their presence, even if small children are able to understand reasoned explanations of where the absent people are.

Phenomenon five: Attachment is the sum total of representations in memory, emotions, beliefs, expectations, and other retained influences and learning from specific relationships in the past. This includes those conscious emotions and expressed senses that can be felt with different people.

Phenomenon six: Once constituted, the attachment processes of adults exist as semi-permanent tendencies with respect to specific attachment figures and in relation to specific others. Once an attachment investment has been made, loved ones cannot be immediately substituted by another person. Even in cases of neglect and abuse, there can be positive emotional investment in attachment figures that continues alongside negative emotions and senses, because there is such a thing as a trauma bond with an abuser.

IWMs show inertia to change and are updated

In Bowlby's work, the picture of the attachment dynamic is that although there is moment-to-moment variable relating with another human being, there are one or more IWM settings, and an automatic, slow-to-evolve tendency to relate and place self in relationship. The existence of one preferred attachment process does not exclude transient changes into other processes according to changes in here-and-now influences, and such a default can be stable across the lifespan (Klohnen & Bera, 1998). Although the attachment dynamic between people in a two-person relationship varies temporarily, short-term variation can also be created by the influence of social contexts and recent experiences, new events in existing relations, and for other reasons. Meeting people outside of the family, who have different attachment processes, can also be an influence on family, work, friends, and partner. These relationships are the affective centre of life. Otherwise, adult attachment

18   ON ATTACHMENT

has a self-perpetuating ability to maintain itself, despite evidence and opportunities to the contrary. The idea of an IWM in childhood is an implied mental model of a care-seeking self and care-giving others (Weiss, 1991). It is taken to all relationships as a predominant potential for intimate relating in a specific predictable manner. An IWM means that significant relationships are encoded in memory and belief as the inter-relation between the two parties involved. Bowlby's own definitions of the IWM are clear:

> each individual builds working models of the world and of himself in it, with the aid of which he perceives events, forecasts the future, and constructs his plans. In the working model of the world that anyone builds, a key feature is his notion of who his attachment figures are, where they may be found, and how they may be expected to respond. Similarly, in the working model of the self that anyone builds a key feature is his notion of how acceptable or unacceptable he himself is in the eyes of his attachment figures. On the structure of these complementary models are based that person's forecasts of how accessible and responsive his attachment figures are likely to be should he turn to them for support. And, in terms of the theory now advanced, it is on the structure of those models that depends, also, whether he feels confident that his attachment figures are in general readily available or whether he is more or less afraid that they will not be available—occasionally, frequently, or most of the time. (Bowlby, 1973, pp. 236–237)

A specific IWM can be a potential default setting, an automatic assumption of how to be defended and how two people should react to each other, that interprets, makes sense of, or gets projected on to the here and now, and into the future of just merely possible meetings with currently known or entirely novel people not yet encountered. Bowlby asserts that an IWM, an interpretation, concerns confidence

> that an attachment figure is, apart from being accessible, likely to be responsive can be seen to turn on at least two variables: (a) whether or not the attachment figure is judged to be the sort of person who in general responds to calls for support and protection; (b) whether or not the self is judged to be the sort of person towards whom anyone, and the attachment figure in particular,

is likely to respond in a helpful way. Logically these variables are independent. In practice they are apt to be confounded. As a result, the model of the attachment figure and the model of the self are likely to develop so as to be complementary and mutually confirming. (Bowlby, 1973, p. 238)

What Bowlby is asserting is that learned inter-relationships between people are at the heart of how to relate. Attachment includes current and possible relations in love, family, and friendship, and successful co-operation as well as attempting contact with others and defending self from disappointment and hurt. Attachment is a primary process in that it is immediate and does not involve conscious thought or inferences of any kind. Its qualities are emotional and automatic. These are involuntary pre-reflexive phenomena of how unconscious processes of the body and the nonverbal basis of the personality create and manage intimate relating. "Every situation we meet with in life is construed in terms of the representational models we have of the world about us and of ourselves. Information reaching us through our sense organs is selected and interpreted in terms of those models, its significance for us and for those we care for is evaluated in terms of them, and plans of action conceived and executed with those models in mind. On how we interpret and evaluate each situation, moreover, turns also how we feel" (Bowlby, 1980, p. 229). These are important central experiences in all domains of life. The idea that meanings come in recognisable wholes, gestalts, or patterns is object-directed: it is the view of a perceiver turned towards the figure and the background that they experience. The term "wholes" in this object-oriented sense refers to figures on a background, when it comes to pattern-recognition and defining characteristics of the cognitive and emotional aspects of lived experience. A whole can be a motivational sequence, of a series of experiences that show repeating patterns that are recognisable as specifically different ways of relating and being able to find a secure base with loved ones and those closest to us.

The received wisdom is that attachment refers to the individual differences that children have. Attachment is evolutionarily caused in that it is a biological potential common to all mammals. This work challenges both these viewpoints with respect to the IWM as the holding of self and other "in relationship with each other" (Bowlby, 1988, p. 120). The interpretation of attachment argued for below is one that considers the contribution of care-giver and care-seeker as a whole, which

20 ON ATTACHMENT

means that the enactment created by both persons form an attachment dynamic is intersubjective, that is, it concerns what exists between people, between subjects (Husserl, 1977; Owen, 2006a).

Two dimensions: anxiety and avoidance

Two fundamental processes in the SSP are the degree of avoidance on reunion and the degree of separation anxiety (Ainsworth, Blehar, Waters, & Wall, 1978, p. 102), that lead to the discovery in four discreetly different ways of separation attaching. The anxiety dimension occurs on separation and the protest made is the infantile way of asking for reconnection with the care-giver. In the anxious process, the signal is large and is maintained in tangling the reunion and being inconsolable with respect to an untrustworthy care-giver. The avoidance dimension is most obvious with a neglectful and indifferent care-giver: the expression of the pain of what should be protest is necessarily repressed, to accept the minimal form of care on offer. The formulation of the motivating forces in attachment notes the following:

- High avoidance on reunion and low anxiety comprise avoidance and promote ostensibly low distress but show a notable blankness of response and hints of repressed resentment and anger.
- The low in avoidance on reunion and high anxious pattern is a tendency to connect with others in a specific anxious way. As individuals, they are inconsolable on reunion and ongoingly angry when experiencing even a temporary absence and reunion.
- The least avoidance and least anxiety group are those who, more often than not, make a secure process with others. This group has the ability to communicate with others and find it easy to be collaborative and create the secure base phenomenon. When they are distressed, they seek and receive caring and emotional restitution. They can re-establish harmonious experiencing with others and simultaneously soothe their own distress.
- The disorganised group is more variable in their behaviours but generally, high avoidance and high separation anxiety are experienced without collaborative peace and harmony with others, and that has major consequences for how they see themselves and get around in ordinary living.

The next section focuses on the explanatory idea of the IWM, a control systems theory reading of getting attachment needs met that is at the heart of attachment theory.

Control systems at the psychodynamic centre of attachment

It was Edoardo Weiss, in 1950, who first coined the term "psychodynamic". This word is not the sole possession of therapists and psychologists; it refers to the innate ability to understand others and oneself that varies according to biological temperament and conditions of distress. All human beings to some degree, even if inaccurately, are psychodynamic when they describe and explain the "manifestations and consequences of the interaction of mental forces within the human being" (Weiss, 1950, p. 1). Weiss emphasises the role of emotions as direct feedback on the success or failure of behaviour in achieving any meaningful project: Weiss was referring to conscious experiences that are "teleological", that concern purposeful aim-oriented behaviour (1950, p. 2). "Every human being is aware of inner driving forces whenever wishes, feelings, emotions impel him to act ... he is also aware of opposing forces which restrain him from acting. When gratification is obtained through action, the driving force is felt to subside; but when action ... is checked by an interplay of emotions, either the initial psychological situation persists unaltered, or new ones arise which must be mastered" (1950, p. 1). The term psychodynamic is equivalent to "psychologically motivated" and demands the ability to understand others and place self with respect to the others with whom we are close.

Similarly, identifying how one mental process influences another is present in control systems theory (Bateson, 1972, p. 109; van Putten, 2009) and is built on the homeostasis model of Walter Cannon (1932). In any one individual, and between persons, there is something like a system, a complex dependent whole, in the cumulative effect of working with attachment processes and emotional regulation, as Bowlby knew: "By the end of the first year the behaviour is becoming organized cybernetically ... the behaviour becomes active whenever certain conditions obtain and ceases when certain other conditions obtain" (1988, p. 3, cf. p. 29). Previous attempts to model the self's responsiveness to intimates and its own distress have been made and become guiding ideas without critical appraisal in therapy and psychological theory. The guiding idea of control systems theory, first expressed in Cannon's idea of homeostasis in *The Wisdom of the Body* as the self-correcting aspect of the physical body, is a guiding principle of the fluctuating relationship between inputs and outcomes and the variable manner in which dynamic movement between states is attained. Homeostasis in biology occurs when levels of optimal functioning are maintained within the many parts of the physical body (Cannon, 1932, p. 24). Under the terms "cybernetics", "feedback", and "systems theory", the teleological and meaningfully oriented view is a psychodynamic type of functionalism that does not make value judgements or consider logic and normality (Bowlby, 1969, pp. 41–45; 1988, p. 3, p. 29). Systems theory explains psychodynamically changing motivational sequences between need and satisfaction, for instance. The idea of control theory appears in ecology, the human body, and technological achievements made for our homes and other apparatus, where it is necessary to have automatic control of an item and the processes that drive it, in order to maintain steady ranges of functioning. But it is not always the case that phenomena follow the steady-state predictions when there are rapid changes in the input to the system that may cause unexpected events.

The most obvious item is a thermostat in central heating but it has to be noted that, according to control systems theory, control can produce satiation, and if that is so, when a drive achieves satisfaction, this decreases the need temporarily. The systems theoretical view has its parallels in electrical and mechanical feedback systems such as the spring and shock-absorber system in the suspension unit of a car or how a gyroscope works. Let us take the example of central heating. When a thermostat is set and the air temperature around the thermostat is lower than the setting, then the central heating comes on until the air temperature equals the temperature set, and then the heating goes off. When the air temperature falls, it triggers the heating to come back on and the process repeats to maintain the air temperature at the desired setting. The control systems view is defined in a figure that notes how feedback operates to control attainment of the set-goal (Figure 1.1).

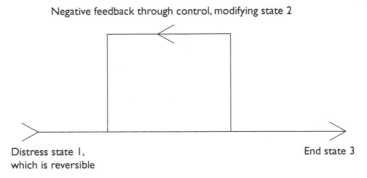

Figure 1.1. Control systems theory.

In human beings, understood as social creatures, the key principle is that whenever the ego acts to achieve its goals (or not), it rates itself emotionally in its ability to act, merely because it is self-aware. This capability is an a priori condition of its ability to change its own state through being aware of what that is, and taking action. This means that the credible estimation of self by self can only really be shown by checking its own effectiveness with respect to any of its purposes. This is done by attending to the evidence of its attainments within a context that works to ensure that it is fair to itself. This is difficult to achieve for any ego fuelled by strong distress.

The key phenomenon that is central to attachment processes is the tendency to be self-correcting across various domains, irrespective of the actual conditions and possibilities around the person. In secure attachment, there is a special type of self-correction that occurs where secure persons tune in to others accurately and are able to communicate with them in effective ways: the "goal-corrected" partnership (Bowlby, 1969, p. 355) and how that relates to perspective taking (Bowlby, 1969, p. 368). Attachment is noted as being a goal-corrected relationship in the sense that mutuality and co-operation can create a harmonious series of calls and responses between any two persons and the sharing of the same goal (Bowlby, 1969, p. 267, p. 351). This marks an achievement of intersubjectivity. The goal is shared between parent and child.

In the insecure and disorganised forms, the attachment thermostat is set, plus there is a tendency to overrule evidence that could improve the quality of the connection and communication. But if improvement does not occur, such sense is omitted even if it is present. In a comparative view, it becomes possible to identify what influences come from both parties' behaviour and compare them to what could or should be, according to some implicit belief and understanding of the secure form. The case of attachment phenomena, moving from unmet need to secure base satisfaction, can be portrayed graphically. Figure 1.2 expresses the means of governance of the attachment system in control theory terminology.

Bowlby noted that attachment initially occurs at the meeting of the necessary internal and external conditions within and outside of individuals who seek satisfaction. It has the aim of moving towards a future state not yet attained, of getting proximity and care from others. The whole process is monitored by innate emotional-relational feedback, which is not only able to select the particular direction of satisfaction to be achieved but also indicate when a sufficient level of attainment has been achieved, and different types of satiation have been produced. The

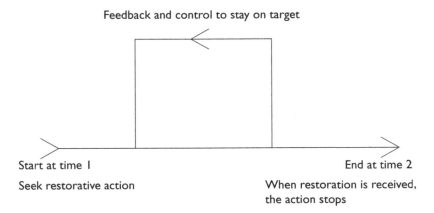

Figure 1.2. Control systems theory as it applies to seeking care and its receipt in any form of attachment.

children with anxious and avoidant patterns received parenting that was slow to respond to their communications and was insensitive and inaccurate in various ways. Disorganised attachment occurs because of parenting and formative experiences that include trauma, abuse, or neglect and chaos (Richardson, 2008). For instance, in the anxious pattern there are calls to the other requesting their help and presence, for the self is programmed to shout loudly in order to get its needs met. Alternatively, the avoidant pattern is a way of requesting minimal contact. Disorganisation is quasi-attachment because a single pattern has not formed properly. Disorganised attachment is most difficult to work with therapeutically and needs greater clarity and collaborative purpose. Being securely attached brings with it the promise of lasting satisfaction and indicates good mental health. The commonalities of the different IWMs are that inherent emotional, relational, and communicational aspects have specific settings and require different corrective conditions if they are to change. The remainder of this chapter briefly notes attachment in its developmental context.

The contextualisation of attachment as part of child development

Experiences up to the ages of twenty to thirty years old are highly influential. However, in the later teen years, just before the transition to adulthood, at twenty approximately, there can be problems with developing a sense of security in new situations that might arise on first leaving the parental home. The contextualisation of the development of children shows that there are potentially protective factors that can conspire to promote or prevent development. Before being carried away with enthusiasm that everything has been understood, following Rutter (1997) and Bowlby (1969, p. 378), a word of caution is required to avoid becoming over-zealous about the explanatory power of attachment: not every relationship concerns intimacy between family and friends. In the context of neighbourhood and society, there is a wide range of social behaviour and attitudes with regard to how people can or should interact. Rutter remarked that the sum total of all relationship influences to date could be considered when attachment is properly contextualised (Rutter, 1997, p. 23). His remarks raise pertinent questions about the overall process of intersubjective influence on the individual across the lifespan. The first thing to be noted developmentally is that the amount of dependence on others that children have, decreases as they mature. What accrues for children is their ability to understand their expanding social world, which is at first most influenced by their early familial and extra-familial experiences. The consequence is that the increasing influence of intersubjective experience will shape the neurological and biochemical aspects of the biological substrate, as well as provide learning of the sort called implicit relational knowledge of how to be, feel, and act, that is, the individual's map of the intimate world.

So, the first relationships that children have are with the selection of persons with whom they have regular contact. When intersubjectivity is the focus of attention, it needs to be noted that there are a range of contributory activities that occur in the family, where the care-giving comes from parents and grandparents, alongside boundary-setting, discipline, play, general teaching of how to be a little person, feeding, bathing, and learning about cultural objects. The quality of attachment can be seen as an emergent property across the sum total of these activities and interactions. Specifically, the advice from Belsky and Fearon (2008) is to regard attachment as a developmental bridge whereby small children learn to relate to adults more generally, as child-adult relating linked with other forms of non-maternal care in the family and outside of it. The wider range of the social contexts surrounding children shows that there are intersubjective influences on the family that may or may not be supportive of an optimal outcome for children and their carers.

When the focus shifts entirely to the function of how individual children deal with the persons with whom they could feel most secure, be loving and joyful with, it becomes apparent, through comparison, how each attachment process is functional in its own way. The conditions of possibility for each attachment pattern are not just the major influences of care from the parents, families, and siblings. To see attachment is to identify it against the greater context of the other learning occurring in childhood and adolescence that, literally, makes the individual. What is shown empirically is that each attachment pattern maintains its own dynamic equilibrium, which has been created by the social context of the family of origin and by the influence of overall upbringing. This may include influences and one-off experiences that may or may not be due to parents, siblings, or grandparents. Disruptive, damaging, or traumatic influences from other children, baby-sitters, school teachers, and unknown attackers, are harmful to attachment.

The next three sections contextualise the background for understanding how attachment patterns are taken forward into adulthood focusing on the social context around the family, the caring for children's needs, and the influence of their carer's contributions. Childhood and being in the family, however that is construed, are formative of a great deal of the adult. The point of the material is to note the conditions of possibility in the making of personality, the living sense of self, and the ability to empathise and relate with others. What is presented below is a series of factors that can promote secure processes of relating and the integrity and unity of self; or if they are absent, then there is an increase in insecure processes of splitting and repression of the self, and failed attempts not to feel or want something (Wenzlaff & Wegner, 2000). It is these latter processes that invoke a psychodynamic account of the qualities of emotional frustration and its defensive management.

The needs of children with respect to their development and mental well-being

The most important aspect of caring for children within the family is to provide love and caring beyond the mere attention to basic needs of feeding, sleep, and cleanliness. One major need that children have is to feel loved and cared for and that their needs are acceptable (Marvin, Cooper, Hoffman, & Powell, 2002). This is the secure base phenomenon, "the provision of a secure base from which a child or an adolescent can make sorties into the outside world and to which he can return knowing for sure that he will be welcomed when he gets there, nourished physically and emotionally, comforted if distressed, reassured if frightened.

ATTACHMENT PHENOMENA AND THEIR BACKGROUND   27

In essence this role is one of being available, ready to respond when called upon to encourage and perhaps assist, but to intervene actively only when necessary" (Bowlby, 1988, p. 11). What it means is that, even before speech, babies have a nonverbal sense of being acceptable in the eyes of their carers and this creates an early sense of self as acceptable to others outside of the family. Secure carers permit children to be themselves and there is the soothing of distress when necessary. If children are distressed on separation, this is soothed. If small children crawl off and explore the room, they can return safely, and carers are aware of the dangers that they might encounter. Children's innate drives are to engage securely with carers, copy adults, and learn through play and exploration. Bowlby phrased three propositions as the outcome of his empirical findings:

> [1] when an individual is confident that an attachment figure will be available to him whenever he desires it, that person will be much less prone to either intense or chronic fear than will an individual who for any reason has no such confidence ... [2] the sensitive period during which such confidence [or its lack] develops ... is built up slowly during the years of immaturity ... and that whatever expectations are developed during those years tend to persist relatively unchanged throughout the rest of life ... [3] the varied expectations of the accessibility and responsiveness of attachment figures that different individuals develop during the years of immaturity are tolerably accurate reflections of the experiences those individuals have actually had. (Bowlby, 1973, p. 235)

Security involves a full mutuality where the care provided to children satisfies them because their adults are attuned to their needs. Problems arise for those for whom this does not happen. However, general emotional and behavioural development concerns the age-appropriateness of the responses of children, as demonstrated in feelings and actions. Although the first social context is initially with parents and care-givers, as children grow the intersubjective influence extends to others outside the family. Development includes the type and quality of specific attachments with new persons, help with the characteristics of biologically inherited temperament, and adaptation to changes in the family such as divorce, changes in baby-sitters and the birth of siblings. Because children copy and respond to their carers, the way to respond to stress is modelled by the parents. Their degree of coping and self-control

28 ON ATTACHMENT

when angry or frustrated, becomes the model for how children do the same and learn how to treat themselves and others. There are a number of other factors contributing to the important topic of attachment. Good health overall includes growth and development as well as the maintenance of physical and mental well-being. The impact of genetically inherited illness, and of other sorts of impairment, should be considered when enquiring about the childhoods of adult clients.

Appropriate health care should be provided in the case of illness, plus access to an adequate and nutritious diet, play with other children of a similar age, exercise, the provision of immunisations and developmental checks, and dental and optical care. For teenage children, advice and information are required on issues that could have an impact on their health, and these include sex education, smoking, alcohol, and drug misuse. The presence of a pro-social family, and social relationships with peers and siblings, promotes the development of accurate empathy (Perner, Ruffman, & Leekam, 1994). Empathy is the capacity to understand the points of view of others, their beliefs and emotions as motivators for why they act as they do. Empathy is a window on the social world. What constitutes positive influences are stable and affectionate relationships with carers and siblings, the increasing importance of the peer group in teenage years, and the response of the family to these relationships. There is research to suggest that the teenage peer group is more influential on children than their parents (Bradford-Brown, Mounts, Lamborn, & Steinberg, 1993; Harris, 2007, 2009).

The sense of self (ego, personality, or identity) concerns a child's nascent sense of self as a separate and valued person who is able to balance being autonomous with being connected to others and the cultural conventions of politeness and social interaction. Children's views of themselves, and their abilities, self-image, self-esteem and the ability to experience self as positive, are important topics. Attitudes of others about race, religion, age, gender, sexuality, class, and disability contribute to individuals' beliefs about these signifiers of identity. Feelings of belonging to and acceptance by the family, peer group, and wider society, including other cultural groups, are necessary, but might be damaged or in conflict because of racism, sexism, and class difference, for instance. Self-care is another topic that is often taught implicitly by observation. It concerns the acquisition by children of the practical, emotional, and communication competencies required for increasing independence. Starting with the early practical skills of dressing, toileting, and feeding, a variety of opportunities arise to gain confidence and abilities, to undertake activities away from the family, and, as they get older, to learn independent living. Despite social anxiety, teasing, bullying, and social or school phobia, carers need to encourage their offspring to acquire social problem-solving skills and the ability to deal with tensions in their peer group. Special attention should be given to the impact of children's physical impairment, if present, and other vulnerabilities, and the social circumstances affecting the development of the ability to self-care. Help should be given to promote individuals to become aware of their needs and get them met (the opposite of learned self-neglect).

The topic of social presentation concerns children's growing understanding of the way in which appearance, behaviour, and impairment away from cultural norms are understood by the outside world. This is an aspect of the cultural and societal processes of norming; for instance, the importance of dressing appropriately with regard to age, gender, culture, and religion. Clashes between the values of the family and those of the wider social sphere mean that children can find themselves becoming bicultural, adopting one way of behaving inside the family and another outside of it, to fit in with the different norms that they correctly interpret there. The term "education" can be used to cover all areas of children's cognitive and emotional development, in the original Latin sense of *educare*, to *lead out* their potential and make manifest their potentials and talents. Parenting, socialising with peers, and enculturation are forms of leading out in this sense. Education about how to be a person occurs in all social environments and is not just what is formally taught in the classroom; it includes opportunities for play and interaction with peers, the chance to have access to books, acquire a range of skills and interests, and experience success and achievement, as well as learn how to manage frustration and disappointment and persist with difficult tasks. Becoming educated requires adults to take the lead and take account of children's starting points and any special educational needs. Such stimulation promotes learning and intellectual development through encouraging cognitive challenge and promoting social opportunities. Being provided with stimulation and interest facilitates cognitive development and makes manifest children's potential through interaction and responding to their questions, while encouraging and joining in with play promotes educational opportunities. The desired end-point is to enable children to experience success in everyday living and school attendance, which gives them the feedback and affirmation that they are on target in expressing their abilities.

30   ON ATTACHMENT

The first context: capacity of the carers to provide parenting

Emotional warmth and love must occur to satisfy children's attachment needs, providing them with the necessary sense of being loved and valued, with a positive sense of their own constancy and individual, racial, and cultural identity. Secure attachment occurs when the requirements for secure, stable, and affectionate relationships, and sensitive and responsive caring, are supplied (Beckwith, Cohen, & Hamilton, 1999; Belsky, Campbell, Cohn, & More, 1996). Physical play and contact, comfort and cuddling in sufficient quality and quantity, demonstrate love, praise, and encouragement and instil a positive sense of agency and self-esteem (Baumeister, Campbell, Krueger, & Vohs, 2003). Children who receive these conditions learn to trust and be confident that they have sufficient inner resources to cope with most situations automatically (the opposite of self-doubt).

Usually, in the nuclear family, it is parents who perform most or all of the parenting tasks. In other forms of family, there may be a number of important carers in the lives of children, each playing a different part that may have positive or negative consequences. A wide range of adults, for example, grandparents, step relations, child minders, or baby sitters, may have significant roles in caring. A distinction has to be clearly made between the contribution of each care-giver to a child's well-being and development. Where children have suffered significant harm, it is particularly important to distinguish between the abilities of the abuser or neglecter and any protective parent or other family members. The parents' relationship with each other can have a powerful impact because of their respective capacities to respond appropriately to their child's needs. For instance, if the parents express violence and conflict in front of a child on a regular basis it creates an atmosphere of anxiety that can become an influence on how to be in relationships as an adult. The quality of the parental relationship also has an impact on well-being, which will be considered more explicitly below. The stability of the family is part of attachment security in that it provides the environment that enables children to develop and can produce secure attachment with primary carers and ensure optimal development. What facilitates this is ensuring that secure attachments are not disrupted, but that they provide consistency of emotional warmth over time, and that the same behaviour among siblings is responded to in a fair and consistent manner. Parental responses change and develop according to children's developmental progress. Children need to keep in contact with important family members who may have left the household; for instance, a father who is divorced from the children's mother and has gone to live with a new partner.

Setting limits and boundaries is another way that the family helps children regulate their emotions and behaviour. A key parental task is demonstrating and modelling appropriate behaviour. It shows how parents cope with distress and interact with others. Providing guidance involves setting boundaries, so that children are able to develop an internal map of moral values and conscience, and enact the social behaviour appropriate for the culture and society. The ultimate aim of parenting is to enable children to become autonomous adults who hold their own values and are able to demonstrate appropriate behaviour with others as a situation dictates, rather than having to be dependent on rules outside of themselves. As children mature, their development requires them not to be over-protected from exploratory and learning experiences, including social problem-solving, how to manage negative emotions, promote consideration for others, and learn effective self-discipline in the shaping of behaviour. Ensuring safety means that children are adequately protected from risk and danger. This could extend to preventing significant harm from contact with unsafe adults and children, and from the desire to self-harm in a wide sense that includes smoking, drinking, and over-eating. The risk and danger from parental mental health should be recognised as another aspect of growing up. This is opposed to parents modelling neurotic anxiety in the absence of real risk.

Outer context: the care and support provided by the extended family, the services within the neighbourhood, professional education, and childcare provision

A family is comprised of biological and psychosocial factors. Family functioning is influenced by who is in the household and how they relate to the children. Any changes in the household composition, with ex-partners leaving and new partners coming, will have major effects. Parents' negative childhood experiences or significant negative life events, and their meaning to family members, will contribute to family functioning. Relationships with siblings, and experiences such as bullying, rape, or physical attack can have powerful effects. If there are

32   ON ATTACHMENT

parental difficulties, an emotionally absent parent, or if the quality of relationship between separated parents is poor, these can create negative influences for children's self-esteem and attachment. The wider family includes those who are allowed into the family by children and carers. This could include blood relations as well as non-related persons and members who are absent but still within the wider family. Their role and importance to children and parents may be influential if they provide baby-sitting or act as role models for the children merely by being present. There are further factors that are relevant in creating a new self in the world, but they pale into insignificance given the central influence of relating that attachment describes.

The following factors also contextualise the individual development of children: housing; employment; income; the family's degree of social integration with the local culture; access to, and provision of, community resources such as crèche facilities and nursery schools; and access to other children of the same age as playmates in the neighbourhood. Further enhancing factors are amenities such as libraries, health centres, and parks, and more organised opportunities to be with other children in nursery schools and breakfast clubs. All these factors serve to create attachment phenomena as well as to provide a background to them. The living sensual body is an intimate part of our existence and the greater the intimacy with others, the closer bodies are together. The care of small children involves getting physically close in order to change nappies and feed them. The closeness between adult partners is physical and sexual, sleeping in the parental bed. The experience of being at home is comprised of childcare and family time and requires negotiating time together and time apart, carrying out the business of family living and earning money. The mind and its intimate psychological life can be understood as concentric circles of less and less intimacy, away from the home setting and towards spending time with work colleagues, friends, family, and neighbours. There are further considerations around the degree to which genetics has a role in propagating attachment phenomena is summarised in the next chapter.

Conclusion

The psychology of attachment is closely related to the conscious experience of love and its disappointment, intimacy, and self-disclosure. The desire to attach includes wanting to be close and connected with other people, and it continues throughout life. The hypothesis of the commonality between child and adult attachment is that the mental processes involved are the same for children and adults, so producing a small number of highly similar aspects of how to be a person and how to manage emotions in self and others, although the relating of adults is more complex and shows greater variability as well as the possibility of self-influence. However, there are more influences in social reality than just attachment patterns, such as the societal roles being occupied. Due to mutual influence and the type of relationship and its context, some persons are taken out of their own process of attaching and, under current influences, temporarily enter another. Universally, in the context of children requiring care, a lack of care and support in an important relationship can be empathised. Parenting should be emotionally intimate and communicate love, warmth, closeness, kindness, and understanding. Both parties concerned should feel connected and respond to each other. When attending to the phenomena of inter-responsiveness between self and other, there are subtle processes of bids to connect and of such connections being prevented (Klinnert, Emde, Butterfield, & Campos, 1986).

Attachment processes are variable because they can be consciously overridden by the ego, therefore altered in the moment, and can be influenced across longer time spans. The phenomena of attachment begin with learning a way of being in childhood that influences later life. Attachment begins an innate, biologically driven need for the receipt of care that later becomes an exchange, a means of dealing with people in different sorts of relationship. From the earliest days of attachment research there has been consideration of the dimensions of this need. The understanding is that the main continua involved are the amount of anxiety felt in relation to being separated from carers, and the amount of avoidance on reunion that is preferred. Attachment is an indicator of the relational personality of current responsiveness to specific others in contexts of influence where unique individuals experience the influence of the current interchange, as well as that of the distant past that provides the ego with its habits and beliefs. IWMs of the qualities of connection between self and other are learned. What pertains to this individual learning is a set of preferences from the past that is taken everywhere, but is open to change and correction by current experience, so that the set of IWMs gained can be altered and grow in complexity and become more accurate. The problem with IWMs is that they are influential and are applied to current situations where they may not be accurate or helpful. Attachment first communicates emotions, from six months of age, and is able to arrange habits, beliefs, and generalisations about self and others in ways that can have lifelong influence.

CHAPTER TWO

The standard interpretation and its processes

This chapter defines attachment for children and adults according to findings from the SSP and the AAI. It defines the four attachment processes in two ways. First, a set of definitions refer to individual differences in mental processes. These mental habits of believing, creating memories, and forming anticipatory feelings and relating, when overused give an impression of what can be called the relational character of someone's personality. Second, mental processes and the tendency of a person to use one particular form should not be confused with the actual moment-to-moment changing dynamic of caring that exists between two persons. Whether or not there is a responsibility of care of any specific sort, from one to the other, it needs to be born in mind that two intimate persons have their own preferences and that what happens between them is the substantial process of attachment. In order to differentiate children and adults, the provision of care to children is called "patterns" and sharing of care between adults is called "processes". They are comprised of verbal and non-verbal social acts that communicate meanings of care and its absence, reticence, neglect, and slowness to respond, and include the vicissitudes between them. What is presented are the findings of empirical research about secure attachment—the optimal sort, two suboptimal

36   ON ATTACHMENT

insecure processes, and fourth, the disorganised sort. Although there is a continuum of strengths of action and reaction and individual variability, only four discrete phenomena appear in connecting with, or distancing self from others, with some variation in the two dimensions of low and high avoidance and of low and high anxiety. The manner of presentation below is psychodynamic in explaining how consciousness and its ego construe their intimate worlds and determine how to live in them. The purpose is to make specific, observable phenomena understood from a first-person perspective of what it feels like between the parties involved in the same process.

The emphasis on process is preferred because it is the most accurate account of mutual phenomena, emotion, and the motivated ways of self-reflexively managing emotions and connections with others, and it explains how the phenomena make sense in an experiential way. It is the role of theory to tie phenomena and experimental methods together into recognisable forms and provide the explanatory power for what is experienced and observable. Attachment is a mode of explanation of the causal links from the past with those of the present (Bowlby, 1973, pp. 414–415). IWMs play their part in a control system theory: these ideas explain the tendency to maintain specific attachment dynamics because of generalisations (due to the meaningful motivating memories, anticipations, and emotion) in self-confirming beliefs about the quality of connection between self and other, that are manifest.

Rather than remain with the Bowlby-Ainsworth model of individual differences, a fuller attention is given to the necessary aspects of interconnections between two parties as processes that exist as a series of telling differences that form four codes that are enacted repetitively between two persons. Once established between the participants, the communication codes require the same interlocking set of roles in order for them to work. The qualitative identifiable aspects of attachment are highlighted and observable in the interaction. The contributions of two parties together comprise the meetings and are recordable between any parties engaged in mental health care of any kind. What is being argued is that attachment is observable in any form of intimacy and distance in emotionally important intimate relationships, in the family, friendship, health care, and the workplace. For any process to take place, each party enacts the same, discreet whole of relating or code of interconnection. While there are individual differences of attachment, the overall encounter cannot be due to just the tendencies of one person. Attachment can only ever be manifest between two or more parties. If the attention is only on one party, then the whole process enacted between the two is omitted.

The topics below start with definitions of attachment, in a way that could be mistaken as characterising the personalities of children in the SSP—a stress test in that it occurs in a place other than the home, with the mother leaving twice and with a stranger involved. It is the standardised format that shows the different types of responses, with the reunion with mother being particularly telling. The standard interpretation focuses on individual differences, which helps narrate the theory, but when words about the repeating psychological process between self and others are understood as potentially variable experiences with others, the core beliefs about self, other, and the world become visible. The next four sections below define patterns of attachment for children.

Secure attachment in childhood

Mary Ainsworth used home observation and the SSP to compare patterns in attachment dynamics. In the secure pattern there is more positive affect among children who manifest gregariousness, autonomy, and intimacy. Secure children explore the room and play with toys when their mother is present. The SSP shows the secure base phenomenon when children explore the room and check with mother by glancing at reaction and returning to her if necessary. On the first separation, children miss their mother and may be subdued in their play. The first reunion occurs with a positive greeting and children initiate physical contact. On the second separation, they may cry and the second reunion may entail physical contact. The key secure phenomenon in the SSP is that when mother returns after being away, there might be some distress expressed, but, if it can be comforted and the connection between the two is re-established, producing the return of play and exploration. It is shown that when the care-giving of parents is reliably sensitive and prompt, it enables children to be active in staying close to mother, maintaining contact, and using positive greetings, and be active when at a distance from her, easily recovering from separation distress and expressing no anger on reunion (Main, Kaplan, & Cassidy, 1985; Sroufe & Waters, 1977).

Children who are secure when they are three years old are likely to express distress and seek help (Sroufe, 1985). Between six and

38   ON ATTACHMENT

eleven years old, secure children display greater social competence (Rose-Krasnor, Rubin, Booth, & Coplan, 1996), are good at identifying and naming emotions (Steele, Steele, & Croft, 2008), and actively seek regulation of distress with a care-giver (Spangler & Zimmermann, 2014). When parents soothe children they also soothe themselves. Furthermore, children who have secure patterns have better self-esteem (Verschueren, Marcoen, & Schoefs, 1996). When there is a habituated secure process, children empathise their adult carers as available for care and support. The other half of the whole is that the care provided is prompt, with appropriate levels of parental communication, shows warmth, and is synchronous with them (Belsky, 1997). The consequence is that it is possible to explore and be emotionally safe and close through fully activating the biological potential. The point is that the emotions felt on both sides of the relationship need to be interpreted in contexts that develop across time. The secure ability to relate can be expressed metaphorically as "secure individuals have lots of good glue". What this means is that there is something self-correcting and self-perpetuating about making satisfying contact that indicates that the level of understanding attained as children (that self and others are reasonable, dependable, and good hearted) leads to becoming adults who have long-lasting and relatively trouble-free marriages and family relations. Such adults experience the positive immediacy of emotional intimacy in many contexts. The phenomena that show secure attaching are those where childcare is high-quality and responsive. Later in adult life, there is the strong likelihood of satisfying friendships and successful secure attachment. What is invested or cathected in others is loving energy and the desire to be close and connected. The cathexis, the type of investment in the connection with another, is metaphorically expressed as "good glue that sticks well". When there are secure attachment bonds both people connect and share a strong bond (whereas insecure attachment types have different properties). For persons who have the tendency to be secure, relationships matter and what is readily provided for them to thrive is loving care and attention, which delivers vitality and a feeling of being bright and alive in the harmony of close and positive social contact. Secure patterns occur where attachment needs are met in mutual satisfaction—a win-win situation.

The primary phenomenon of the secure base is one of full and sufficient provision and receipt of care, love, and verbal and nonverbal communication (Figure 2.1). The establishment of appropriate levels of contact occurs with respect to the ages and roles of the adults

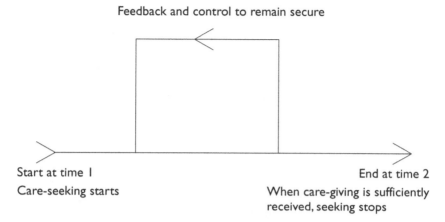

Figure 2.1. Secure attachment.

involved in providing care. In secure processes from infancy onwards, the biologically based drive to be cared for elicits the drive to care from others (and vice versa). So satisfactions are mutual and subtle cues exist and are learned as a language of looks, requests, initiating friendship, tacit agreements, and implicit understanding about their importance. When there have been good-enough secure patterns for children, it is possible later in the lifespan to invest love, friendship, and trust in others (more often than not). There is the expectation that needs will be met and that others will oblige and negotiate mutual satisfactions. There is not much need for defences. When necessary, the self-disclosure of one's needs is unproblematic because they feel likely to be responded to with help from other persons. The conditions of the possibility of the secure pattern include absences of fear, anger, and terror from parents, and permission for children's own self-soothing and problem-solving.

Anxious pattern is caused by unpredictable care

The anxious pattern concerns an intermittent ability to be cared for due to unresponsive and under-involved care that has consequences for self-soothing. In the SSP, anxious children are focused on their mothers throughout, with little or no focus on the room or the toys. Even prior to the first separation they may be wary, distressed, angry or passive. They may immediately be distressed on the first separation and remain angry and distressed with tangled resistance to attempts to soothe them on the first reunion, with no return to exploration and play. Anxious

40   ON ATTACHMENT

children grow up in an environment of unpredictability, insensitivity and unresponsiveness (Weinfield, Sroufe, Egeland, & Carlson, 2008). The distressing qualities of uncertainty, disappointment, and the difficulty of placing trust in another who is in a position of care provision is experienced as lack, care is in short supply and varies in its quality. Children with the anxious pattern are likely to be ambivalent in their play with toys and passive and withdrawn socially. Children who have been frustrated and cannot achieve autonomous emotional regulation, or have received intermittent caring, may over-use protest in order to regain connection. However, anxious children are the most fearful and inhibited in their exploration with toys and peers. Maternal absence and reticence to care promote attention to her that decreases play and exploration and can promote distress (Cassidy, 1994; Cassidy & Berlin, 1994).

Carers who provide unpredictable care show ambivalence for their children who cry prior to separation, are distressed during it, explore little, and are wary of the stranger, and on reunion they tangle attempts to console them (Figure 2.2). In the SSP, when the mother returns, the child is inconsolable by her attempts to soothe distress, and may express outright resistance to being consoled. Being unable to permit soothing and unable to soothe themselves co-occur in children who are demanding, needy, anxious and uncertain of themselves as well as uncertain of how worthy they are to receive care. A bigger communicative signal is used to get parental attention and pre-empt the possibility of their needs remaining unmet. The anxious quality of distress is twofold. There is a state of anguish or anxiety about disconnection, motivating protest and moving forward towards the carer, with demands and big signals to elicit care. The second movement is a step backwards, away from the carer on reunion, in the continuing rejection, implied criticism, and expression of protest that also functions as a call for care. Protest anger occurs when children remain angry at a lack of care for a period of time after the misdeed has first been criticised. This is interesting because it shows the use of anger as a communication that the resentment is justified and continues without forgiveness or calmness, even when care has been provided. To speak metaphorically, the protest keeps a score; whereas if forgiveness and relaxation were the case, the score would have been settled, as evidenced by less distress and anger, and would constitute a different equilibrium. The higher self-consciousness, the self-consciousness of their own needs and abilities, are interpreted as being insufficient because the equilibrium in the anxious pattern is one of expecting insufficiency and inconsistency as a matter of course. The

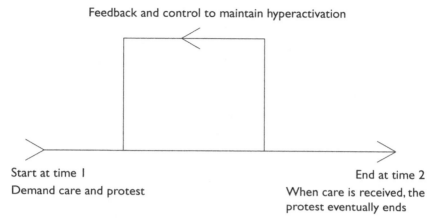

Figure 2.2. Anxious attachment.

core pattern is that if others are unpredictably available then there is an automatic hyperactivation of protest and demands that are addressed to carers (Bowlby, 1973, p. 57).

This suboptimal pattern has its own psychodynamic motivations: anxiety in children shows in their attempts to express anger that they have been left uncared for when they should not have been. There is also an anxious pattern of defence where energy is mobilised and there is vigilance for the possibility of the carer stepping back and reducing the level of intimate contact that has been supplied so far. There may be sudden protests and measures used to maintain contact with others. However, the emotional world is confused between good and bad senses of the same self and other. Ambivalence is the order of the day, perpetuating vacillations between a good and a bad sense of self, and a good and a bad sense of the other, expressing volatility and anxiety. The cathexis, the type of investment in the connection with another, is metaphorically expressed as "glue that sticks hard and then suddenly fails".

Avoidance in children is due to receiving minimal caring so producing unmet need

In the avoidant pattern there is intrusive, controlling caring and excessive stimulation leading to a reversal of the desire to express needs over-assertively, as in the anxious case, which leads to a repressed and notably absent desire to connect with carers. In avoidant attachment, instead of wanting to gain closeness, a more general repression

42 ON ATTACHMENT

or compartmentalisation of the emotional life has the purpose of maintaining psychological distance, because of previously receiving minimal and begrudging caring (Cassidy & Kobak, 1988). The key phenomenon in the SSP is that children do not seek proximity before separation and they focus on the room and the toys away from mother. They are ostensibly accepting of separation because they do not cry when it happens, unless alone. They can be comforted by the stranger and engage in superficial joyless play with the toys. On reunion with mother, children ignore and avoid her, turn away or look past her, and are otherwise blank and emotionally unresponsive in comparison to the other children. The phenomenon is an absence of connection with comparatively little or no contact-seeking and little influence between mother and child where one would expect there to be such. But this is not the only consequence of the force of repulsion that children feel is necessary to maintain the minimal amount of care they get. Empirically, avoidant children are less socially competent than others and liable to be aggressive and victimise playmates (Greenberg, Kusche, & Speltz, 1991; Moss, Parent, Gosselin, Rousseau, & St-Laurent, 1996). Avoidant children grow up in an environment of persistent lack of attention from adults who are also intrusive and can provide excess stimulation (Belsky, 1997). Children may have been threatened or punished with the insistence that they must be self-reliant and their legitimate requests for help may have been scorned (Hesse, 2008); or they have been punished or rejected for wanting to get close, and they learn to see their care-seeking attempts as futile, so there is a behavioural omission in comparison to the secure and anxious patterns. Avoidance in children is created by parenting and caring from adults that was in short supply. The biologically driven authentic needs of small children are persistently ignored, so their self-contained reactions are due to parental neglect. Children who exhibit avoidance learn the necessity of neglecting their own needs and attempt to repress distress, so there is a form of repression and splitting within a still-unified self.

In the avoidant pattern there is not enough caring available so children reduce their expressions for care and contact in order to receive the minimum that is capable of being received. The distress of avoidant children is motivated by a taught anticipatory sense of absence and disconnection. Specifically, it is empathised that others will be absent, so it is expected that relationships will be uncaring and distant, or cannot be maintained, or are often lacking or get broken. Thus, the avoidant pattern maintains only superficial contact with others and a

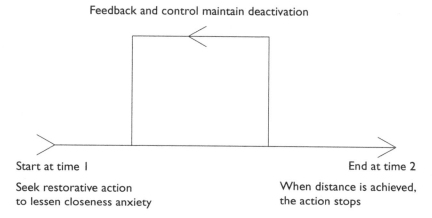

Figure 2.3. Avoidant attachment.

low investment when connecting with them. The core pattern is that if others are unavailable, then self deactivates its attachment attempts (Bowlby, 1980, p. 345, Figure 2.3). Depending on how the nature of the bond is made and tested, the cathexis or emotional investment in the other is one of "glue with little sticking power".

The understanding of avoidance is that the biologically based attachment drive is repressed in what becomes an automatic defensive desire for minimal intimate contact. The avoidant pattern is accustomed to this type of discomfort, and may fail to recognise when a positive offer of care and intimacy has been made. This suboptimal pattern is one where repression of the need to attach operates, so permitting superficial non-intimate or pseudo-intimate relationships. Avoidant attachment is a dysfunctional way of protecting self in a harsh and lonely environment by repressing the biologically driven need for closeness and contact, which in consciousness overall, means that there are continual disappointments circulating. The distress remains alongside attempts to manage it away from conscious attention, as it is both painful and disapproved of by the ego who designates its own desire to be close as inappropriate neediness or weakness.

Disorganisation in children

Disorganised attachment occurs frequently in the personal histories of those who have experienced fear-induction and the survivors of sexual, physical, and emotional abuse and neglect (Alisic, Jongmans, van Wesel, &

Kleber, 2001). The major phenomena in children are freezing around the mother, huddling in a corner, or falling to the floor, the absence of responsiveness, and the expression of simultaneous anxious ambivalence and avoidant ambivalence in the SSP (Main & Solomon, 1986, 1990, Figure 2.4). Behaviours include crying and clinging, plus looking away from mother, alongside more organised behaviour that is classifiable as belonging to the other three patterns. Requests for help are addressed to mother on her return and may co-occur with freezing and appearing continually distressed. Research on disorganised attachment shows it has the definitive aspects of confusion towards attachment figures, plus anger with peers and adults (Carlson, 1998; Hesse, 1996; Hesse & Main, 2006; Main & Hesse, 1990; Waters & Valenzuela, 1999). The core pattern is comprised of simultaneous approach and avoidance plus fast oscillations between approach and avoidance. In disorganised attachment, there can be a failure of the insecure attachment patterns noted above, because each can be briefly begun but is not continued: the disorganised pattern is in disarray, with dissociation present and the possibility of children attempting to be controlling and defiant.

However, the overall form of the movements between states features moving and changing the self: the defensive dysfunctional effect produces a fragmented and confused quasi-unified form of self in one physical body. In later childhood there can be role reversal and attempts to give care and be punitive and controlling. The pre-reflexive experiencing of the disarray is that consistent motivational sequences and meanings are hard to achieve. Children with disorganised patterns can express, at different times, discretely different ways of being a self with

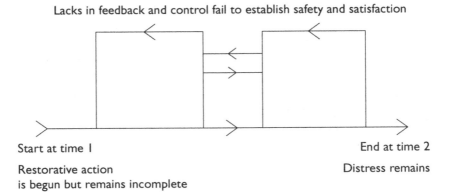

Figure 2.4. Disorganised attachment.

others. There is more dysfunction in the disorganised non-achievement of attachment. It is a co-ordinated but highly ambivalent form of self-understanding and other-empathising. The self is fragmented, shattered into different ways of dealing with the very same self and other people, and its own feelings and perspectives are confusing. Strictly speaking, disorganised attachment shows that there is the absence of the attainment of a control system because hyperactivation and deactivation operate and the attempts at attachment behaviours are highly ambivalent.

The dysfunction has a purpose, for what occurs are identifiable phenomena and complex interactions of the two suboptimal patterns of anxiety and avoidance. There is cycling between the suboptimal forms of hyperactivation and deactivation without attaining the object-constancy or object-permanence of the sense of self or the other. The language of referring to objects has previously been a standardised way of speaking about the many senses that the same person can have (Akhtar, 1994; Solnit, 1982; Tyson, 1996). The answer to stress and feeling cornered in disorganisation is that there are strong defences that can prevent the sense of continuity of being a self altogether. What can arise are multiple links between fragmented contradictory actions.

The next section defines attachment processes in adults with particular attention to the psychodynamic processes between the two halves of a pair in a two-person relationship as derived from research.

The developmental psychology of adult attachment

In order to explain the connections between the empirical psychology of attachment and the process of making conclusions from it, it is necessary to return to a wider view of what happens in researching and drawing justifications for practice. This section explains the relationship between research and conclusions, to orient the reader towards understanding what makes the difference between acceptable and unacceptable justifications. Empiricism is the justificatory basis for action in therapy and mental health care. Yet there are varieties of experimental designs and statistical tools used for the psychology of attachment. Something needs to be stated about their different standards, otherwise bare claims might give the incorrect impression that all empirical findings are beyond reproach. The Open Science Collaboration (2015) is engaged in a meta-analysis of replicability in psychology. Unlike natural science, psychological being is not entirely governed by

46   ON ATTACHMENT

natural causes. Psychological cause produces outcomes that are socially and egoically influenced, as well as having natural causes. For instance, if there were no choice and free will, therapy and mental health care would be impossible.

In short, the results of empirical work entail error bands that need to be born in mind when comparing studies and their replications. Errors are due to a number of factors. Possibly, the cohorts of persons in each study are not representative of the general population at large, or cohorts of participants are incomparable between countries. Then there are the problems of measures that quantify completely different phenomena that become mistakenly included under the same scope of enquiry; for instance, attachment between specific adults versus general beliefs and expectations about people in relationships. The measures used may have been incorrectly or inconsistently administered, so studies, ostensibly about the same population, are incomparable. In addition, the phenomena themselves may be time- and context-dependent and not easily quantified by the measures being employed.

Psychological empiricism deals in meanings, motivations, and the influence of the past, and in current contexts that introduce variability, even in well-designed experiments. The developmental psychology of attachment uses interpretative principles when it attends to attachment phenomena in the homes of children and the lives of adults. For children, it has to be noted that general developmental processes, the socio-economic status of families, and the general context around childcare in different societies, make a big impact. When it comes to making conclusions about adult attachment then the most important literature are those studies that correlate with SSP, home observation, and the AAI. What presents as suitable material are longitudinal studies and research into long-term partnerships and marriage. It is then necessary to identify the qualities of what constitutes good research and how to conclude from it in order to justify practice. In this way, hypotheses can be shown to be untrue according to investigation into one part of a whole, or the interaction between two factors, one that is a cause and the other taken as an effect, all else being kept the same. If a theoretically predicted outcome is due to a specific cause and is observed in an experiment, and this occurrence is more frequent than chance, then a hypothesis may stand (because it is not yet falsified). What this means for the psychology of attachment is that methodological and epistemological meta-commentary on measures and psychometric properties is required to gain the attachment theory community's agreement on the quality of findings. Clearly, low-quality findings cannot be used to justify practice. In addition, if a hypothesis cannot be tested, then the subject lies outside of science and is classed as a cultural belief of no scientific importance. The in-depth quality assurance of attachment studies is long overdue. Rather than jumping to conclusions about what it means to work with attachment theory in practice, time should be spent stating the methodological conditions for the possibility of high-quality study of attachment phenomena (Crowell et al., 2002; Waters & Rodrigues, 2001).

With these thoughts in mind, let us look at some of the findings from SSP and AAI concordant research between adults in long-term marriage and cohabiting partnerships. So as not to get lost in the assertions being made, let us be clear about what the phenomena are. First, De Haas, Bakermans-Kranenburg, and van IJzendoorn (1994) showed that there is no connection between inherited temperament and AAI results. Second, because of the early quality of experience of secure base creation and usage in the home, then the type of parenting supplied has specific influences on what can be seen in the SSP, as well as what can be researched in home observation or ascertained through measures such as AAI and its modifications. One modification of the AAI, secure base script analysis (SBSA) works to capture the contributions of empathic attunement, the exchange of care-giving and seeking, and the overall quality of assertiveness in the interaction (Crowell, Pan, Gao, Treboux, and Waters, 1998). SBSA gives numerical scores about varying degrees of verbal and nonverbal congruence and empathic accuracy of caregiving in couples with respect to the one in the care-seeking turn. What AAI measures is the retrospective quality of adults in relation, mainly, to the mothering received.

One measure that can be given to adults about their current relationship satisfaction is the Current Relationship Inventory (CRI) by Crowell and Owens (1996). However, CRI is not fully concordant with the AAI. Haydon, Collins, Salvatore, Simpson, and Roisman (2012) found it fifty-eight to sixty-four per cent concordant. Another group of researchers found it between forty-seven to fifty-six per cent concordant (Owens et al., 2008). However, there are a number of influences in adult life that contribute to what is being measured, that might be influenced by factors other than mother–child and father–child attachment.

Attachment phenomena themselves are variable (Rutter, Kreppner, & Sonuga-Barke, 2009; van IJzendoorn & Bakermans-Kranenburg, 2014). The point of the Ainsworth and colleagues 1978 study was to kick-start empirical research by making some ideal theoretical conclusions so that

48   ON ATTACHMENT

psychometrics can be used. The proper understanding of theory with respect to everyday research and practice, is that the ideal usages of ideas need to be monitored to make sure that colleagues are in agreement with them. In the forward-looking direction, SSP is inaccurate in predicting adult attachment (Grossmann, Grossmann, & Waters, 2005; Rutter, 2006). In the retrospective direction, of looking back into childhood, AAI and CRI suggest some interesting findings that need careful consideration.

Freud claimed that "the root of a mother's importance" is "unique, without parallel, laid down unalterably for a whole lifetime, as the first and strongest love-object and as a prototype of all later love-relations for both sexes" (1940a, p. 188). Bowlby supported the prototype idea that the quality of parenting received creates a foundation for partner-choice and attachment in adult life (Bowlby, 1969, p. 82; Haydon, Collins, Salvatore, Simpson, & Roisman, 2012; Crowell & Waters, 1994). The influence is one of soft psychosocial cause (not natural cause) where the IWMs from childhood influence adult relationships. But the study of marriage and long-term partnerships, by Treboux, Crowell, and Waters (2004), suggests various trajectories according to individuals' attachment history (secure or insecure) in connection with their current experience of marital satisfaction (secure or insecure). There were two conditions in the Treboux, Crowell, and Waters (2004) study. When stress is on, those who have had insecure parenting experience the repetition of the insecure IWM and a lack of the secure base in their here-and-now relationships with their partners, with consequent distress and low self-esteem. When under stress, those individuals who had received insecure parenting (and might be guessed to have "little to give", as it were) were less distressed than those who had received secure parenting. Alternatively, those who had secure parenting and had a secure relationship, when under stress, still felt positively about their relationship, experienced some conflict in it, but used the relationship strongly as a secure base to discuss how they felt and receive comfort, as might be expected. The improvers, those who had had insecure parenting but were able to create a secure relationship when under stress, did create a secure base to a lesser degree, experienced conflict in the relationship, and were distressed and felt bad about themselves—but they were able to cope, as evidenced by their current secure base creation and usage. This suggests that even if there is just a small amount of secure base creation and usage, in the here and now, what transpires despite there having been insecure parenting, is distress with coping for the improvers.

The earned secure couples cope in the here and now despite the parenting they received (Fox, Kimmerly, & Schafer, 1991). It is almost the reverse for distressed couples, who did have secure parenting, but whose here-and-now attachments are marginally positive. It is shown that having had a secure childhood did not act as a buffer for couples in current relationship distress. They feel marginally okay about themselves currently, but having strong distress and conflict in their current attachment was not moderated by their good attachment in childhood. It is findings such as these that are taken as further evidence for the hypothesis that the processes being measured are semi-permanent: they show inertia to change *and* they are open to change because of the context of life circumstances around the couple and family, due to the input from current partners, their context and life histories.

Another relevant finding that comes from Crowell, Treboux, and Waters (2002) is that their cohort of couples, who were studied before and after marriage and cohabiting, were given a three-way classification according to the AAI. Of them, twenty-three per cent were found to have two secure partners, forty per cent had one secure partner, and thirty-seven per cent had two insecure partners. The findings showed that only twenty-three per cent shared the secure process; seven per cent shared the anxious, and twelve per cent shared the avoidant processes. The remaining fifty-eight per cent had different IWMs in operation within the same couple.

What is also noteworthy is the use of retrospective analyses of adults, looking back into the childhoods they have come from. The findings of Haydon, Roisman, Owen, Booth-LaForce, and Cox (2014) were that, on the one hand, if mother had been insensitive, then avoidance was supported. But on the other, if father had been unavailable, anxious and avoidant processes were supported. Moreover, there was a gender correlation such that men had a tendency to be avoidant and women a tendency to be anxious in attachment. One piece of research found that those with the secure process in adulthood express joy, have a sensitivity to empathise, understand shame, and experience little distress (Magai, Hunziker, Mesias, & Culver, 2000). Adults with a secure process did not experience the withdrawal of love when they were little. However, those with the anxious process in adulthood did experience the withdrawal of love as children, are sensitive to facial expressions of disgust, experience anger and depression, and imagine closeness and connection. Those with the avoidant process in adulthood are likely to be sensitive to empathising disgust and deny experiencing anxiety. The disorganised process is linked to anxiety and expressing shame. They experienced punitive parenting and are sensitive to empathising anger in others, and seek the approval they themselves had not received. Finally, adult avoidance has been linked to the quickest empathic understanding of faces and social situations but the least responsiveness to what they empathise (Maier et al., 2005). This suggests that the learning in avoidance-producing parenting leads to adults who lacked access to the secure base as children, experience heightened physiological distress during the AAI itself, but continue in their inhibited responsiveness to others, even though their empathic abilities are intact.

Finally, papers on the rates of transmission between the generations, show that there is a large amount of variation according to the cohorts used. Papers on the connections between SSP and AAI reveal the following variations. The usual way forwards when understanding statistically derived information is to be more trusting of the largest sample sizes as well as the most rigorous and telling experimental design. The meta-analysis by Verhage (et al., 2016) on a four-way classification of mothers in comparison to a four-way classification of their children retrospectively, showed that every adult process indicates a distribution of every child pattern. When considering the findings of Verhage and colleagues, what appears is that the secure process is transmissible to secure infants, yet the other three patterns occur. This suggests that there may be further influences operating. Similarly, the anxious process is also transmitted and some infants become secure, and the other three patterns occur. Something similar happens with avoidant and disorganised processes in adults.

One way of making the mental processes clear in research and practice is to consider how they create coherent, multiple views of the same person, or fail to do so. This line of interpretation adopts some of the early emphases of attachment theory (Ainsworth, 1969) and connects to the perspective called object relations (Diamond, Blatt, Stayner, & Kaslow, 1993) and object constitution in phenomenology (Owen, 2006b, pp. 322–324). The terminology for this perspective is as follows: the understanding of the same person, or interaction between people, is addressed as an object of attention. This is not a value-laden term but merely a technical way of describing the forms of attention that both cohere and coalesce in the secure sense they make; or they potentially conflict and remain incapable of becoming united, due to the different views of the same person or event, that cannot be united.

The remainder of the chapter takes definitive comments from the CRI and the AAI that are read through the lens of identifying the mental processes of empathy, the identification of the self in relationship, and a perspective that comments on the style of the constitution of the object: this means that what is being abstracted are different types of empathic understanding. The lowest levels of accuracy and representation are those where the accounts made do not tally with what was felt, and what necessarily occurs in practice. The more sophisticated and accurate understandings are those where there are more complex additions of the relevant pieces of why people feel what they do, what motivates them, and how they see others and themselves, in relationship.

What psychology and therapy theory notices is that any relationship between two people is comprised of a range of senses in dynamic interplay with each other. A genuinely detailed account of what comprises the greater manifold of being in a long-term marriage or cohabiting relationship is that the forms of inter-relating and empathising of the other are only properly understood when they are placed in historical and meaningful contexts. Two persons in interaction are understood as having an adequate account of their relationship with each other, when both of their contributions can be held in mind at the same time, so that the dynamic interplay can be described. What this means is that mutuality, reciprocity, and the inter-weaving of each person's stance towards the other needs to be present in order for the account of one of them to qualify as adequate. To account for cause and effect in psychological terms between two people means understanding the object of a relationship, as something that unfolds across time. In couples, what they say and feel are necessary parts that comprise the whole. People do not stand alone. They want to achieve something. They come from somewhere and are headed somewhere else. To attempt a qualitative study of couples in long-term relationship necessitates the ability to have a theoretical meta-commentary on the nature of such inter-relating. For SSP, CRI, and AAI, and other investigations into relating, demand the ability to discuss and quantify the specific forms of representation being used. What is expressed in the SSP, CRI, and AAI scoring systems are ways of allocating numerical scores to varying degrees of the four major types of attachment. A view that spans these systems for quantifying the strengths and presences of the phenomena sees the processes of attachment itself. However, when looking across the scoring systems the following definitive processes are read from the guidelines for scoring. The next four sections define adult attachment processes.

52 ON ATTACHMENT

Security in adults

What the CRI defines as being the quality of a secure base between adults is as follows. When the focus is on assessing the strength of the individual difference called secure attachment, it correlates with thoughts and feelings that express a balanced clarity about the partner, the state and future of the relationship, and the quality of self in relationship. Because what is being assessed is the tally between appearance and reality, it is important to understand that senses between two persons are in the spotlight. For the secure process, the good news is that the empathised senses are likely to be accurate. When there are experiences of rejection, divorce, trauma, and loss of an attachment figure in childhood or adolescence, the distress has become sufficiently resolved for it to be able to be talked about it in a coherent way. This shows that despite the distress felt in the telling, there is coherence about the lost object and what is felt can be said. When there are criticisms about a partner, then the comments are evidenced and well-balanced, with the partner's strengths being included, and the comments placed in a context. Clichés and jargon are not used. The qualities of the comments are fresh and nuanced. What is clear is that the relationship is positively valued, with plenty of appreciation expressed. There is confidence and optimism about the couple's future.

The empathic constitution of the sense of the partner is a unified manifold of senses that occur about the person. The manner of speaking and being aware shows flexibility of attention during a secure process, alongside the ability to integrate disparate senses. Secure adults are good at explaining how their past has shaped them. Their verbal style is collaborative and coherent, irrespective of the positive or negative scenes being recounted. The descriptions made are balanced and consistent. When the object of attention is an adult partner, there is the constitution of a unified object of the other as a well-balanced description comprised of their positive and negative qualities, and showing forgiveness and compassion for their misdemeanours and weaknesses, whilst not losing sight of their strengths. The manner of narration is congruent and relaxed with slow or fast speech that shows equal ease with negative and positive content. When the same object or event is discussed, the felt-sense gained about the speaker's experience is that it is a unified well-formed whole where the views of others, from their perspective, also count. Further, persons in a secure process are able to express their own shortcomings and it is acceptable for them to ask

THE STANDARD INTERPRETATION AND ITS PROCESSES   53

for what they need, and depend on others, and state that they miss their presence and support. If there are shortcomings about self, these can be expressed and are accepted maturely: persons in a secure process accept themselves as imperfect. There appears monitoring and meta-commentary on their own biases, idiosyncrasies, and apparent contradictions and failures of memory, and there is an open attention to the differences in perspective between different persons.

Anxious process is related to short-term frustration and remaining distressed

What the CRI focuses on is the specific quality of the ambivalence about the relationship, the partner, and the self in relationship. There are multiple senses of the objects of attention being described. These are often positive and negative senses of the same person and the meaning of their differing intentions towards the speaker is explained. It might be the case that the earliest experiences of being a child and growing up in the family of origin are improperly described, more so than more recent experiences, where there remains difficulty in pleasing parents who may be critical and have high standards that are hard to achieve.

To make a comparison, unlike the anxious processes defined above, what happens in the secure process is that there is a bias in empathising the other, making sense of the relationship, and oneself in it, which in the anxious manner, is skewed. Regardless of the contributions of the other, what is brought to the relationship include the following: selves in anxious process experience anxiety, anger, confusion, and attempts to control the partner. The anxious self may express her needs clearly but then doubt (privately and to the partner) that her needs will be met. Idealisation exists in that the quality of being in love is praised and valued but the emotions expressed include the view that the current relationship does not, and perhaps may never, get close to the ideal. What this suggests is a naive and immature view of what adult long-term relationships should be. Given that partners are not empathised as separate persons in their own right, but rather exist as an extension of the anxious self, an ambivalent codependence can occur. On the one hand, there is doubt that the relationship will last long-term and problems in it are denied. On the other hand, the empathic understanding of the partner and the relationship is inaccurate with respect to the evidence of the partner's view and capabilities. The anxious self tends to be unassertive and so does not wield proper influence in the relationship,

54   ON ATTACHMENT

tending to contain her emotions, anxieties, and targets for the partner to achieve. This coexists with attempts to please the partner whilst not getting her own needs met. The key process of fluctuating ambivalences about other, self, and the relationship, produces two phases: there are temporary moves forward, towards the other in anxious and needy ways, except to the point where there is felt to be too much closeness by the other person, or the tie is understood as potentially too weak to be maintained; then there is criticism and rejection, leading both partners to step back, which introduces a temporary preference to be distant, and can be followed by the anxious person's desire to be close again.

In the AAI (Hesse, 2008), the anxious process either shows itself in persistently being focused on childhood and earlier senses of attachment figures, even when a question is not asked about them. The character of object constitution of a partner is the generation of ambivalent senses of an attachment figure, expressed in contrary senses where the parts do not fit together properly. The sense of anxiety and anger expressed from events years ago is still burning hot when it is expressed. Or, if not expressed, the emotions are still present at an implied level. The picture of the self is one of self-blame. The interviewer is given the impression that the accounts consist of well-rehearsed clichés being repeated once more. The verbal style is one of expressions that are long-winded and excessively detailed, that include irrelevancies and grammatically tangled clauses. The content of what is expressed is overly detailed and the emotional tone is anxiety and anger. The verbal style is passive, vague, and contains broken references to what is being discussed and indicates that the speaker is enmeshed in his own position, and has difficulty seeing the perspectives of others. Answers to questions may include more recent senses of upset and conflict with parents, and other attachment figures.

Avoidance is the attempt to build self-containment and deal with absence of connection

The CRI notes that repression of attachment emotions is the focus, so that individuals who score high in avoidance are poor care-seekers and poor care-givers. In short, any relationship with one or two avoidant persons in it is not collaborative in the way that the secure, and even anxious relationships, are. Persons who are stuck in the avoidant process have closed down their attachment systems and may find it difficult to awaken them. For them, closeness is not a valued achievement in anything other than a superficial way. The technical terms are that attachment is decathected, deactivated, and derogated to indicate that the persons involved have given up on the possibility of loving, warm intimacy and are managing to get through without. Their speech also shows a form of ambivalence of its own peculiar kind. In comparison to the anxious person's speech, avoidant ambivalence concerns senses about the same person or event that are indifferent. Their other tendencies are to repress and dismiss their attachment figures and experiences in a general way.

One tendency in the avoidant process is to claim invulnerability and deny problems. This is added to the superficial emphasis that the partner is an ideal person also. However, the understanding of the relationship is faulty in that when problems are admitted, they belong exclusively to the partner, and are alleged to cause no problem to self. When pressed, there is no evidence cited as to why the partner is ideal and the attitude of thinking and feeling about him or her is dismissed, with the admission that the partner is not thought about much. The quality of the long-term relationship is one of pragmatism. There may be claims that the relationship is satisfactory or good but there is no evidence to support them. Accordingly, the style of empathising the other and understanding the relationship is inadequate and a specific sort of ambivalence occurs where a gloss is paraded with nothing to substantiate it.

In the AAI, repression appears as poor coherence with a particular character of denying and censoring accounts, with the repeated insistence on absent memories, alongside obvious contradictions to what is professed. The character of object constitution of the empathised sense of the parents includes idealised senses of them, added to by further senses that are negative, but the discrepancies are not commented on. The overly positive and abstract semantic verbal content expressed is not reflected by further explicit and implied senses of rejection, neglect, and abuse. Contempt towards attachment itself, and contemptuous refusal to discuss an attachment figure and related scenes, may be the content of brief responses to AAI questions. Repression appears because the ego is narrated as strong, independent, and normal, with little or no mention of distress, neediness, or depending on others, which indicates that avoidant persons defend themselves against expressing distress. Persons who have a tendency to the avoidant process generally lack memories but these might be followed by accounts of the past. Alternatively, such attachment-related verbal content is given a positive value in one part of the conversation, only for it to be contradicted in the same

56   ON ATTACHMENT

discussion. In short, there is a persistent focus away from attachment in the personal history and the genuine implications of actual events.

Disorganisation in adults

Disorganised attachment in adults is an amalgam and less coherent than both the non-optimal insecure forms. The process maintains weak amalgams of the ego-states or sub-personalities in connection with others, with a weak overall cohesion between them. The defences exist because of overwhelm by neglect and trauma in childhood. There are many intense experiences that have not yet been unified into the creation of robust and resilient senses of self and of others (Hammersley et al., 2008). These serve a function of managing the pre-reflexive experiences, by continuing the lack of integration between parts of self (Dillon, Johnstone, & Longden, 2012; Johnson, Cohen, Kasen, & Brook, 2006). In the AAI, disorganised attachment in adults shows itself in discussion of attachment issues when there has been loss, trauma, and abuse that interrupt the usual steady flow of speech to produce lapses and interruptions in normal logic, long silences, or eulogies about a dead parent, for instance. Such lapses and silences may co-occur with verbal behaviour that is also apparently secure, anxious, or avoidant. For instance, deceased parents are discussed as though they are still alive or were killed because they felt something. Because this process is more complicated, only the most salient details are mentioned below.

1. The process entails severe ambivalence to the point of there being failures to connect with others and cope with distress. There are ongoing simultaneous approaches and avoidances plus fast oscillations between them. In total, disorganisation features ongoing distress, ineffective approach, and ineffective big signals to gain contact, ineffective avoidance, and non-empathic responding to others' distress. Disorganisation comprises both the anxious and avoidant strategies. When both are in play it leads to states in control theory called zeroes and poles. Zeroes are when the system stops or functions only in a limited way. Poles occur when there is chaos (van Puten, 2009, p. 7).
2. The result is rapid cycling, disoriented and aimless relating when others are present and absent.

THE STANDARD INTERPRETATION AND ITS PROCESSES   57

3. Splitting of the self can occur with dissociative phenomena related to trauma and abuse. Despite their differences, the net effects of physical and sexual violence are varying degrees of inner tension produced between contrary motivations, thus showing dissociation, repression, and ultimately the full splitting of the ego that can produce dissociative disorder not otherwise specified (DDNOS) and dissociative identity disorder (DID). These processes and end states concern various forms of fragmentation, either of the ego or of loss of memories, for varying lengths of time, and loss of access to various experiences (Boysen & VanBergen, 2013).

In the strongest forms, each dissociated identity has entirely different relations to other persons and psychological objects in the world. This clinical picture is one where traumata have occurred and non-egoic processes outside of the direct control of the ego co-ordinate to help it deal with what it expects to happen in its social world. The anticipation is that catastrophes and conflict might occur, and there are extreme defensive changes between the senses of self and of the empathised other, as ways of managing unbearable distress. These emotional-relational states are over-modulated and under-modulated, and lack soothing from others and self-soothing. The territory can show a number of selves who engage with strong and persistently inaccurate senses of empathised others (Bowlby, 1973, pp. 204–205). Disorganised attachment is related to a spectrum of distress and attempts to manage it, right up to trauma-induced psychosis, trauma-induced bipolar, and DID (Shevlin, Dorahy, & Adamson, 2007). Disorganised attachment can be explained as a fragmented self that attempts to act in a cohesive way but persistently fails to maintain its proper unity and coherence.

For instance, three senses of self might co-exist in relation to specific ways of empathising others. One sense of self could be due to abuse in childhood where there was violence, trauma of various sorts, neglect, or repeated ignoring and rejection of a child's needs. The parenting and adult contact received was severely dysfunctional in a variety of ways. The process gets replicated in the ongoing production of the continuing map of the world as a dysfunctional self in relation to mis-empathised others, felt to be untrustworthy and attacking. The psychological world is felt as extremely harsh, even in the absence of current evidence to support such conclusions. A second sense of self could be more functional, and this could have been created with respect to early relationships that

58   ON ATTACHMENT

were functional and caring. The concomitant behaviour and emotions for the adult self will also be, temporarily at least, positive and accurate, but only until anxieties or meanings arise that cause one of the other senses of self to occur, and, with that the process changes altogether. Alongside the above two senses of self, there could be a third sense of self which might also be functional and, to some degree appropriate, because of having related with other children or siblings or another person in the family, school, or neighbourhood, who acted as a role model for how to act in a decent way. The problem of disorganised attachment is that there is no integration of the discrete ways of being a self and dealing with others. Specific meanings and motivations can cause sudden large changes between these ways of being, relating, and managing distress. This discrete changeability functions as defence in that the overall process provides relief for what is felt to be unbearable threat or the prospect of it.

The next section summarises the processes once more in the specific cases of when they are shared on both sides of a relationship.

Developing the attention to processes

By way of comparing and contrasting the four processes, what needs to be emphasised is that attachment between adults refers to variable processes over and above a checklist of merely categorical definitions of what is entailed in one sort or another. The point is that the standard interpretation of the Bowlby-Ainsworth model of attachment is that it becomes too easy to want to make a fixed diagnosis of a person's traits, which is a reification that goes far beyond the evidence. On the contrary, the most accurate way to represent attachment professionally is to understand that the same two persons (and the same individual) can participate in a number of changing, even short-lived, transitory processes, all the while consciously wanting, and unconsciously engaging in, a process that they find themselves drawn into. The way to refuse reification, and attend to long-lasting and momentary changes between processes, is to bear the following comparison in mind. It is true that individuals have their own tendencies to enter into one or more forms of attachment because of their IWMs. However, for any IWM to be enacted it has to be shared between people as a type of communicational code. When emphasising the repeating forms of connection between self and other, the actions of both parties have to be co-ordinated in the same way in order for them to be enacted. When there are changes between

THE STANDARD INTERPRETATION AND ITS PROCESSES   59

observable processes between people, they are accompanied with the valued senses that each has for the other. When there is clarity of empirically tested understanding of repeating processes, that have definitive features and require co-ordinated operations between self and others, it is the case that both persons empathise the other's perspective and value each other, the details of which are most generally ambivalent in their myriad forms, although they show distinguishable types of process and emotional investment. This emphasises the processes between the senses of self and other involved in the standard developmental interpretation of attachment stated above. Because the focus is attachment in adulthood, what is being summarised is a comparative view across the definitions.

In the secure process between two adults, it is safe and easy to invest positive emotion in the other: there is a phenomenon of mutual attraction and positive connection because goals between two persons must be in alignment in order for conflict to cease (Bowlby, 1969, p. 355), another example of the synchrony required in a goal corrected partnership (Bowlby, 1969, p. 372). However, the principle being stated is even more necessary, because for any process to be enacted at all, it must be shared between both parties. In the secure process, whatever the real-life faults of the two, others are valued as overwhelmingly positive. Therefore, the mutual process involved is between two mutually positively investing persons who hold each other in admiration and respect (Owen, 2009, p. 67). Because both persons find the other lovable and trustworthy, and feel the same way about themselves, there is little or no resistance to expressing any topic or disagreement. Accordingly, all emotions that accompany these topics are fundamentally acceptable. In addition, while the unconditional acceptance of the topics of concern may not follow, overall, all topics and emotions are acceptable. The first pragmatic consequence is that within the secure process, it is comparatively easy to resolve a dispute or difference of opinion, and forgiveness follows easily after anger and disappointment, for instance. The communicational habits of the long-term secure process include continual rebalancing of the relationship as well as rebalancing of the mood and emotions as one whole occurrence. One immediate consequence of secure process is that emotional good health is likely. Mini-disputes and tensions are dealt with quickly so that vitality is easily felt, and negotiation is easy to achieve and provides proven gratification. Congruent and authentic communications enable this continual

60   ON ATTACHMENT

rebalancing, which shows a further implied phenomenon: part of being able to discuss any topic and to accept accompanying emotions implies the occurrence of two-way co-regulation and co-influencing that maintains strong mutual valuing on both sides of the relationship. The senses of self and other are maintained as positive, and both parties prove themselves skilled in continuing in this fashion, and both can put the brakes on each other, in providing calmness to the other through verbal discussion, and so provide calmness to themselves when helping the other. The implication of co-influencing between the two is implied and only becomes noticeable in comparison to the insecure processes noted below. In this emphasis on understanding, when the focus is on repeating psychological processes, such an analytic attention compares the constituent elements, and makes their wholes become more apparent. The most definitive features are identifiable commonalities across the full spectrum of findings about children and adults.

Despite the universal fact that all relationships are ambivalent (in that the sense of the other will never be permanently good or bad, even when the other is valued clearly positively in the secure process), it is easy to accept others' perspectives and use them to help oneself through valuing them. The consequences are that it feels safe to be intimately connected *and* apart. The innate gyroscope within the secure process is that it rebalances itself easily around its set point of mutual positivity and this expectation gets proven in actual experience: intimate relationships are relaxing, enjoyable and reduce tension between partners as part of the deep joy that good quality relationships supply. For people in this process, it is abundantly obvious what the benefits are of valuing specific other persons as good. They are likely to help you with one of your problems and you would gladly do the same for them.

When the anxious process is given the comparative treatment, to indicate its inherent implied aspects, it shows how the process is different. The anxious process promotes schizogenesis, a type of splitting between its participants (rather than a unification, as in the case of security). The cycle of pulling the other in and then pushing them away, is powered by a longing for connection that is thwarted because a number of implied parts create the anxious whole. The overly strong demand for connection, alongside a fear of abandonment and blame, power a demand for the other that can feel all-consuming. But from the other's perspective, it may not look attractive at the moment of its expression because of the excessive amplitude of the calling itself. Because the

THE STANDARD INTERPRETATION AND ITS PROCESSES   61

process is shared, there arises retaliation, turn-taking, mutual longing, neediness, demand, anger, and rejection. There is mutual preoccupation about the motives of the other that support forward-looking worry and backward-looking rumination—without forgiveness of the other or acceptance of the self. Unlike the secure process, it follows that there is great variability in the senses of self and other, with potentially fast and unpredictable changes in the topic of discussion and emotions. The valuing in this type of mutuality features ambivalence between rapid vacillations of good and bad. What follows are repeating cycles of an unworthy unlovable self grasping at a positively valued other, who, if he or she steps away or refuses the demand, becomes valued negatively. Or, if help is supplied, it can be resisted, criticised, or perversely frustrated if the other is still being valued negatively in angry protest. However, what is implied in this whole is that in the variability of anxious ambivalence, there is an accompanying sense of stress and low trust in the other, and with these go further consequences. The frequently variable senses between the pair exist alongside a much greater variability of the emotional tone of the relationship that contributes to mood problems, and the ability to maintain calm rationality and openness to the other.

The anxious process features rapid movements between intense neediness, rejection, longing, dealing with the consequences of rejecting the other, self-doubt, and the accrual of hurts and betrayals, which mean that this process is tiring. The implied consequences are that there is difficulty in getting resolution of outstanding issues, so ongoing disputes are maintained, which is stressful. (Clearly, when there is calm intimacy, disputes are more likely to be resolved). Persons in an anxious process can be out of synchronisation with each other, so that positive gestures designed to please the other lead to criticism, tangles, resentment, and frustration—and fail to please them. For the giver of positivity to the other, it is disappointing to feel that it is impossible to please them. Accordingly, it is hard to care, trust, and invest positively in the other. Anxious process is a recipe for emotional dysregulation, and accompanying moods of anxiety, or anxiety and depression, occur because distress is mutual and liable to continue without adequate rebalancing. This process maintains itself through ongoing disruption and failed attempts to be positive that are thwarted.

The avoidant process has a different type of low-energy schizogenesis: one that maintains splitting between the parties. The mutual orbit is distant and insufficiently close for the type of hot angry action of the anxious sort. The relationship that is shared remains at a distance. The consequences of the lack of intimate communications and positive investment between the pair are the starting point to bear in mind. The process is co-ordinated at mutual distance and excludes a positive sense of the other for this pseudo-intimacy. Rather, the process concerns avoidance, distance and defensive withdrawal, the cruelty of indifference. There is no genuine authentic communication in the avoidant whole because the other is not valued, their perspective is frequently seen as wrong or misguided, and this is why it is ignored. The immediate consequence is that there is little resolution of disputes and no forgiveness either. Because there is impaired mutual empathic failure and ongoing irresolvable disputes, there is little or no mutual influence. What this promotes is resistance to raising sensitive outstanding issues because the record of accomplishment to date is that the self's perspective is unacceptable and wrong according to the other, and vice versa. Over time, this lack of mutual empathy increases the resistance to speak about current, unresolved issues. The expectation for the future is non-achievement of resolution and refusal of the other's view as valid, so there becomes no point in attempting negotiations and no way of resolving the felt tension between them. In comparison to the other two processes commented on above, the next implication that appears is that the avoidant whole of the deactivated reactions between the pair means that some topics and their accompanying emotions are present but are unspeakable. They are banned from the shared agenda but still circulate within both persons' consciousnesses. This creates distress that must be repressed because there is no point in voicing one's distress or one's genuine perspective, because it is expected that neither will be accepted as valid. The overused remedy is to maintain distancing and the repression of felt distress. But it follows that mutual contempt and loneliness occur as a result. There are speakable, safe, and neutral topics and the accompanying emotions form a narrow band of acceptable discussion. The ambivalent senses of self and other are either valueless, defensive positivity in the face of contrary evidence, or both self and other are valued negatively. The process maintains psychological distance.

Finally, the disorganised process is like the anxious and the avoidant processes combined. There are defensive ways of dealing with distress that include performing solo activities, physically, emotionally, and mentally avoiding one's distress and that of the other. The process has high drama and frequent occurrences of strong ambivalent positive and negative senses of self and other that cannot be unified but remain as fragmented pieces that are hard to tally cohesively. Self, others, and the world do not make sense. There is no clear map of the world to negotiate, and there are ambivalent and confusing senses of the attachment figures in it.

The biopsychosocial view of attachment according to behavioural genetics

One of the most scientific experimental designs is the investigation of monozygotic twins who have been adopted and reared in different families. This is a way of comparing the strengths of nature and nurture at work (Allgulander, Nowak, & Rice, 2007; Fearon, Shmueli-Goetz, Viding, Fonagy, & Plomin, 2014). When it comes to nature and nurture as co-occurring types of cause in attachment, the biopsychosocial way of understanding is to know that the whole variance in individual differences is due to hard biological cause plus soft nurture from the shared family, peer, and neighbourhood forms of psychosocial influence around individuals. A recent summary of the behavioural genetic perspective is that attachment is only weakly heritable and the psychosocial inter-generational cause is the stronger force at work (Verhage et al., 2016). The specific influence of genetics is expressed in the idea of heritability, a numerical measure of individual differences in attachment, which is the average ratio between nature and nurture. Biological cause can, on average, be estimated by comparing the attachment processes of adopted monozygotic twins. When identical twins are raised apart, the differences between the overall social contexts are shown. For instance, in the case of intelligence, regressive analysis shows that the major factor of cause is hard biological cause; whereas soft psychosocial cause, the sum total of influence due to shared social environment, accounts for a lesser percentage of the variance. The data for attachment shows that the sum total of the meaningful psychosocial influence from context (parents, siblings, the neighbourhood, and schooling), when compared to the whole of biopsychosocial causes, indicates that psychosocial cause is strongest. It is safe to assume that the shared environment is sufficiently similar for children in the same family. This means that the amount of variation of a psychosocially expressed factor is entirely due to biological cause in the case of monozygotic twins

64   ON ATTACHMENT

who grew up apart, when divided by the total amount of variation due to all biopsychosocial causes in the "environment" (which refers to the total of epigenetic, nutritional, prenatal, and intersubjective causes of the factor). This creates a ratio of genetic cause divided by the sum total of causes (Fearon et al., 2006). This ratio is a measure of the degree of heritability of the genetic cause for the factor on average with respect to a sample.

The experimental design is genuinely scientific because the deoxyribose nucleic acid (DNA) for monozygotic twins is constant and unchanging, whereas the psychosocial components vary. This allows for the estimation of the strengths of each type of cause in relation to the total set of differences expressed in the psychosocially meaningful world. When estimations of heritability are stated, it promotes understanding of what can be achieved through psycho-education, therapy, and mental health services. The findings suggest an inevitable set of consequences for how people can be responsible for their own well-being and that of others. For adults, what follows from assertions of empirical conclusions about the relative strengths of the three types of cause operating is that each ego is responsible for itself in the sense that it is charged with the quality of its own destiny and how its uses information for its own well-being and that of its fellows. The ego can choose to accept its own genetic inheritance, and, whatever the psychosocial causes, understand itself and others sufficiently well to produce ongoing coping in social contexts. What is significant is to assume generally that the role of biological temperament also decreases as a proportion of the whole set of influences. This means that the amount of heritable vulnerability to manifest biologically caused temperament decreases with age, as the amount of positive corrective influence from the social sphere increases across the lifespan.

Conclusion

The definitions above achieve two things. The first is to bring together into one place the research findings that show empirically, in connection to intimacy and its absence, that there are four discrete patterns and processes. What these findings mean is that the social milieu around any one of these four types is made sense of in radically different ways. The point for contemporary psychology is to contemplate these findings because they indicate the full set of instances of what it is to be a

THE STANDARD INTERPRETATION AND ITS PROCESSES   65

relational being. It is the responsibility of psychology to be precise about empirical findings that suggest that there are counter-intuitive forms of being conscious and connecting with others, intersubjectively and empathically. There is potentially one unified structure of consciousness in general; and four processes occupy it and comprise an infinite continuum of vicissitudes in ways that need further research. The full spectrum to be considered includes the phenomena called repression, splitting of the ego, dissociation, psychosis, and the alterations in mood and manner of relating that suggest there are continua in responding to emotions and other meanings.

Attachment is at the heart of the psychological life, therapy, and the labour of caring and compassion in all types of mental health work. The insecure and disorganised processes are frightened and inhibited by emotions and possibilities. Only secure attachment maintains its coping balance through the ability to investigate what is really the view of the other, and deal with its own and others' distress, by making itself open to it and finding mutually corrective experiences: that is, it is self-correcting. Similarly, when there is a secure process in therapy there is discussion and relating leading to the mutual identification of inaccurate beliefs, dysfunctional habits, and faulty ways of looking at mis-empathised motivating evidence. Clients need to acquire new motivations for new actions. The half of the whole called "the client" is the one who self-discloses and receives help and caring. The half called "the therapist" is the one who leads and puts pieces of the clients' account together into an understandable pattern and interprets it to explain key motivations via attachment theory. The purpose is helping clients deal with their lives more functionally outside of the clinic. As will be seen below, applications of these ideas arise in helping clients find their own self-correcting experiences, regain their balance, and fend off other possibilities that perpetuate their distress.

The accuracy of empathy on the part of therapists, and the means by which they are able to check that empathy with their clients, keeps both on track. Therapists have maps of what should be happening. For the moment, readers should not jump to the conclusion that all is understood by presenting the process interpretation above. Rather, these assertions should be taken with a pinch of salt as regards their truth until they are empirically demonstrated. It is probably better to regard them as working hypotheses that need empirical support and require proven application, for the ultimate test of any psychological perspective is whether it predicts consistent outcomes. What psychology offers is a map of how to relate parts and wholes. Empathy provides some sense of what the other person is feeling and therapists motivate clients to act in one way or another. (Although it has to be noted that sometimes the sense empathised by both parties is inaccurate with respect to the perspective and intentions of the other). There is a need for clarity of treatment and for getting clients into positions where they can use what is being offered. Part of the skill is making sure that clients are able to tolerate the ambiguity, worry, and possible disappointment that having therapy may activate.

CHAPTER THREE

Psychodynamics, motivation, and defence

Just to look back for a moment, before progressing on to new topics, a summary needs to be made of what has been stated so far. Chapter One explained the issues that surround attachment theory. Chapter Two noted the standard interpretation of attachment as individual differences, and then commented that lived experiences of attachment concern the connection between people. This chapter concerns what Bowlby saw as the psychodynamic understanding of human being. In order to arrive at a psychodynamic understanding of attachment, in the way that Bowlby began, it is impossible to progress without understanding the type of thinking that Freud began. Bowlby's comment that IWMs are "representational models" about actual attachment figures needs to be unpacked in detail to understand what he was referring to (1980, p. 55). The comment that "psychoanalysts from Freud onwards have presented a great deal of evidence that can be best explained by supposing that it is not uncommon for an individual to operate, simultaneously, with two (or more) working models of his attachment figure(s) and two (or more) working models of himself" is a major conclusion (Bowlby, 1973, p. 238).

Because there are connections to Freud in this chapter, and in Chapter Seven on practice, then some introductory remarks are

68   ON ATTACHMENT

required to explain the selection of topics below. The sequence starts with explanations of the original definitions that support understanding attachment as meaningful motivational sequences of behaviour. Because the standard terms in this debate are frequently assumed to be clear, when in fact, they are not, it is best to explain them. Bowlby explained what he meant by considering what co-occurs with adult attachment processes.

Psychodynamics as variations in direction and across time

Psychodynamic refers to change in meaning and emotion "that describes and explains the manifestations and the consequences of the interaction of mental forces within the human being" (Weiss, 1950, p. 1). The root sense of "dynamic" just means that a quality varies across time (Ellenberger, 1970, p. 289). Psychodynamics is primarily being aware that people are motivated by experiences that are similar to what we call love, anger, and fear. Psychodynamic motivating forces create interactions between the ego and intimate others, and motivate the parts of psychological achievements of attachment. To be psychodynamic is to see that there are regular processes between people, and within them, which can be observed and discussed. Consequently, psychodynamic explanation is about representations, or better, specific links between mental processes necessary to move between various states in what are called formulations of the causative factors across time. These causative factors are the meaningful experiences that motivate the actors in any scenario to express the attachment script or IWM, to connect with the terminology of the research literature. Accordingly, to make comments on the relation between the technical terms and the lived experiences they refer to is required in order to make commentary and analyse the regularly observable processes. Such a position is called meta-representational because it requires understanding and commenting on representations, the associations of sense that are implied in the attachment processes, or indeed any defensive or coping reaction. The basic reason why people act as they do is that the dynamic movements are motivated between states that accumulate tension and let go of it. The referents of the words "tension" and "relaxation" are emotional, breathing, and bodily-based modes of meaningful relating, and are valued as good or bad.

Psychological motivations can be seen in relation to differences between states and across spans of time. These differences in meaning concern not only the actuality of the present predicament but also involve an orientation to what has been and what could be. When considering trauma and the ongoing distress that continues from it, for decades after its beginning, the difficulties at starting recovery show the long-term effects of what is counter-factual and not perceptually present. Mental distress concerns what is felt and interpreted about what exists. Anyone who had similar prior experiences would experience something similar.

What is being urged is an attention to repeating processes of distress and its management that begin at some earlier point but self-maintain over much longer periods, because they are unsoothed, undamped, and do not dissipate without intervention. The psychodynamic attention identifies, across persons' lives, the different contributory parts of the greater picture of a life that unfolds socially, in context. The psychodynamics of what happens in the secure process is that persons create around them an interpersonal field, where care and attention are freely given and received (in the direction of attending to the needs of others, and permitting care to be received). When there is a compassionate attention to self, it means that the secure self keeps itself in an optimal condition for everyday functioning. Being kind to oneself, understanding personal needs, and getting those needs met, keep the self fit to support connecting securely with others. The outcome is that not only are there secure connections with others but there is also a sense of autonomy, which manifests in the ability to explore. What is entailed is the possibility of being able to return from exploration to the welcoming arms of a secure base. In control systems terms, secure IWMs express negative feedback of the sort described in the running of the homeostasis of the physical aspects of the body, or a central heating thermostat. In the case of good mental health, security shows that the way of being in the optimal case is being able to deal with its own distress and maintain its sense of unity and connection. Differences and the potential for conflict are accepted and lessened, whilst promoting satisfaction, congruence of expression, and harmony with others, with a peaceful unity of self.

The work of the dynamic unconscious is a comparative process where two or more goals are considered, and these can be pulling in different directions, producing anxiety and tiredness, leading to depression. Those who have suffered profound trauma can find themselves becoming different selves when under stress, and need an account of

70   ON ATTACHMENT

how their personalities respond to the stress. Such experiences make little sense to the people who have them.

The idea of defence is derived from Freud's notion of *Abwehr*, used in the sense of fending off, defensive actions of the ego and its consciousness that are triggered to preserve the current state (1920g, 1923b). Defences are used purposefully and automatically, and sometimes through processes of forgetting and managing conflict. This led Freud to acknowledge that the ego obtains relief when it chooses short-term pleasure over distress (Freud, 1911b, 1915c, 1925h, 1926d). This is equivalent to what is called negative reinforcement in behavioural theory (Walker, 1984). The terminology of defensive exclusion is a way of commenting on the failures of information processing in that meanings about what is subliminally present, and potentially experience-able, somehow persistently fail to enter consciousness (Bowlby, 1980, pp. 69–70, 230–231).

Defence can be understood as attempts to prevent awareness or to break reference to any distressing object of awareness, a repeating process, such as defensively being focused on a new topic, or removing a troublesome topic from one's own view and the awareness of others (Owen, 1998). Frequently, the ego and its consciousness are involved in holding on to the good aspects of an abusive parent, and so omitting attention to what the parent did because the full realisation of the damage and the negativity of the abuse towards themselves is simply too awful to be considered. This is often why the bad memories are not thought about for decades and it is only when something changes that the bad memories resurface. There are increasing degrees of broken reference: preventable distressing objects of attention are frequently about the connections between self and others, repressively demanding the avoidance of what is felt to be unbearable. This is repeated day after day, year after year. There are a number of approaches to defence, including experimental approaches that put a cognitive stressor on participants in order to understand how they react in this condition (Baumeister, Dale, & Sommer, 1998).

Ellenberger explains that for Freud, the process of *Verdrängung*, repression, keeps a trauma unconscious, even though it is still linked to a conscious symptom (Ellenberger, 1970, pp. 497–498). The attentive reader of Freud knows that he used the term *Verdrängung* in several different ways. Briefly, repression was the more all-encompassing term, more than defence. Repression was a term first used by Breuer and

Freud to refer to the effects of their cathartic method. In brief, repression in Freud's early writing means being successful in keeping something unconscious and attempts to do so, where representation of a whole experience is banned, or appears infrequently because the attempts at banning it are intermittent in their ability, and, from time to time, show what it is that they are meant to be hiding. Often because of cultural taboos and the feeling of personal stigma, social conventions apply that demand the banning of specific representations, in a broad sense of the word representation. Most often, what is being banned are the memories and distressing experiences in the aftermath of trauma, possibly sexual abuse, violence to children, or other shocking events, where there was both the remembering and the forgetting of actions that were highly stressful, shaming, or in many other ways, anxiety and anger provoking. When the process of repression is successful, the whole object is split so that the emotion is kept stored in the physical and sensual personal body, Freud thought, while the split-off part of the original whole is forced into the general storehouse of memories, the most of which never resurface, because they are unimportant and merely about humdrum ordinary life. However, Freud and Breuer's cathartic method and the evidence of the ability of people to feel relief after remembering were important. When something traumatic was remembered and told to a professional who was external to the family, the telling of the past horror to another person was found to be genuinely healing.

So on the proviso, that the client population were young women who had suffered exposure to experiences that were genuinely unable to be discussed in polite society, then the core meaning of repression for Freud was that prior perceptions, and the ability to remember them, become unobtainable and the quality to which the original remains inaccessible is variable. When the original association of the whole perception occurred, what Freud observed was that to varying degrees, and in varying ways, the inability to remember is accompanied by varying qualities of not being able to feel, to remember bodily, or understand one's mood of anxiety and depression. The problem is that not only are the experiences confusing, but the person doubts his own identity and sanity, because he finds that his own emotional life no longer makes sense, so it becomes hard to discuss it with anyone. Furthermore, Freud believed that repression is undone when speech in a confidential relationship allows the improperly felt but unspoken events to be expressed. Breuer and Freud found that after remembering and

72   ON ATTACHMENT

expressing something horrific, the return of the understandable whole of experience provided healing through self-knowledge. The alleviation of distress occurs when the recombination of the previous parts occurs and the story is told. Repression and defence have been refined since Freud's time, because it is frequently true that past trauma can be very conscious. While repression is only one form of defence, it is worth noting how a person's ego and passive unconscious work together. The ego and consciousness have a specific type of relationship in happiness, mature coping with adversity, and otherwise managing anticipatory anxiety about uncertain outcomes in important relationships.

Rudolf Bernet, a philosopher and psychoanalyst, has done much to clarify the relations between repeating mental processes in Freud (1996, 2003). Bernet has explained repression, pushing down or pushing away, as the means by which a composite object of a conscious sort, with emotion as part of its sense, becomes separated in such a way that the ego loses parts of itself in splitting, where emotion and the visual and conceptual aspects of the original whole object get broken apart (Freud, 1915d, 1915e). When Freud wrote that the representations (the internal dialogue, speech, or memory) are repressed into the unconscious, what he meant, explains Bernet (2003), was that such previously conscious aspects become an unconscious quality of experience, in the sense that they are defensively forgotten, unwanted, or disowned by the ego and its consciousness, and this has a subliminal effect. The relation between ego and consciousness is really a partnership. Passive unconscious primary processes provide fast responses to the immediate situation in a type of participatory sense-making that includes the sensual responsiveness of the body. The most clear passive process is emotion that automatically accompanies the awareness of any object of attention, person, memory, relationship, or futural and imagined situations.

Psychodynamics of attachment

The comments above set the scene for understanding attachment. In order to understand Bowlby, it is necessary to return to the original thinking of Freud, because, in the wider view, there are two types of event occurring with respect to memory. While it is easy to assume that everything that happens is easily memorable, more broadly, the ability to remember something at will is the exception rather than the rule. For more often than not, a great deal is forgotten. The same applies to thinking through what are the comparative differences between those adults who were loved and cherished as children, and those were have been damaged in childhood and adolescence. What appears are increasing senses of breaking and fracturing, of being unable to hold together opposing tensions, and being unable to co-ordinate contrary anxieties and desires, and hold together a unified self. Problems with mood show that unity is being pulled further apart, and the ego feels increasingly split because of conflicting aims.

Bowlby rightly noted that trauma and attachment co-occur. For him, trauma causes a clear set of repeating patterns for adults, and there is further dissociative between aspects of the one person. Bowlby argued that lighter versions of dissociative moving between distress and the means of reducing it, are common for everyone in various ways. The least version of intrapsychic conflict is to feel tension between parts of oneself, because the ego can identify two opposing wishes that it has. For instance, wanting to be fit and wanting to smoke is a case where the different currents between the two parts are felt, where in extreme cases the tensions are of far greater intensity The most basic observation is to be aware of what it is to be conscious and be self-conscious: there are self-reflexive attitudes towards parts of oneself that are in opposition. Bowlby's formulation notes that attachment-related experiences necessitate a movement from non-understanding to understanding, and imply that the new, improved understanding produces a broader and stronger blossoming of attachment satisfactions.

Bowlby's ideas on defence and defensive exclusion concern a specific manner of interpreting the evidence that appears within intimacy. Defence and defensive exclusion are automatic, involuntary, and co-occur with egoic purposeful attempts to limit distress as a type of self-protection. Bowlby preferred the conclusion that splitting within the ego and its consciousness, and the tensions that it feels within parts of itself, are formulated when he refers to the work of the psychologist, Ernest Hilgard, who theorised the activities of hypnosis. Hilgard's explanation of hypnosis concerns three parts of self, which are required to change between one ego-identity and another, through a co-ordinating aspect of an implied and interpretable, hidden observer. By invoking this image, Bowlby suggests that there is the ability to move between opposing perspectives, within one person and across time. The control systems insight that Bowlby used is a way of explaining a self-maintaining bias, in that the ego and its consciousness elicit specific reactions from others

74 ON ATTACHMENT

and self maintain. Bowlby believed that the unconscious organises the repressed aspects of self, because Hilgard's (1974) explanation of hypnosis suggests that there is an automatic co-ordinating aspect of consciousness at work (Bowlby, 1980, p. 59). The psychodynamic view forwarded by Bowlby accepts Freud's idea of splitting. There are various possibilities of dynamic changes in repression and varying degrees of what Bowlby (1980, pp. 345–349) called "segregated systems", a compartmentalisation, a mental avoidance, which is part of a continuum.

It is important to discuss the combinations of insecure attachment, defence, and ego splitting in a value-free way. The explanatory worth of the observation about defensive exclusion and the *Ichspaltung* has its worth as follows. The form of *Ichspaltung* in the survivors of physical and sexual abuse account for people who experience dissociation and depersonalisation, and gain the diagnoses of personality disorder, DDNOS, and DID, who when under intense distress, feel themselves to become a different person, as a defensive reaction to stress (Freud, 1894a, 1896b, 1940e). The *Ichspaltung*, the splitting of the ego, occurs when the tension is too much to bear within one consciousness, and the result is that two egos and worlds of others appear: the senses of disparity within one ego and consciousness are replaced by two or more new unities (Bowlby, 1980, pp. 345–349; 1988, pp. 113–115). However, the same process of splitting is part of all the other cases: repression, forgetting, and voice hearing, and fragmentation of the personality into multiple senses of self. Defensive exclusion occurs where a sense of oneself, or that of another person, is omitted. However, the *Ichspaltung* works to maintain a status quo of inertia and bias. When the amount of violence received is low, defensive exclusion maintains a unified self-reflexive sense of personhood. In the situation of much higher levels of violence, which promote *Ichspaltung*, division has taken place, as exemplified by DDNOS and DID, and those cases where defence, fugue, and dissociation become extreme (Bowlby, 1980, p. 59). The strongest dissociative phenomena are present in DDNOS and DID. Dissociative splitting is most obvious after experiences of torture, multiple rape, and prolonged violence, particularly during childhood. However, full splitting is most prevalent in those cases of gross rape, abuse, maltreatment, poverty, and ineffective parenting that produce the toxic soil of poor mental health.

Bowlby specifically comments that defences include a non-phenomenon, an absence or blank within pattern-matching and identity constitution, in that there is an ability to block awareness and omit understanding others and self, to such a degree that parts of personal experience, so that the information, goes missing or fails to exist. What Bowlby asserts is that to have defences is to entail loss and the inability to experience a memory, so that the memories are unobtainable. This type of event happens when children are under stress or suffer violence, and gain the set of experiences called PTSD. In PTSD, there are presences of flashbacks and nightmares that replay what has been lived before. When overwhelm has been present for six months or a year, for instance, then there is the tendency for anxiety and defensive avoidances to produce a narrowed, overly defended lifestyle (Bowlby, 1980, p. 64). What occurs is a package of tendencies. Defence and dissociation co-occur and trauma produces a set of reliving associative stresses, long after their first occurrence.

Defence and repression as part of development

Defence as part of attachment is understood when Bowlby draws readers attention to the observation that what happens in one part of consciousness can be measurably slowed down because of a cognitive load being placed on another part. For instance, the subliminal meanings of speech can be associated with responses of hyper-vigilance to repressed traumatic memories, and subliminally mentioning distress can slow down, or interrupt, other abilities (Bowlby, 1980, p. 53). Bowlby interpreted this as evidence that the personal web of meaningful experiences is disturbed when distress is mentioned.

There are empirical views on the nature of emotion and its relation to choosing a lifestyle (Baumeister, Vohs, DeWall, & Zang, 2007). In studies that ascertained the degrees of inability to recall attachment-oriented memories, it was found that the greater the degree of avoidance, the more detail was unrecallable in an experimental parallel of attachment experience. The experimenters concluded that this was due to a failure to encode memory in the first place (Fraley & Brumbaugh, 2007). The reading made of these experiments is to take the idea of defensive exclusion as the loss of senses between self and other, and the quality of relationship between the two, as a central feature in attachment psychopathology. In order to understand properly what is being asserted, a mainstream understanding of defence needs to be cited. The *Psychodynamic Diagnostic Manual* notes four levels of mentalization in the original French sense of noting variations in the ability to avoid

76   ON ATTACHMENT

openness, to defend against accurate mental representations, and the failure to represent or mentalise what others and self feel and intend (Marty, 1991). The four levels are:

- Openness is "an optimal capacity to experience a broad range of thoughts, affects, and relationships and handles stresses with minimal use of defences that suppress or alter feelings and ideas" (PDM Task Force, 2006, p. 79).
- Defensiveness involves avoiding specific objects of attention and their accompanying emotions, memories, thoughts, ideas, and understandings such as intellectualisation, rationalisation, and repression. Reaction formation is the denial of one's own negative aspects, in order to save one's self esteem by controlling the expression of socially unacceptable impulses and personality traits, and the attempt to appear in a completely different light altogether (Fenichel, 1945, p. 146). Psychodynamics explains the worst cases of avoidance and displacement, in the sense of being a priming of frustration in one context, for instance, that is carried over and discharged in another.
- Restricted narrow lifestyles, and rigid forms of relating with others, may indicate overly defensive and habit-oriented forms of living. If there are severe restrictions, they may constitute the next higher level for defensiveness and repression. These include egoic disavowal, denial in the refusal to accept facts, the refusal to accept the actual consequences of a cause, and blaming others and contextual circumstances for one's own choices. Automatic processes include projection, splitting, and acting out. Isolation is the creation of a barrier through artificial compartmentalising to permit discussion of only one instance of a mistake (rather than the full series of them). The psychodynamics of isolation concerns prideful self-esteem that is too threatened by a full admittance of addiction, for instance, and the latest admission to rehab is claimed to be the last one (which is in fact repeated next year by a new admission).
- A strong level of defensiveness can be seen in delusional beliefs and trauma-induced psychoses. In trauma-induced psychosis, memories keep returning, and are so powerful that they require some means to deal with their accompanying emotions and meanings. Strategies such as grounding and safe-place techniques need to be employed.

PSYCHODYNAMICS, MOTIVATION, AND DEFENCE 77

What the above means is that it is possible to determine increasing qualities of the ability to reverse defence and repression, to understand and soothe oneself, given that the recovery from trauma is more difficult without help from loved ones, professionals, and the community at large. In the avoidant and disorganised processes, there is more than the disappearance, or better, an attempt to make the innate biological need to connect with others disappear. However, what is of interest is the type of self-relationship that is being enacted. Specifically, traumatised people often make harsh demands on their own abilities and put pressure on themselves that they would not apply to another person. Frequently, they make the judgement that their actions, and they themselves, are outside of the social expectations of others. This creates feelings of alienation, shame, and self-directed anger. By definition, ambivalently valued objects are both positive and negative, and consequently for self, self-identity changes to become in-part taboo, with stigma attached to it, as well as good self-esteem. It is inevitable that there is forever the likelihood of the return of the repressed, and guilt and shame, anxiety and self-reproach. Such experiences occur alongside the inner tension when the ego disapproves of a part of itself.

However, when considering the developmental view across childhood and adolescence, a variety of perspectives agree that the links between trauma and defence are the major factors in understanding attachment processes. The following two figures compare how a secure process (Figure 3.1) compares with the suboptimal and traumatised inheritance (Figure 3.2). In diagrammatic form, the figures portray the differences between psychological distresses that lead to coping and recovery (Figure 3.1) and those problems that are obscured by repression, dissociation, and defences as part of the reason why problems are maintained (Figure 3.2). The arrows below indicate where one form of sense leads to another.

For people who present themselves for professional help, what has not happened is a self-correcting re-balancing of the system. Dependent on the type and severity of impact, distress self-perpetuates. However, every time there is an expectation that there will be distress and that is disappointed, it should lead to a lowering of the estimate of the frequency that there will be distress. When corrective experiences are absent, it leads to the psychological problems becoming an accepted part of self identity and that acceptance may last for decades before the problems are properly confronted. In the case of an ongoing excessive

Figure 3.1. Good mental health sustained.

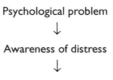

Psychological problem
↓
Awareness of distress
↓
Defensive exclusion of distress and attempts at breaking awareness of it, prevent corrective experiences
↓
Psychological problem maintained and lifestyle narrowed leading to impairment of role, self-esteem, and mood problems

Figure 3.2. Psychological problems modified by defensive exclusion maintain imbalance.

sensitivity to distress and the over-estimation of its occurrence, this leads to avoidance. In the absence of actual distress, what should happen is that relaxation returns, and confidence in the abilities to deal with the amount of real threat should increase. Specifically, all the times that expected distress is disappointed should lead to better accuracy in dealing with real uncertainty, a better estimation of the level of threat, and a better and more confident understanding of how to respond in a way that works well.

When peoples' lives are close to overwhelm, and there is a strong sense of crisis, for those who are risk averse, threatening possibilities warrant a narrow, overly defensive lifestyle. People with positive personal resources are able to create self-governed influence, even when distress and overwhelm are strong. The more general problem is that when distressed, empathy and rationality can fail, temporarily disrupting the usual responsiveness of thinking, feeling, and acting (Levenson & Ruef, 1992). A number of things happen when emotional overwhelm occurs, including increases in impulsivity, anger, and defences, and decreases in understanding causes and emotions, and lesser abilities to rationalise the distress felt and begin self-soothing. In the case of the splitting of the ego, there are two explicit sets of conscious experiences of self and other that are either absent or inaccurate. The next section considers the detail of Freud's way of looking at the psychodynamic motivations between two different points in time.

Inter-temporal choice

In Freud, the handling of short-term and long-term risks and rewards across time, falls under his interpretation of dualities, such as the pleasure and reality principles, repression, and the return of the repressed in repetitious ways, and other aspects of trying to explain irrational behaviour that is strongly motivated (1911b, 1920g, 1950a). Similarly, at the heart of attachment theory is the phenomenon of the ability to accept and understand distress, and react to it. Those who have received sufficient healing attention are able to self-soothe and soothe others.

Psychodynamically, Freud's insight was that immediate satisfaction for wishes and desires was, he thought, a mistake, and long-term solutions were always preferable (Breuer & Freud, 1895d, p. 157, p. 166; Freud, 1950a, pp. 358–359). Freud's original point was that he observed a telling opposition between short and long-term satisfactions. This formulation of the balance between desire and satisfaction, the ability to achieve and bear the frustration of non-achievement, appears in the case of erotic imagination versus gaining real, sexual satisfactions with a partner (1911b, p. 223). Another example Freud cited was that religions ask their adherents to renounce short-term pleasure in favour of the delayed gratification promised in an afterlife. Freud formulated that something similar happens in explaining different levels of commitment to education (1911b, p. 224). This same observation is generalised to understand the tension between risk and gain in the short-term, as opposed to different risks and gains in the longer-term. All these cases share the perspective contemporarily called "inter-temporal choice".

80   ON ATTACHMENT

The original intuition behind the focus on inter-temporal choice has been subjected to empirical enquiry where delayed gratification was explored. Four-year-olds were presented with a marshmallow by experimenters. They were offered a second marshmallow if they could wait fifteen minutes (Shoda, Mischel, & Peake, 1990). The experimenter left the room while the children made a decision whether to eat the one marshmallow and not wait, or to distract themselves from the immediate gratification, and get two as their reward. The experimental period continued when there was then a follow-up when they had graduated from high school, to see what their academic performance had been in the intervening years. What was discovered, twelve to fourteen years later, was that there were remarkable differences in academic performance. Those children who had been able to control themselves showed higher measures of social competence, assertiveness, and greater confidence and persistence, and better abilities to deal with frustration. However, the one third who had eaten the single marshmallow almost immediately after the experimenter had left, presented a completely different picture as adolescents later on. The immediate gratification adolescents were more avoidant of social contact, and more stubborn and indecisive. These same adolescents had lower self-esteem and were more easily upset by frustrations, more prone to envy and jealousy, expressed more anger, and were more likely to be unreactive when under stress. The students who employed delayed gratification had higher academic scores than those who could not bear short-term frustration.

The general principle is that people with distressing and traumatised meanings can respond to their emotional and meaning-related imbalance, by preferring a short-term solution to the longer-term view. There are the short-term risks and gains generated when distress is avoided. However, avoidance sustains the occurrence of further longer-term risks and gains. For instance, if there is a risk of having a panic attack on the street, then the gain afforded by avoidance of the street, means that occurrence of panic attacks is lessened. However, the consequence of such an interlocking set of beliefs is that agoraphobia may ensue as a new risk. When avoidance is repeated it makes it more difficult to go out of the home, and the ego finds then that further risks are entailed. It is irrational to want exclusively bad and damaging outcomes, yet people who self-harm, for instance, may tell themselves that they need their self-harm to go to sleep at the end of the day. The pain and bleeding are a reasonable price to pay for the benefit gained. For them, self-harm is less bad than not sleeping. Therefore, from their perspective, the meaning of the pain is not only that it distracts them away from the distress they feel, but also that it is necessary for sleep.

The short-term motivator of the possibility of limiting distress becomes a driving force for a number of defensive processes that can quickly prevent, reduce, or minimise distress in the short-term but may give rise to unintended consequences that are destructive. In the longer-term view, there is a second set of risks of the unintended consequences of short-term defensive solutions. What defensively motivates the ego is getting the quick fix of gain over the distress of hallucination, emotion, meaning, imagination, anticipation, and pessimistic conceptualisation. Freud believed that the primary gain of a psychological problem lessens anxiety and conflict, through creating a lesser problem, in preference to encountering an even worse one. Secondary gain is the relief caused from entering the sick role itself, where the ill person gains the power of weakness, through the threat of even greater weakness, which, Freud reckoned, can be used to demand that their needs should be met (Freud, 1905e, p. 44). This is a suspicious view of motivations because what it means is that if there is such success, it rewards the illness behaviour. The next section provides some more details about what happens in dissociation and the problems constitutive of DID.

The dynamic relation between the ego and its passive consciousness

Dissociative phenomena cover a wide range of experiences. Some of these are experiences of selective attention, that when the ego is focused on driving, for instance, the mind wanders to survey something else. This is not a hazard, and there can be faultless driving and extended periods of inattentiveness to the road while the driver's mind is in part engaged elsewhere. Similarly, the other types of experience that comprise the picture of dissociation within a personal history of trauma are temporary amnesias that indicate that there have been lapses in the usual felt-experience of flowing unity, temporal continuity. These include being approached by people who are not currently recognised, addressing the person in question by another name, or insisting that they have met before. One of the most frequent dissociative experiences is coming to consciousness in a new place and feeling startled because one has no memory of how one got there. Waking up in different

82   ON ATTACHMENT

clothes, and the failure to recognise people who are well known, are related indicators that there has been a change of awareness during the last few hours. Other experiences that are frequent with dissociation concern depersonalisation and derealisation, and changes in the abilities to execute tasks and roles. Another classic expression of change in awareness concerns looking at oneself in a mirror and not recognising oneself, and interpreting one's own body and self as unreal.

What Bowlby meant by "defensive exclusion" (1980, pp. 44–74) is that one or more senses, of self and of other, are not remembered when they have actually occurred. Psychologists would call this a bias, or a negative hallucination, in that something that was perceptually and empathically present leaves no accessible trace in memory. Bowlby's explanation of defensive exclusion, of senses of self and of other, is that although there are current potential distressing events, or the attachment relationship produces a threatening event, through deactivation or omission, distress does not become felt because the "link may sometimes be missing, or the wrong link be made" (Bowlby, 1980, p. 67).

One form of dissociation is when there is the spontaneous occurrence of an observing part that imagines experience outside of its body. The imagined perspective occupies an external point of view and looks down on itself, which is likely when the ego is emotionally overwhelmed. The strongest versions of the phenomena of dissociation are when persons realise that they have two or more personalities who inhabit the same body. This phenomenon, previously called "multiple personality", now DID, is well documented and has been known since the time of Pierre Janet (Ellenberger, 1970, p. 127, pp. 359–364; cf Breuer & Freud, 1895d, p. 12). Janet called it *"désagrégations psychologiques"*, a part of autonomous splitting of consciousness of the sort that happen in trauma and hypnosis.

On neurology and consciousness and in relation to meaning

In support of the idea of defensive exclusion, and associated lacks of awareness and action, this section makes contact with the message gained from the case of Sydney Bradford in neuroscience. The impact for the understanding of social life and the ability to hold contrary senses in mind is found in the parallel case of the difference between having the physical faculty of vision—and the experiences of visual object constancy and understanding of visual depth and perspective. Sydney Bradford, from Wolverhampton, UK, received corneal

PSYCHODYNAMICS, MOTIVATION, AND DEFENCE 83

implants at age fifty-two, which fully returned the vision he had lost at ten months of age (Gregory, 1998). The story that Richard Gregory tells so well is that although it was expected that surgery would successfully correct the physical structure of the cornea and give him vision, it was unexpected that it could not give him meaningful vision. Mr. Bradford was never able to understand the visual impressions of height, depth, and complexity, which did not register for him. The fact that Mr. Bradford was unable to interpret some aspects of his vision reveals a huge difference between the natural hardwiring of the brain, the eyes, nerves, and its visual cortex (as living properly functioning systems) and the lived experience of being able to understand visual meanings and impressions of object constancy. The unexpected inability of Mr. Bradford to interpret some aspects of the visual world with the acquisition of sight shows the role of implied learning. Implied learning in this sense refers to the ability to learn through play and general development that becomes an automatic part of visual perception.

However, the usual visual understanding of objects is easily taken for granted. Even after some years of exposure to the seen world, Mr. Bradford was unable to understand items at a distance, and preferred to get close and touch them in order to reassure himself that they were the same as the things that he knew by feel, when he had been blind. The understanding of perspective, distance, and the Necker Cube illusion never occurred for him, and the fact that things get dirty and tatty after use was unexpected and depressing. Similarly, it is possible that although, as in the case of Mr. Bradford, the hardware is working, people with attachment problems may not be able to interpret and understand some aspects of social life.

The implication of the case of Mr. Bradford for attachment is the possibility that in the learning of the IWM in childhood some shared objective meanings about intimacy and distance, its difficulties and its successes, may not occur. In parallel to learning visual meaning, the psychological learning of shared attachment understandings must also play a role in making mutual understanding. The telling insight is to understand that for the successful enactment of attachment, a communicational code has to be shared between persons. The social unconscious makes itself apparent when expectations are momentarily broken, when something attachment-oriented is assumed by one person in the relationship, and not other. When attachment processes are shared between two people, they operate seamlessly when one process is occurring. For processes to

84　ON ATTACHMENT

be mutual, both parties must be co-ordinated, in that the bids of one are responded to by the complementary and confirming responses of the other. Thus, attachment processes are acquired and maintained codes of communication that share references between self and other in compatible ways, which ensure the co-ordination of shared scripts.

Closing discussion

The strong point of the all-inclusive psychodynamic view is that it makes clear that we all occupy a place within the spectrum of forms of damage received and how to respond to them. There are continua of splitting and repression, awareness and defence, association and dissociation. Humans live with compartmentalisation and felt tensions, due to varying conflicting motives, through to dissociation and DID. The problems of discord and loss of the senses vary but exemplify the defensive purpose of pre-empting anticipated negative events, by switching between parts of itself, and altering relations between others. What happens across all versions and severities of repression and defence concerns problematic loss of control brought about through being emotionally overloaded. This impairs functioning of the basic abilities to be a parent, to work, and leave the home and function.

Defence for Freud was connected to the tripartite view of the relation between aspects of the ego, superego, and its consciousness. The ego, originally *das Ich* in Freud, is the "I" who "is part of consciousness and controls perception and motility ... is a self-preservation drive ... is a reservoir of libido ... is the cause of repression ... conforms to reality, is to some extent identical with the reality principle ... a reaction to the drives it constitutes the basis for character formation [and] carries out reality testing" (Wyss, 1966, p. 121). The "I" is subjectivity and refers to the choosing and deliberate aspect of consciousness, and the self-reflexive relation that people have with themselves. Various types of self-reflexive relationship can be noted. These include guilt, which has the function of making the ego act more socially appropriately in the future. Shame has the function of an inhibition, to maintain limitation and avoidance. When considering the possibility of opposing forces that prevent distress co-occurring, one combination is the state where there are two hypotheses: persistent self-doubt and lack of confidence can exist in the face of abundant evidence of positive abilities. How persons appear to themselves can be explained through an inability to recall those experiences of the self's sufficient performance; and a persistent inability to trust others and believe they are emotionally available can be explained by a similar inability to retain positive empathised feelings about them, their perspective, and intentions, even when persons did act and feel positively about the self, and openly said so.

It is worthwhile to note that people frequently treat themselves in a far harsher way than they would treat their friends and loved ones. The *Über-Ich*, superego, is the introjection of familial and cultural norms where "a child's super-ego is in fact constructed on the model not of its parents but of its parent's super-ego; the contents which fill it are the same and it becomes the vehicle of tradition and of all time-resisting judgements of value which have propagated themselves in this manner from generation to generation" (Freud, 1933a, p. 67). Most people want to do well, and conscience can drive excessively high standards, which cannot be attained and produce tension. However, the point about the superego is contemporarily best related to the wider sense of self-awareness in relation to the sense of self, for a potential audience of others, in what is called the Dunning-Kruger effect. This can be summarised as the general principle that persons who are more self-critical and self-aware have higher standards for their own comportment, whereas those who are less self-aware, and have lower standards, are blissfully unaware of their low performance (Kruger & Dunning, 1999). Accordingly, the superego is obviously manifest in those who have high standards for themselves, who are bound up with improving their own reputations in their communities, to the detriment of authentic understanding and relating.

Within Bowlby's thought, there is a genuine attention to the phenomena that are manifest between people and continue to exist across time. When there is violence, the aftermath concerns how to make a recovery from a negative impact that makes people become more fragmented and tense, until they can no longer bear the opposing currents, and are taken to breaking point, literally. There is the intention to honour the actuality of traumatic experiences by understanding that the more violence people have suffered, the more fluid they can feel themselves to be. In addition, one of the main dimensions of understanding is to note how strongly the memories and distress reappear in intrusive imagery, body sensation, and other experiences, the majority of which never get voiced. However, it is safe to assume that talking about distress is only one way of incorporating it into the greater weave of life.

86   ON ATTACHMENT

Defences begin as mixtures of active choices, values, aims, and decisions, plus passive automatic pre-emptive absence of anxiety and distress. These are repeated so they become automatic. Lived experiences of attachment are embedded in the ordinary cloth of experiences that unfold across contexts of time and perspective. Bowlby believed that what gets excluded and repressed are meanings, and that all processes of tension, shared by unified selves and traumatised dissociated selves, have the same basic shape. The same forms of dissociation in consciousness is shared across humanity, but most easily noticed in the clinical picture of the survivors of violence and trauma. There are very many of these and it would not help to exclude anyone from the full family of resemblances concerning what can be called PTSD in personal development. All instances of the attachment processes co-occur within a form that is immutable. The unifying schema across secure individuals, disorganisation in the intimate life, DID, and psychosis, is that we are all created out of a number of parts. In addition, to speak metaphorically, the orchestra of parts can be fully in tune or not, as the case may be.

The splitting of the ego and its consciousness, across time periods, and between increasingly disparate aspects of the self, is common to all people alike. The commonality is that all share the quality of experiencing felt tensions and frustrations between self and others, and within personal experience. In a sense, others are always with us, they are always in expectations and memories, no matter the quality of what actually happened between us. In short, a psychodynamic approach notes that everyone is split, and distributed across space and time and between people. What differs is that there are different types of being split, which have different emphases. The purpose of the detailed route is to appreciate the details of the sections above, and adopt the psychodynamic understanding of attachment, for various pursuits. The meaning of "defensive exclusion" (Bowlby, 1980, p. 45), not remembering experiences between oneself and others, plays out in many ways. Bowlby's ideas on the psychodynamics of repression and the operation of various sorts of defence need to be made clear in relation to the IWM as the assimilation, or introjection, of what is taken as a model to act and feel in future relationships (Pallini & Barcaccia, 2014). An equivalent interpretation of the same experience is a generalisation: learning from observable relationships makes a role model of how to be (Fairbairn, 1952), which is a social learning that can be represented as a number of specific self-other connections.

Conclusion

Neuroticism and trauma-induced psychoticism are perfectly normal reactions to violence. Human being splits when it is faced with genuinely unbearable tension. In the strongest cases, the dynamic unconscious enacts two or more egos rather than one: the horror of what happened then, and what is happening now, cannot be held together. However, all lesser instances share a similar tendency when the fragmented multiple parts of a unified ego alter their relationship to manage or prevent something being felt. In the cases of the greatest violence, the usual sense of being a single cohesive person, with inner tensions, produces splitting in the ego, to become two or more egos: in this way trauma indicates the maximum extent of how one ego and consciousness can become fragmented. The spectrum of instances of the increasing effects of violence is witnessed most visibly in the effects of physical and sexual violence on children who seek help as teenagers and adults. The key to understanding increases in vulnerability is to note greater sensitivity to distress, and to increasing difficulties in receiving self- and other-oriented emotional regulation. Attachment processes show changes in increasing damage that are apparent when detailed attention is given to the onset of relationship problems and the full range of psychological difficulties. Good mental health is the generation of positive psychological capital, that is, reasons to be cheerful due to one's satisfactions with others, and the relative absence of negative experiences of psychological poverty.

The consequences for therapy are that approaches to personality and psychological problems need corrective experiences of recovery where the ego learns how to steer towards its own chosen destiny, as it sails across the stormy waters of life. What therapy should provide is a "corrective experience" to "undo the effect of the old" (Alexander & French, 1946, p. 23). This is read as meaning that experiential antidotes reduce distress, broaden the lifestyle, and manifest potential in achieving the good life. The good life means establishing balance and being able to look back over a life well spent, and having plenty of attachment satisfactions to contemplate.

For epistemological reasons there is something unsettling about Bowlby's propositions. Bowlby encouraged experimentalists and practitioners to entertain a lack, where there could be intimate connection, and accept explanations of lack, loss, and failure to experience something that those who had secure childhoods readily do. Value and gratitude rest on learning from reflection and analysis, and being able to apply corrective experience that is tailored and works. The observation is that despite being capable of rationality, the human being is most often irrationally motivated by emotional representations that could be better managed. The balance between ego and consciousness (including its primary unconscious processes) can be stuck where the motivation towards secure attachment with others is caught in varying demands, fear, and rejection, in confusing ways. However, the good news is that it is possible for the ego to struggle with its conscience and promote satisfaction of its attachment drive.

PART II

THE ROLE OF ATTACHMENT IN REDUCING DISTRESS

Introduction to Part II

This part explains a manner of interpreting attachment phenomena as processes in relation to the theory and skills of emotional regulation for self and others. It argues for formulating specific relationships between psychological processes and objects. It is important for theory to express qualitative phenomena accurately and experimental methods also force the sharing of conceptual validation and justification. Attachment explains lived experience and the developmental influences of the past that propel the current emotions and forms of relating in self-perpetuating ways. Attachment has existed since mammalian life began. Good parenting has also been manifest in past generations who produced secure intimate relating regardless of being able to identify its current empirical definition. However, since Bowlby and Ainsworth made the implicit explicit, it has become possible to specify the previously tacit processes and emotional regulation that exist in pre-reflexive understanding, and therefore it becomes possible to respond consciously to problems of intimacy and distress. Whether the responses are tender and timely, or come with hatred and violence, intimate responding is based on the model of the parenting received. To say that attachment was unconscious and now is conscious misses the point that it is possible to do something without knowing in detail how oneself has come to learn and achieve it. It is just obvious to a person who habitually provides secure parenting how to look after children, for instance. They have seen it demonstrated and it is the norm.

To discuss these matters further, Chapter Four makes some basic comments about what is revealed when attachment is understood as a qualitative phenomenon. Chapter Five discusses emotional regulation between self and others. Chapter Six explains a control systems theory view of distress and mental health.

CHAPTER FOUR

Meta-representation and motivation

This chapter makes theoretical remarks on what it self-reflexively means to know the necessary conditions of what it is to feel, relate, imagine and be aware of attachment between people. Understanding any psychological process requires detailing the links to objects of attention to understand how something is problematic, know where the emotions and meanings come from and explain them. To do this, the importance of meta-representational accounts of psychological experience is explained. Bowlby held that "the brain builds up working models of its environment but that in order to understand human behaviour it is difficult to do without such a hypothesis" (1969, p. 81). The working model is an explanation about the setting of self-relating with others made from influential attachment experiences. In order to explain the consequence of the idea of mental modelling or mapping in this way, the first task is to set the scene and introduce motivation to act and meta-representation between implicit choices in attachment. One thread that runs through the chapter is the need to be clear and formulate the meaningful and observable aspects of the processes between two persons in an attachment relationship. The two halves of the whole enacted by self and other are co-ordinated to produce one process. In order for one process to occur in a goal-corrected partnership, there

94   ON ATTACHMENT

is mutuality, working together in a collaborative way to create what happens between the pair. Similarly, in therapy and more generally, when two people share a goal, the same process can exist for both of them and be co-ordinated between them. If this were not the case, there would be conflict because a common goal had not be agreed and there would be a tension with confusion and conflict occurring.

Attachment requires synchrony and simultaneity of the various forces in the relationship. The same code of verbal and nonverbal total communication of a process is enacted and properly co-ordinated between participants. Given that attachment is important psychologically, then the task is to be precise about what the connections are and understanding the conditions in which processes remain the same or change. Although there can be automatic changes in the dynamic, it is the case that relationships with specific others tend to find their own level.

Defining meta-representation

Meta-representation is the "ability to represent the *representing relation itself*" (Pylyshyn, 1978, p. 593, original italics). "Meta" means about, so meta-representation means being able to discuss and specify how objects, for consciousness and its unconscious processes, are apparent in any instance. For instance, meta-representation of attachment occurs in any discussion of the relationships between an IWM map and its territory. A focus on understanding meta-representation means a self-reflexive ability to understand the different ways that the processes and objects of attachment appear in multiple manners of being aware, some of which are emotion, behaviour, attachment relationships, fixed format experiments, or film. The point of having a technical term for this awareness is that it pinpoints what happens and can specify how an IWM is linked to implicit and unconscious mental processes. Meta-representation necessitates the formal ability to reflect and compare different perspectives on the cognition and affect of self and of others that begins at approximately four years of age, where children understand and can explain *how* they know that others believe something mistakenly (Perner, 1991, p. 92). It supports the ability to hold in mind implicit differences, and explain how another has false beliefs. For instance, how it is possible to judge between one experience of Mummy as angry with me as opposed to how Mummy usually is with me, a distinction between one sense of the other person and how she is more generally.

Meta-representation marks how persons can change their perspective through experiencing, and explains, for instance, how observable behaviour can be based on a false belief. Similarly, attachment comparatively shows different types of wholeness in its four processes. This is also a meta-representational achievement simply because the constituent parts, self, other, and their relationship, are being discussed. One informative way of thinking like this is to account for the differences between times past, present, and future in order to find out about the links that lie there.

Meta-representation is the ability to understand understanding itself: different forms of awareness give multiple senses of the same objects of attention and the processes between people (Perner, 1991, p. 6, p. 40). The abstract terminology covers a large number of specific possibilities. The media from which meta-representation can occur are thought, emotion, observable behaviour, discussion, writing, or symbolic diagramming, for instance. Meta-representation is based on the ability to be aware of mental sense and the forms of mental processes employed. Associated terms are meta-cognition, awareness about awareness, reflection, and mentalization. When one form of awareness is directed towards another, understanding the intentional relationship leads to "being able to reflect on validity, nature, and source" of mental representations and pre-reflexive presences (Main, 1991, p. 128). The meta-representation of attachment concerns comparing its forms in theoretical explanations. Thinking something about what oneself feels, or feeling something about what another person can imagine, are two examples, although there are very many other possibilities. Meta-representation is part of the ability to be psychologically minded and read others and oneself as being motivated by emotion, and meaning. Meta-representation involves the ability to empathise what motivates and causes others to act as they move between different psychological states.

Meta-representation in attachment identifies specific relations of mental processes in relation to varying senses of an object. For instance, care-seeking and care-giving share a goal when the reactions to each other occupy the same set of emotional and relational processes. The attachment dynamic is shared when the goal of the motivational sequence of the current behaviour is the same for both persons, by

96   ON ATTACHMENT

assumption or by explicit agreement. Once this is achieved, it becomes possible to compare formally how different psychological situations are given sense according to different attitudes of approach to them. Meta-representation involves meta-cognition that happens when any explicitly conscious senses are compared about the same object. In short, being aware and reflecting on one's own experience, or that of others, forms the basics of a qualitatively based study of representation itself. This is a way of stating some fundamentals that inevitably concern interpreting the mental, emotional, and other types of lived experience that people inhabit.

People are, to some degree, able to reflect on their own experiences and understand themselves through being self-reflexive and self-aware. However, the ubiquity of what is being identified in the term meta-representation is more extensive. Iso Kern and Eduard Marbach define meta-representation in the case of pictures, for instance, as understanding that "an externally perceived picture or model as a simple object *represents* (dasrstellt) something in a certain way, and to understand that another person as another subject represents something in a certain way, namely *figuring or representing something to herself* (sich etwas vorstellen), would seem to be rather different modes of consciousness" (2001, p. 75, original italics). Kern and Marbach are referring to the fundamental ability to empathise persons and their psychosocial objects, and refer to processes between people. For instance, empathy represents what others' views of objects are and it is due to previous social learning across the personal history. Specifically, in thinking and communicating about attachment, the constituent elements of varying senses of self, other, and the relation between them, get frozen in time with early set points often having dominance over current actuality.

Children above three years of age begin to be able to judge that other persons can be motivated in different ways (Perner, 1991, p. 87). This is a developmental achievement that supports the understanding of multiple perspectives on the same thing and involves the means of choosing between alternative actions and outcomes. For instance, a meta-representational account identifies how current and merely possible scenarios are presented in terms of the psychodynamic relation between the ego, its passive or anonymous emotional syntheses that automatically make emotional representations, and the emotions felt about something. Considering the aims of defences reveals some telling differences between the ego and consciousness as a whole.

META-REPRESENTATION AND MOTIVATION 97

Psychodynamic pushes and pulls *in general* need to be made explicit because comparisons between actual and merely possible counterfactual states of affairs are how individuals navigate each other and the shared world. What enables describing and explaining the manifestations and consequences is meta-representation. There is a necessity to account for one's own ability to self-consciously know how psychological explanations are made and can be retold differently, or be told through different forms of communication altogether. Interaction is due to psychological processes with respect to meaning within the caring of intimate relationships. The point is that whilst psychologically minded, emotionally intelligent persons have the innate ability to empathise others and grasp their directedness towards the objects of their attention, meta-representation is the formal and explicit ability to reflect, analyse, and contrast these senses.

Meta-representation across time

Meta-representation of two different outcomes, at sooner and later times, holding both outcomes in mind, is how decision-making is achieved. Inter-temporal choice demands the meta-representation of short-term fixes as opposed to long-term rewards where the latter often require calmness and dedication to achieve a more skilled and less conflicted outcome, as Freud knew well (1911b). Control theory is the leading model for emotional regulation, to understand the inner working of the ego and its consciousness where there can be conflict in knowing how to deal with a variety of options. Exemplary cases of meta-representation occur in the inter-temporal choice between a quick fix of pleasure or distraction at time one, the short-term, as opposed to the delayed gratification of longer-term adaptation, at time two. Short-term fixes deliver a quick reward but incur cost and risk. Examples are activities such as smoking and drinking to receive pleasure and cheer oneself up despite the inevitable consequences and risks involved. To choose the short-term fix is to prefer instant rewards to longer-term risks and costs. In general terms, the positive function of short-term fixes is that the ego enacts the defensive fast option to gain pleasure or reward itself through avoidance, a negative reinforcement.

Freud hypothesised pairs of opposed tendencies in an effort to theorise how objects can come into and move out of conscious apprehension. Within the pages of "Formulations on the two principles of

98   ON ATTACHMENT

mental functioning" (1911b), he claimed that neurosis and psychosis are defences away from perceptual reality. The primary process of self-gratification begins in infancy, and through time children learn to live within their limits. However, across years of maturation adults should come to know that to make real change requires sustained effort in the real world. This pragmatic observation is at the root of his theoretical tension between the pleasure ego, who wishes and gains satisfaction by imagining satisfaction now, as opposed to the reality ego who strives for usefulness and protects itself in the long run. Any decisions that provide short-term relief rather than addressing root causes, and the best interests of the individual-in-relationship, are related to how problems are generalised across the domains of life, potentially producing greater imbalance, with knock-on effects for mood and self-esteem. However, distress, repressed memories, and representations sometimes cannot be permanently repressed and, from time to time, the dreaded event occurs. Freud argued that while the memorial representations are stored away, they might from time to time reappear in consciousness in connection with new emotions, whilst the previously conscious emotion contributes to mood problems (1915d, pp. 154–156). Such variability in containing and not expressing distress is a genuine phenomenon. However, the direction of the cure is to value an outcome sufficiently to commit to long-term satisfactions, and cope with their non-achievement and frustration along the way, in order to make socially acceptable satisfactions through work, effort, and self-management (Freud, 1926d, p. 159). Therefore, the direction of the cure is towards *decreasing* childish satisfactions, the daydreams of narcissistic and short-term pleasure through quick fixes, and the schizoid use of the imagination, for instance. The moral of Freud's cure is that the way to sublimation and the actualisation of a person's potential inevitably requires delayed gratification that is synonymous with maturity.

The negatives involved in defensive choices are the valuing of short-term relief over delayed gratification and may be linked to emotional reasoning. One variety of emotional reasoning is "I feel like pleasure therefore I will have it", or other versions of "Because I feel ___ I will not do ___", and many others. Problems occur when the ego identifies itself fully with how it feels or makes rules about how to behave when, for instance, it feels distress. This is another situation where it is required to go further into the wholes of experiential evidence that are contained within attachment. Emotions are bodily felt and can become conscious senses of objects of attention, irrespective of whether there is a current perceptual object present or not. Some aspects of attachment function in relation to wholly imagined, anticipated, or remembered senses that are available to no one else. What appears is that emotions can be used to set rules for behaviour. In emotional avoidance, it can be a preference to avoid the possibility of distress and showing that one feels it to others. Distress leads to behavioural aversion, whereas positive desiring leads to seeking something out. The closeness of belief and emotion, particularly in small children, means that emotional reasoning exists, such that feeling something (such as induced shame about oneself and one's needs) stands out as implicit beliefs about how the person should act in intimate relationships. The idea of emotional reasoning is that the felt-motivations towards something genuinely gratifying, and away from something genuinely worthy of avoidance, is that emotions are often by far the most important factor in how decisions to act are made. When there is felt distress in association to some current or possible state of affairs, then the choice to avoid that distress can be the only factor used in assessing how a decision is made. The negative consequences of smoking and drinking are well known and there can be no attention given to the negative triggering of distress that begins a motivational sequence of attachment or defensive behaviour. There is a medium-term cost of a hangover from drinking too much, and also the longer-term problem of addiction; if many hangovers do not lead to a change in behaviour and problem-solving, then the medium-term negative consequence of hangovers is accepted as a reasonable price to pay for the short-term outcome of relief provided.

Another example that involves meta-representation occurs where the ego acts through an inaccurate understanding of its own needs as regards its physical and mental health. If an ego chooses to let go of its self-control, and discount its highly desirable future of delayed gratification in favour of the short-term fix, then this type of choosing with active and passive aspects, needs proper understanding. The point is that it is still a matter of interpretation to work out to what extent the avoidant and reinforcing aspects of the personality in addictions are due to the pleasure-based activities of drinking and drug taking, for instance; or whether they are defensive due to trauma in the personal history; or whether there are other motivating factors that mean the balance-setting is stuck in an unhealthy way, where there are more risks than benefits. Often logic is not being applied to problem-solve and

100 ON ATTACHMENT

work persistently to redress the balance towards well-being. What these examples show is the importance of differential diagnosis of distress by using concepts about experiences to interpret unique combinations of imbalance and disharmony, in meaningful and experiential ways.

Meta-representationally, there is a progression through the four types of attachment. In pro-social secure processes, there is the tendency to be accurate in the interpretation of self (insight or self-understanding) and of empathy, and feel safe and secure. In the anxious process, there is protest, anger, and demand, when the focus is an anticipatorily empathised distance or disconnection from the carer. In avoidant process, the brakes are on to prevent connection because it is anticipated to be disappointing and, hence, the self's desire for care is repressed. In the disorganised process, there is disarray and changeability, which are the means of managing what does and might happen. The sorts of psychological objects pertinent to attachment are fundamental experiences of recognising the following forms of meaning as they happen.

- When there has been actual threat to the well-being of self, from infancy onwards, right across the lifespan, the insecure and disorganised processes are likely to form. Insecure care-giving in itself is likely to promote emotional dysregulation, with the unmet attachment needs of children affecting adolescents and adults.
- When distress is felt due to a sense of threat, recognising if a valued attachment figure is available to help is functional. This is someone who is well known and who has superior skills (in the case of infants), or who is a peer (in the case of adults), who is wise, sympathetic, and helpful. If no other person is available, then memories and inner resources of positive experiences can be brought to mind as examples of how to deal with emotions, problem-solve, and act in the current situation. Secure care-giving in childhood provides the legacy of emotional regulation for later adulthood.
- When attachment figures are close, a key phenomenon is recognising whether they are emotionally represented to be psychologically available (in the sense that they are empathised as being able and willing to provide contact, or succour of some sort), which would ordinarily lead to satisfying psychological contact with them (or not, as the case may be).

However, some natural causes of psychological problems are irreversible, such as the physical effects of ageing on the brain and the biochemistry of the body. In the biological register, the medical model is apt. However, the proper understanding of any intersubjective context requires a view of the common set of characteristics of what happens between any two people, to be used as a template to notice other differences and similarities. Naturalistic explanations differ from psychological ones because they specify natural causes. In recent years, there has been enthusiasm for explanation involving mirror neurons that goes beyond the function they have neurologically (Heyes, 2010a, 2010b). Psychological explanations specify how motivations to do x are preferred over doing y via comparing thoughts, feelings, and behaviours, and are recognisable by the public, theoreticians, researchers, and practitioners in their own experience, and comprise a starting point for empirical interventions. Psychological explanations of both problems and answers involve meta-representation.

Motivational sequences as the behavioural outcome of meta-representational comparisons across time

Rather than maintain an abstract level of attention, a few examples are required to explain specific cases. Psychological change is not just about beliefs or merely about behaviours. In a wholistic attention, the pieces of the whole are ways of living that cause an imbalance to remain. If the whole under consideration is the ego plus its future anticipations, then the relationship that the ego creates with its own future is one where it could imagine a worried catastrophic future full of mistakes and difficulties. If so, then consciousness automatically responds with emotions of anxiety and depression that could result in impairment of the ego, in its ability to function. If the ego is anxious and reads this emotion as requiring defences to protect itself, then it avoids or overuses defences to protect its comfort zone. This is an overly defensive response that promotes its own classical conditioning of anxiety with its psychological objects and rewards itself through the negative reinforcement of avoidance of distress (when it should be doing the opposite of coping, tolerating distress, and recovering).

One way of getting a grasp of attachment problems is to ask oneself where such problems and resources are located. The answer provided below emphasises that the defensive insecure processes that persons overuse are indeed individual differences enacted in triggering contexts; and developmentally, the problems are driven through memories, anticipations, habits of sense-making, and overused skills that

102　ON ATTACHMENT

come from past contexts of childhood and the family of origin, where damage occurred. Current attachment problems are located between the learning that is played out socially in the current moment and socially acquired learning that has engraved an IWM on the individual's heart. Discussion promotes reflection and highlights key psychological objects and processes in the lives of clients.

Let us take attachment as it is lived. The automatic quality of emotion that influences the ego is involved in beginning motivational sequences of meaningful behaviour in relation to others. Contrary to the general conclusion in developmental psychology that meta-representation begins in the fourth year (Perner, 1991, p. 88), it seems that attachment is an automatic process that makes distinctions about emotional communication and beliefs about the caring received before the explicit ability to indicate true from false beliefs. From six months of age, prior to the child's ability to meta-represent explicitly, attachment research suggests that meta-representation is taking place but that it operates at a level that does not involve the infant's ability to choose. Meta-representation in attachment exists because the insecure forms bear a relation to the secure base phenomenon even though they cannot achieve it. Infants know what to expect and alter their behaviour and communicational expressiveness accordingly, so much so that it becomes a generalised way of dealing with their needs with respect to care-seeking. The automatic quality of emotional connections between experiences is that associations of motivation, action, and sense, are forms of conditioning that connect pieces of the whole in the four characteristic patterns. Infants become adults who have early IWMs within their repertoire of responses.

Internal working models

IWMs are maps of relational habit, belief, and emotional understanding about the psychological world, a set of representations of care and self-other interactions (in memory, pre-reflexive retained influence, and habits of thought, emotion, anticipation and relating). The metaphor of maps of an attachment world, starting with the family of origin, is a means of formulating the influences in contemporary here-and-now relationships. The four forms of IWMs describe the phenomena of the pre-reflexive habit of seeking intimacy (or not) according to memories

META-REPRESENTATION AND MOTIVATION   103

of the senses of self and other, and the relation between the two. It also
has to be noted that Bowlby was wary of using the idea of a map for
referring to the type of modelling because he was afraid that it conveyed
the image of a reified ability incapable of being updated, when in fact
they can be updated (Bowlby, 1969, p. 80, p. 112). Meta-representation
is involved in mental modelling and it has to be noted that Freud concluded on the same in his last work, *An Outline of Psycho-Analysis*:

> The yield brought to light by scientific work from our primary sense
> perceptions will consist in an insight into connections and depend-
> ent relations which are present in our external world, which can
> somehow be reliably reproduced or reflected in the internal world
> of our thought and a knowledge of which enables us to "under-
> stand" something in the external world, to foresee it and possibly
> alter it … we infer a number of processes, which are in themselves
> "unknowable" and interpolate them in those that are conscious
> to us. And if, for instance, we say: "At this point an unconscious
> memory intervened", what that means is: "At this point something
> occurred of which we are totally unable to form a conception, but
> which, if it had entered our consciousness, could only have been
> described in such and such a way." (Freud, 1940a, pp. 196–197)

The passage is a place where the motivational model of the world of
self-other relations is noted. Something similar is at the root of the idea
of the IWM concerning the relationship between the "inner world"
of the mind in the "outer world" of social reality noted by Bowlby. In
attachment theory, the guiding idea behind Bowlby's use of "model"
came from the philosopher Kenneth Craik who posited that the territory mapped is a general one as to how to understand the new, in terms
of the already understood. "By a model we thus mean any physical or
chemical system which has a similar relation-structure to that of the
process it imitates" (Craik, 1943, p. 51). By "relation-structure", Craik
meant, "the fact that it is a physical working model which works in the
same way as the process it parallels" (1943, p. 51). And in the general
discussion of how the consciousness of any animal can model reality, it
appears as though "the organism carries a 'small-scale model' of external reality and of its own possible actions within its head … it is able to
try out various alternatives, conclude which is the best of them, react to

104   ON ATTACHMENT

future situations before they arise, utilise the knowledge of past events in dealing with the present and future, and in every way to react in a much fuller, safer, and more competent manner to the emergencies which face it" (1943, p. 61). Craik's understanding of maps of the world was the forerunner of Bowlby's idea of the IWM that represents childhood actuality (Bowlby, 1969, pp. 81–82, p. 354; 1973, pp. 241–243, p. 418), and the development of multiple models of interaction with respect to the same relationship (Bowlby, 1973, pp. 237–241, pp. 361–63). Understanding that there can be multiple possible understandings of the same situation aids comparison between the secure and the insecure patterns and highlights their different ways of attending to evidence.

The explanatory idea of an IWM is the model for self and other connections to be understood when making emotional sense of self and of others currently. The phenomena described by attachment theory include the tendency of children and adults to rely on the generalisations of how to get help, in the context of how they emotionally represent their world. In the secure process, care is supplied until satisfaction is gained; as Bowlby put it, the "conditions that terminate the behaviour vary according to the intensity of arousal" (1988, p. 3). The naturalistic tendency in attachment theorising is to link publicly observable phenomena to the view of Darwin's ideas of evolution as biologically caused. Whilst this is the naturalistic view and acceptable (with some stipulations), the problem is that it does not tend towards defining the phenomena as psychological processes, and explicating them in relation to the psychological objects of recognisable interactions. Ultimately, what researchers and therapists want is proven theoretical understanding to formulate attachment problems and understand the conditions of possibility of change. Ellenberger is clear in stating that it was Freud who began the developmental formulation that childhood makes the adult (1970, pp. 489–491). The distal onset of psychological causes in childhood and the family of origin leaves its mark in beliefs, and emotional triggers. Attachment is a substantive influence that produces the adult intimate lifestyle of relationships with partner, children, and parents, and affects family and friends where mood, self-esteem, personality, and psychological problems co-exist with the person's successes in life. Figure 4.1 summarises the most general set of causes from the past into the present in the making of any IWM.

However, one reading of the evidence on divorce, loneliness, and lack of purpose is to note that unmet attachment needs cannot be fulfilled

META-REPRESENTATION AND MOTIVATION   105

Distal onset of an attachment IWM pattern with distressing associations of sense
↓
Current trigger or triggers create distress and prime attachment needs with
effects on mood and self-esteem, and inhibit exploration
↓
In adulthood if there is a current secure base then contacting it and
its learnings decreases distress and increases problem solving.
(But if there is no current secure base nor the ability to access personal
secure resources, then distress and defences operate in recurrences of the
insecure process and its emotional associations impair functioning in
a variety of contexts.)

Figure 4.1. The intentional relationship between distal causes of attachment problems and contemporary triggers and processes.

through any other means. Problems of emotional regulation, and an excessive sensitivity to upset, are caused through the laying down of habits and beliefs across the lifespan that are recalled as signifiers of personal identity (Ellenberger, 1970, pp. 489–500).

Meta-representation of motivational sequences in attachment

Experiences with psychological objects can be mapped through ideas of motivation (Husserl, 1989, p. 241, p. 243). Let us take the example of individuals who are prone to the anxious process. When they encounter stress, they easily feel over-stimulated, emotionally dysregulated, and there may be persistently ineffective attempts from others to soothe and emotionally regulate them. Persons who have the tendency towards anxiety are highly sensitive to distress. If it is too easy to be in contact with past relationship pain and disappointment, then current conflict with another can easily promote the remembering of past distress. Anxious process is where self actively resists caring at times, being indifferent to positive approaches from others whilst expressing neediness; they protest at real and merely interpreted lacks in caring, for they can believe that they are not being cared for when they are. Hence, the anxious process concerns the back and forth motions towards others and trying to unify ambivalent senses of self and others accordingly. Specifically, the ambivalent doubling refers to a needy, demanding, self seeking contact, plus a rejecting, angry self refusing contact.

106   ON ATTACHMENT

For adults, avoidant process has ambivalence when there is the occasional permitting of closeness, although letting others be close is itself a source of anxiety and self-doubt. The beliefs of the avoidant process expect others to be unresponsive, unavailable, or invasive. This produces self-containment, the repression of attachment-related emotions and experiences. Inhibitions create a low investment in keeping away from others for fear of disappointment. The failure to approach others intimately appears in comparison with the other forms, and provides some clues as to how psychological distance is maintained.

For disorganised attachment, though the patterns are more complex in that there is sudden, and sometimes simultaneously expressed, attraction and repulsion: freeze, fight, or flight. Also, because the meta-representational ability is not fully formed at an intellectual level until about four years old (Perner, 1991, pp. 82–102), it is not always clear how these influences get summated in childhood or in later years, when young adults leave home and live outside of the usual family influence (Carlson, 1998).

However, leaving home for the first time can show a young person's map of the world clearly, because the territory has changed and they use the old model in the new context, where it may not suffice. The change to adulthood is noticeable because that is when the map of the world needs updating. When children become adults and leave home, they are taking their old map of how to be attached, to a new psychological territory. So there is plenty of scope in this transition to find evidence to show how it no longer fits the new territory. The maps of the world of the lived experiences that are currently understood are unique in the sense that there are many variations in the transient variables with other identifiable permutations. People have their individual maps of the world, their social learning, and their mixture of contributing variably, which communicate and express their way of living. The social learning comprises the IWM map that begins with attachment in the family, or families of origin, at around six months of age.

Individuals carry within them their stylised map and consult it when automatically engaging or egoically making explicit decisions in higher secondary-process thinking. When stressed, it is more likely that there is pre-reflexive engagement without deliberation, and habitual and well-rehearsed motivational sequences are employed from their repertoire. There are numerous repeating circumstances and new situations that require skilful and well-practised responses. The metaphor of the map is useful because it is about a relationship. It is not the map specifically that is most interesting but the use of it altogether, in that the quality under consideration is the moment-to-moment dynamically changing relationship between the attainment of needs that are desired and clearly sought out; as opposed to those threats that need to be avoided; and in relation to a number of further abilities, being aware and checking what satisfactions are gained from the current lifestyle and how rationality and irrationality coexist in the same person. The quality of the map and its use are made apparent through the metaphor of the map in a way that emphasises the overall process of how to check how the ego is oriented currently, in an all-encompassing sense; with respect to how the person would like to be in his interpersonal relations and treat himself. Similarly, the context for understanding therapeutic relationships, is the role of the insecure forms as opposed to the therapist's ability to maintain a secure relation between self and others.

Learning theory of a specific sort is required to understand how the attachment control settings are stuck in four different ways because something counter-intuitive occurs. Logically, in Leon Festinger's theory of cognitive dissonance, for instance (1985, pp. 5–8; cf. Weinfield, Sroufe, Egeland, & Carlson, 2008), it is rational to assume that persons work to decrease a state of distress, incongruence, and anxiety, in preference for overall congruent relaxation. But this is contrary to what happens in the two insecure forms of defensive attachment and disorganisation. Contrary to Festinger's rational assumption, what attachment research shows is that forms of dissonance, compartmentalisation, splitting, or incongruence coexist with other rational states in the same consciousness. These fragmented states coincide within the same consciousness and are structurally similar to the most extreme cases of DDNOS and DID. Everyone is united *and* split and can hold within themselves strongly different approaches to others whilst experiencing personal integrity and agency. Indeed, states of incongruence have a tendency to perpetuate in some circumstances (such as avoidance, repression, dissociation, and DID) when occurring with substance use and abuse.

Conclusion

When the current social context overly influences the self and places demands and uncertainty on it, then emotions—the representational

108   ON ATTACHMENT

form that is within the sense of one's living body at any moment and in any context—can be called meaningful-relational sensations. When there are problems of anxiety and distress, these include fear about something current, or anxiety about something possible, if they are not discussed in an honest and open way; when they are about a current relationship, the lack of discussion is a factor that prevents attaining balance once more. On the other hand, if the ego were to be in a more regulated process with its social context, then there might be social anxiety before an important social event and fear during it. However, as long as there is no avoidance, staying in the anxiety-producing situation works to produce habituation (through accepting distress, impairment, and risk), relaxed responses, and good functioning, and that alters the total set of meanings. It is only the secure attachment process that produces the relational ability that follows the assumption that Festinger made: there can be the promotion of congruence, an increase in the sense of personal integration, and the reduction of incongruence. The two insecure sorts show processes of maintaining ineffective states.

Because an aim for therapy is to increase security and promote self-disclosure, the need is to enable co-ordination between people as regards their comfort with intimacy. This is often noted as setting boundaries but in fact, what is being negotiated is the setting of wholes that have different functional reasons for handling connections in the psychological environment. Each attachment process has its own way of engaging with others according to the IWM setting when, under stress, for instance, or due to other means, there can be a movement away from a more open and robust way of engaging with self and others. When the habits of relating and thinking occur in one of two insecure processes, despite inertia to change, they are open to understanding and the possibility of correction. When a therapy states that it is contextual or relational in its approach, it gets to grips with the details of individual repeating relationship problems and uses the therapy relationship to help the public alter their manner of relating. Moment to moment there are the senses that both parties have of each other. Yet it is necessary to go a step further because any sense of an object is just one out of a manifold of many others. When translated to human relationships, this means that when any party in a relationship empathises the other, or interprets itself in relation to the other, what happens, and what it is interpreted to mean, feel, and be, could exist otherwise. In attachment, there are various positions on defence with respect to meta-representation, the ability to be aware of and reflect on a psychological situation, and represent it to oneself and others through speech or writing. Meta-representation creates the ability to reflect on different actualities and possibilities, and compare them.

Defences operate with respect to specific sorts of threatening objects that get updated across the lifespan, such as how to deal with conflict, disappointment, the risk of being let down by friends, family and loved ones, and other examples of what happens to one's investment of love and attention in another person. Similarly, there are problems of how to deal with unwanted positive attention from others and how to deal with others who wish to be over-close or over-distant. The remarks above need further empirical enquiry to determine how the control settings in attachment become stuck and can change. The good news is that through understanding generally, and the new understanding gained through therapy, clients can work on their own habits and beliefs concerning attachment.

CHAPTER FIVE

The good life is correcting imbalance

This chapter assumes that all brands of therapy aim at improving self-managed self-care, long after the sessions have ended. A useful part of self-care is learning how to self-correct distress and connect with others to receive further soothing, create problem-solving, and take corrective action. This chapter is about the commonalities that can be observed when considering the themes of control systems theory, and rebalancing various types of neuroticism and psychoticism that belong to the ego that require them to be properly understood. If the understanding is inaccurate, problems will be compounded. With the image of control systems theory, Bowlby replaced Freud's idea of *Trieb*, inherited biological drive, with ideas of automatic self-governance (Bowlby, 1980, pp. 56–58). Socially learned generalised pictures of self and others, expressed in the idea of the IWM, and in how relationships should be enacted, are interpreted (Bowlby, 1973, p. 236). The learned senses of self-other connection in IWMs refer to specific attachment figures and can become influential for a current attachment process that is elicited when individuals are under stress. The ideas of homeostasis, control systems theory, goal-corrected relationships, and self-regulation are formulated below. Therapy and mental health work encourage the re-setting of disorganised and insecure attachment. The topic of

112   ON ATTACHMENT

self-correcting influence is explained below. The key phenomenon is that persons who have received secure caring as children are likely to be able to problem-solve and comfort themselves, whereas others who have not, are more likely to attempt to soothe themselves in varieties of suboptimal ways, and this in itself can reduce or prevent problem-solving simply because distress limits empathy and accurate insight. In effect, clients come for help saying "I am doing something where the negative consequences hurt me, but I keep doing it because of the short-term gains it gives me. I have not been able to change my behaviour or exercise choice in this area, but I would like your help, to help me change what I am doing."

Belief, emotion, and habit are basic parameters in attachment work. Clients know that some aspect of what they do in their relationships is unhelpful, but there is something about the problem that is maintained and repeated by the ego and its consciousness, that makes sense automatically. Defences have some sort of benefit, such as gaining the reward of reducing distress through the negative reinforcement of avoidance or similar. The question is how to achieve negative feedback and create corrective experiences through instances that tip the balance in a positive way. People come for help because they cannot make an impact on how they feel. They want to experience a good mood and a good sense of connection with others, but they are stuck in a different set of achievements altogether. Part of the problem is that the map of the world is not being checked and updated with respect to its objects and contexts. To cut a long story short, one reason why there is the trade of therapy is to promote the self-correcting resource within persons, and help them attenuate their distress and impairment (Gross, 1998). The sequence below sets the scene by discussing the dynamic forces around defences and their undoing, before introducing the need for openness and awareness. The good life for attention concerns the ability to notice distress and to do mature activities that help tolerating distress. The next three sections discuss issues that lead to understand the role between defensive exclusion and mindful awareness.

The good life: secure awareness and rebalancing

The image of the good life needs to be clear because it requires much motivation and constant reminders to support the flexibility, persistence, and learning required to reach long-term goals. The good life is

THE GOOD LIFE IS CORRECTING IMBALANCE   113

being secure most of the time with partners, family, and friends, and where relationships are important in service industries. Attachment is a genuinely comprehensive understanding of human reality in that the way towards having quality time with the people we care for, does have a shape and form that is known. If it is the case that a person's current relationship with partner, family, and friends is strained, in that their partner seems to be pulling away in reality, through actual distancing behaviour, then the feelings that are current bear a specific relation to how attachment existed in the family of origin. A testable hypothesis is to be precise about how current low self-esteem, anxiety, depression, and stalemate in a current relationship relate to the long-term way that intimacy has been lived. Feeling uncared for in the past, and having had no one to turn to in the home and at school, makes children become adults who have difficulties in discussing their partners' behaviour with them. The relationship they are in suddenly becomes a no man's land. Problems exist but when they cannot be discussed, and what is intimate may not feel safe or trustworthy. The theoretical point is that if it is impossible to make testable hypotheses then what was done to past generations through violence, abusive step-parenting, and messy divorce, continues into the next generation.

The incentive towards getting professional help is to reduce distress and speak about it for the first time even though it is often shame-provoking. What adds to resistance is the stigma of having a mental health problem. The stigma associated with asking for help may require lifting a denial that has existed with the distress. This is one factor that holds people back from getting help. Also, self-disclosure begins a process that focuses more on the distress (rather than less). After the initial phase of opening up, the value of having therapy should be felt. Now, not only are there changes in the meaning of aspects of childhood, but distress and stigma should feel less. The word "should" is used because the path of positive change is being defined where not everyone can tolerate the distress that basic explanation includes. One general aim of therapies is to promote self-soothing through helping people understand themselves, and take new actions to look after their needs. Those restrictions in the personality and lifestyle called "personality disorders", and those who repress their own needs for love and care, may have difficulties promoting their own well-being.

Good mental health is informed by understanding. The good life is achieved through applying helpful actions to create a suitable lifestyle.

114   ON ATTACHMENT

The role of the professional helper is connecting with clients to help them make their own self-managed self-care and become able to offer care as well. Good mental health is not the absence of distress. The good life that therapy provides is a version of stoicism; valuing the ability to cope with distress flexibly promotes resilience and robustness. Good mental health copes with emotional overwhelm in relation to how the ego positions itself in its social contexts, and copes with the senses of disconnection and alienation it can feel from others, its own unmet needs, and values. This is important because prolonged distress impairs the self's potential for experiencing good contact with others. Life is such that there will always be suffering, illness, challenges, setbacks, bad luck, unexpected events, and novel situations. The good life is being able to adjust to negative events through calming distress by using inner resources, looking to the future, and consulting with others to problem-solve and manage distress. One source of understanding the good life is found by consulting the empirical research about people who have had a childhood where their parents cared for them and comforted them when they were distressed. Persons from secure childhoods are liable to have good mental health because they innately know how to act in ways that are autonomous *and* connected with others. The way of understanding this has happened is to see it as the blossoming of an innate control mechanism where, if a person is momentarily out of balance, then there is an automatic fast-acting return to balance.

For the moment, however, it should be noted that the self's picture of itself in its world has a large number of consequences. How self treats itself and how it becomes possible (or not) for others to engage with it, occurs through subtle differences. Sometimes the tiniest of enquiries about the other—or the showing of interest by others, or the pitch of voice, the quality of nonverbal expression—make "doors open", metaphorically, between people or make them close. The mapping process for the constitution of the senses of any object is built on the way it has been treated previously. Experiences of verbal, emotional, physical and sexual violence leave their mark, and the vacuum made by these shocks on the previously created wholes of meaning, can destroy a confident assumption of the degree of kindness about persons in general.

It is helpful to understand that the habits of mental processes are brought into play automatically. These include well-practised attempts at solutions about counterfactual possibilities that may never happen. There could be avoidance of distress that is also merely possible and not actual because the object that the distress is about is perceptually absent. Some forms of distress related to attachment insecurity are more related to the self, whilst others are more related to other persons. However, if there is low trust in the helpfulness of others, and their intentions are habitually empathised as being negative, then genuine problem-solving may not be attempted.

When people defend themselves against their distress and try to avoid, distract, or reduce it through their own inventiveness, sometimes the defensive acts do little or nothing to deal with their impact and beliefs. In most cases, defences do not problem-solve or provide long-term relief. However, when defences have not worked, and attempts at solutions have brought negative consequences, people begin therapy after a long period of having tried to take control of their distress, and repeating problems in relating. Self-correcting influence is the means of getting the client's ego and consciousness, to gain the freedom from repeatedly being stuck in the same old problems. Distress recurs because the ego's previous attempts to prevent them are used once more but they may no longer work. Changes away from distress and its maintenance can be clearly defined with respect to presenting problems in the proper use of theory for practice.

Dynamic equilibrium between coping and defence

As noted above there are some basic definitive distinctions between distress about the timeframes of the past and future, as opposed to fear felt in relation to current perceptual objects. A defence pre-empts distress about possibilities and motivates protection. However, false beliefs create real anxiety so there can be false alarms when there is no real risk, but only its possibility. The fending off employed may not be about anything actually current or perceptually present. So the way to grasp defence is through the idea of meta-representation across time (Owen, 2015). But defence is not positive coping. Defence occurs when a non-actual event is connected with a sense of meaningful threat in association, a link or an implication. Coping is when persons use their personal resources to manage strong negative emotion, even if the distress is not removed or substantially decreased. One means of coping is to know that self is strong enough to get through distress. In fact neurosis and psychosis are remarkable in that the fending off achieved by defence is

116   ON ATTACHMENT

mainly addressed to the mere possibility of what might go wrong (not about things that are perceptually present).

The outcome of emotional dysregulation as a type of misrepresentation is vexed indeed. In the worst possible cases, it can mean the difference between life and death. In summary, the original writing on the attachment way of interpreting the psychological world understands that the empathy of motivations, and the estimation of the availability of others, can be aided through applying reasoning. The guiding idea of a control system concerns the homeostasis of the human body that is the model for the IWM, and the self-reflexive habits of emotional regulation, and their lack (Bowlby, 1969, p. 57). It needs to be emphasised that there are four ways in which the control setting of the IWM, the default attachment, can be stuck and over-used in relation to a person or situations where different kinds of behaviour would produce better results (Bowlby, 1973, p. 369). However, the rationality that applies knows that people protect themselves from different things because their attachment is aimed at different outcomes. Each attachment process has a different setting according to how one type of psychological contact is sought and others are prevented. Moreover, because they are biopsychosocial in origin, and relationships and stress have biological consequences, then biopsychosocially, physical and intersubjective effects around human beings are involved. This is not to say that attachment cannot be changed, but in some cases, the phenomena may be generalised over increasing portions of a person's life. If the neurological and biological damage is pervasive because the damage has been in infancy, then change may be hard to achieve.

Understanding how choices are made after the first occurrence distress is a learning concerning how intelligent, educated rational people make decisions of the defensive sort. Previously, explicit choices concern incentivised decision-making about risk and reward, which when repeated, become a series of automatic behaviours with no awareness of their origin and history during their execution. Given that the central role of pre-reflexive understanding, belief, and the emotions form avoidance, defences rationally push away from something dreaded, and pull towards things that are false relief. These become a part of the relational self, and with overuse, there is the accumulation of increasingly complex problems across the lifespan. Let us consider an example of defences in adulthood.

THE GOOD LIFE IS CORRECTING IMBALANCE 117

Sometimes in adult life, there is no actual precursor of anxiety problems. Let us consider an example. Claustrophobia is an anxiety about being hemmed in by other people or being caught within physical constrictions. However, after careful questioning, it can be found that many people who have claustrophobia have never had an actual experience of being physically trapped. What actually happened is that the person is so vigilant about being hemmed in that the feelings of anxiety get associated with the mere possibility of being hemmed in and how bad that would be, but there might be no actual experiences of being trapped and unable to move. Thus, defences include types of safety behaviour, mental action, and avoidance. In claustrophobia, current avoidance exists with respect to the mere *possibility* of being trapped and unable to move. The anticipated catastrophe in the anticipatory imagination of the ego, of the possibility of being unable to move, is the source of a series of avoidances that narrow the lifestyle and make ordinary functioning more difficult. The slightest possibility where a claustrophobic person might be hemmed in or feel trapped, becomes the source of excessive attention and misattribution. With an over-focus on the negative evaluation, the person becomes out of balance through worry and anxious anticipation, and the physiology of anxiety becomes a contributory factor concerning his evaluation of himself and his emotions. Such negative attention highlights the self-interpreted inadequacies of self, and makes a previously automatic and assumed ability, the focus of worry and rumination that maintains the problematic functioning, rather than it being possible to reflect, overrule the automatic ability, and correct it.

The path of courage towards healing requires delayed gratification and coping with distress in the short term and the long term, and requires the patient application of skills when something that is wanted urgently is unobtainable. There are most frequently a number of well-valued outcomes available. For instance, behaviour is more likely to be congruent with values, an expression of authentic personality and good self-esteem, when self-responsible behaviour is chosen. To work hard and bear pain, without an immediate positive reinforcer, requires valuing oneself and ones' abilities, and employing rational problem-solving, rather than permitting oneself to be distressed without end. The most basic process is to use awareness, reflect and interpret problems, and act to solve or minimise what constitutes any triggers for distress (which could be understood as a need for cigarettes and a double scotch). Rationality about distress is best attained when the person is relaxed and can put a stop to the distress by using their awareness of it to reduce it. Distress is an important message that needs to be acted on in the right way.

Future coping is the prize to be won. Emotional and social intelligence show in being able to think about them in such a way as to motivate clients into wanting what is in their own best interest. Frequently, there are irrational motives that are clearly chosen to support self-harm and self-medication, and the excessive desire for certainty and safety, in ways that narrow the lifestyle. Self-harm does deliver short-term relief, as do alcohol, drug, and food binges. But these options are irrational in that they cause short- and long-term harm. Healing occurs through the ego understanding itself in relation to its meanings, its personal potential and social context. Through help, the ego can become more active in caring for others and itself. Change in the conscious meanings from distress towards improvement and acceptance demands change in the balance between the ego and its non-egoic processes and biological drives. The key phenomenon is to understand that human beings are not entirely rational creatures and that, particularly when under stress of any sort, people are liable to do irrational things for emotional reasons. In light of the comments above, a wider understanding is that people who are distressed lose their ability to rationalise their emotions, empathise, interpret themselves accurately, and consequently, are likely not to act for the best.

Merely growing up in a family and culture teaches common-sense ways of what are sufficient, good enough, and resilient forms of coping and defending, in relation to specific objects. This is because coherent identities appear across manifolds of sense. The aim is being able to identify events and processes between oneself and another as secure and capable of meta-representative comparison—with inadequate and incoherent forms of intimacy that are insecure. The full spectrum of manifold appearances means that a comparative qualitative analysis is required that defines how to recognise each form. The need to be open to clients' needs and provide care that is gender-, age-, and culture-appropriate is necessary because of the complex embedded nature of the human being. If treatment planning and interventions are tailored to individuals' maps of their worlds, then they are more likely to be effective in mobilising abilities, coping, and the specifics of how to live as part of family, religion, and culture. The necessity of reviewing meetings at assessment, at the end of each meeting, and particularly during the first few meetings, adds awareness of clients' mental states and helps tailor the approach taken. Finding the perspectives of clients, on what they feel is happening in each meeting, is another major part of the ability to tailor the care provided, according to abilities, level of readiness, and general needs. The remaining sections comment on awareness and how it is used to promote self-soothing and emotional regulation in concrete ways.

Awareness and openness

Following Daniel Goleman (1995) and Jon Kabat-Zinn (1994), there are three steps in self-awareness when employing emotional and social intelligence. Similarly, Paul Gilbert uses a neurological model, mixed with the idea of compassion from Tibetan Buddhism, to create a means for understanding the influence of biological drives, ways of dealing with felt-threat through manifesting compassion and increasing kindness and understanding towards self and others. These are offered because distress is a tension to be released through self-soothing and providing soothing to others when they need it too (Gilbert, 2010). The three most basic steps are:

1. Awareness and acceptance of current emotions concern permitting self to feel, rather than defending against unwanted feelings by choices that prevent full emotional representation to occur. The most basic awareness of emotion is supplemented by further permissions to vocalise and express distress, and place trust in others in the anticipation that they will be helpful. (On the other hand, a problematic occurrence is an inability to feel one's own emotions, by unconscious processes or egoically, by distracting the ego away from what is felt, because of being afraid, or expecting that self will be overwhelmed and damaged by emotion). What is felt has to be named and specified by the speaking ego. The unconscious speaks when distress is experienced with respect to an object that can also be thought about, to produce an entirely different sense of it. To the logical mind, if the distress is understandable it can be noticed that the emotional reaction is too large in comparison to the logical size of the problem.
2. Engaging in active problem-solving is one means of regulating the self's distress (as opposed to having no functional responses to a problematic situation or responses that have negative consequences).
3. Engaging in seeking care from others, or other forms of effective coping, can draw on inner resources of feeling loved and cared-for.

120   ON ATTACHMENT

The formative past experiences of being able to trust that the self has enough within it to meet most of the demands placed on it, also contributes to self-soothing and lessening distress.

No matter what the cause of current difficulties, what is required is for the ego to take charge of itself responsibly, and decide to rethink its current distress and beliefs, and give itself some new options. One new quest is to understand how consciousness filters out evidence to the contrary of its biases. Theories concerning the incentive to act in one way or another need to be understood within a functional or teleological view of the repeating problems. Specific senses of the words "dynamic" and "equilibrium" are cited. This means that homeostasis is oriented across time. For what raises its head is the question of how to interpret motivations arising out of the psychodynamic pushes and pulls that are felt in relation to the total situation of the beliefs used, and their consequences. Thus, psychodynamic considerations meta-represent current actualities and mere possibilities; for instance, being clear about which emotions arise with which attachment processes, and in what circumstances. Interpreting the processes involved defines the attachment problems verbally or on paper, before working to see if attachment relationships can be different. Psychodynamic motivations are emotions and habits of dealing with distress that are felt meanings that encourage action for a variety of reasons. The importance of appealing to, and motivating, the free will of clients to begin change, is to increase self-care and improve their ability to manage distress, care for others and connect. Theory and clinical reasoning justify the psychosocial skills of practice in relation to the lived experiences of providing and receiving care. Psychological help requires the assessment of hope, motivation and its encouragement in the face of difficulty. In this respect, belief is seen as a central topic for overcoming persistently negative senses of self, others, and threat. The remaining sections note the changing relationship between the ego and its consciousness and how to improve emotional regulation.

The ego's responsibility to correct itself

The ego is capable of recovering its well-being through understanding the specifics of its own unique personal history. Thus, causes that might be reversible include relating with others (for instance, choosing not to

THE GOOD LIFE IS CORRECTING IMBALANCE   121

be hostile, callous, or destructive, even if angry); choosing not to damage self and others, and choosing what to focus on with the ego's attention (not the over-focus of anorexia, worry, shame, rumination, or some topic of thought and feeling that prevents the restoration of balance).

Finding how to cope through learning to understand attachment leads to the idea of attaining earned security (Pearson, Cohn, Cowan, & Cowan, 1994; Phelps, Belsky, & Crnic, 1998). Earned security refers to those people who have recovered from non-optimal and disorganised types of attachment. Earned security shows that it is possible to increase the relative proportion of secure processes in a person's life. The picture of good mental health is the ability to make many small steps to pre-empt distress through communication, and other means of becoming automatically self-correcting, so placing self in a harmonious relationship to its own needs, and those of others. When this happens, emotional and social intelligence is made manifest. Persons who exhibit psychological mindedness in their lifestyles share the benefit with others. What follows is a model of how clients can move between distress, defence and crisis across their lives and is once more the subject of further attention in the next chapter and Figure 6.1.

When following the control systems idea, five distinctions appear: the first steady state of mood, functioning, and felt-value is a balanced mood, a steady state of optimal functioning that features positivity between self and others. Challenges to the ability to cope are met positively. Persons in the secure process cope when they are distressed by adjusting quickly.

In relation to toxic meanings, there is distress, an out-of-balance, emotionally hijacked and overwhelmed state that includes anxiety and self-doubt in reaction to various situations and the interpreted meaning of them.

Coping is feedback about the difference between distress and what could lead to balance, through a variety of means including successfully recovering from distress. It includes problem-solving to use inner and outer resources. However, if coping and recovery do not happen, two more states ensue.

If coping is not achieved and distress continues, what operates are defences that are ineffective, with the use of inaccurate negative feedback. (Or with positive feedback, that makes distress worse). However, the rule of thumb that appears is that often the defences employed do not attenuate distress.

122   ON ATTACHMENT

Finally, if defences that are ineffective are overused then crisis occurs, and if that exists without further intervention, there can be no return to higher quality states of functioning.

To use an old-fashioned term, a nervous breakdown is really a state of exhaustion brought on during a long period of time when individuals are exhausted, depressed, and overwhelmed. Many experiences of depression occur after a prior period of anxiety, so this type of depression can be understood as emotional exhaustion. Depression may also be an expression of loss, where what is lost is some valued aspiration, what could have been, or what might have been. Either way, after an extended period of distress persons can become unable to function in their roles. This is a crisis in functioning that can be rectified to promote a return to a more relaxed state of coping. If there are repeated instances of crisis across the lifespan, these effects accumulate in personality functioning because the problems of relating to others, and dealing with the inevitabilities of stress and change, belong solely to the individual.

The next section comments on the link between theory and practice in Marsha Linehan's (1993) dialectical behaviour therapy (DBT), where she uses the behaviour therapy view of learning to create a model for the self-soothing of distress. DBT is cited because it forms an exemplary case where it is easy to see how the processes governing distress and coping operate. The point of mentioning DBT is that it makes the general case clear. The good life is being able to deal with one's own distress and that of other persons. DBT employs negative feedback to decrease distress rather than increase it. Negative feedback is the case in the thermostat example where central heating systems operate successfully at required settings.

Dealing with the personality factor of neuroticism in dialectical behaviour therapy

DBT first began as a specific type of treatment for borderline personality disorder, which refers to people who react with excessive distress to small upsets, and may harm themselves as a means of calming their distress. DBT has developed and broadened its application to other types of problem where distress, and ineffective means of dealing with what causes it, continue unabated. DBT has gone beyond merely helping people provide their own emotional regulation and helps with personality functioning and other psychological syndromes. Thus, DBT presents

THE GOOD LIFE IS CORRECTING IMBALANCE   123

itself as an effective treatment for emotional overwhelm or emotional hijacking, where intense and persistent distress occurs (and defences that are ineffective lead to increasing overwhelm and crisis, the inability to function because of emotional exhaustion). Before treatment, there may be intense distress without reaching a means of coping, self-soothing, problem-solving, or asking for help from others. Emotional dysregulation, high neuroticism, and psychoticism, are the end result of an excessive sensitivity to specific objects plus a lack of self-soothing as a necessary long-term aspect of the personality. What the absences of understanding and of self-soothing show is highlighted in comparison to the abilities of secure attachment noted above. Secure self-soothing is likely to work on managing distress and returning to coping. Positive coping and the basic toleration of distress are addressed in a highly pragmatic and didactic way in DBT.

DBT is a formulation-based treatment practised after clients have given informed consent to the principles of the treatment. This means that it is directive in its relational process and explicitly problem-solving in reaction to frequent suicide attempts, self-harm by cutting and extreme forms of defending against distress. One focus is breaking chains of associations after a trigger that has an emotional meaning, impulse, or motivation, that otherwise would lead to self-perpetuated high distress, long after the trigger is over. The focus for the treatment is attending to and decreasing risk, starting with homicidal and suicidal tendencies when distressed, then attending to potential motivations for suicide and self-harm. Three key aspects of the problems that it treats are when persons have been overwhelmed for long periods of time in the absence of finding ways of coping with how they feel, when their defences are ineffective, and when crises are frequent.

In brief, the onset of borderline personality disorder is in part due to an inherited biological temperament to be sensitive and easily distressed (Kuo & Linehan, 2009). In addition, there may have been a major failure of parenting or of the education and socialisation of children, producing insecurity, shame, or low self-esteem in teenagers and young adults. There could be the occurrence of alexithymia—an inability to feel and be aware of emotions and speak about them, and express and negotiate emotions in any relationship, through discussing them. The result is that persons with borderline personality disorder do not know how to express how they feel to themselves or others, not because of the other's unapproachability, but because of their own difficulty in

124   ON ATTACHMENT

understanding their emotions, feeling and expressing them, and so asserting themselves and gaining feedback.

Another aspect of the constitution of the neurotic personality might be that self-soothing, the discussion of emotions, and their negotiation, were never sufficiently well-modelled by the family of origin. When adult clients were children, they may have been raised in an environment of criticism, in addition to the verbal and physical violence of the invalidating family. Children were not allowed to feel the way they did and their righteous cries of protest were dismissed with scorn. "Shame on you for asking for what you need!" This type of upbringing generates an internal critic, a tendency to empathise self-criticism in relationships generally, and produces a way of treating itself in a harsh critical way, by being punitive and unfair to self. Sometimes this is experienced as an internal voice in precisely the same tone as the parental critical voice, or the internal voice repeats family mottos that are unhelpful. This is a way of identifying how young persons were told they should feel and be.

Other experiences of an internal critic occur when adults feeling as though they are being watched by an audience, and feel they receive harsh judgments from critical others. The original sense of criticism, coming from being watched by an actual audience, observed, and harshly evaluated, has been generalised and extended for decades, long after the original criticism ceased. A final phenomenon associated with the internalised sense of self-criticism is experienced as anxiety and threat due to the self's own unachievable standards of behaviour. This is a phenomenon of paranoid anxiety about self and is related to empathic anticipations of criticism. Therefore, powered by anticipated criticism, there arises self-doubt, unnecessary self-limitation, and inaccurate beliefs.

To learn to regulate away from distress and towards rebalance, it is necessary to cue reparative action. Another aspect of recovering from distress is asking for help, care, and understanding from others when necessary. Any tendency for reluctance in verbalising their emotions should be reversed and persons can increase their emotional intelligence, and become able to name and negotiate negative feelings with others, and become more socially skilled. The key problems of borderline personality disorder are:

1. There is an excessive sensitivity to distress that produces large negative impacts and states, and defences that are ineffective, so crises are

frequent. In some cases negative impacts are entirely the result of the meanings produced by interpretation and implication, rather than being recordable facts about what has happened.

2. There is an absence of self-soothing when distressed, leading to long periods of anxiety and shame, maintaining distress, defences that are ineffective, and crises which could be frequent.

3. The solutions that clients attempt either do not work or have high costs and unintended negative consequences. States of defences that are ineffective are dysfunctional, and may become part of the personality, and lead to crisis states, for example, frequent experiences of self-harm, temporary psychosis and multiple suicide attempts.

In diagrammatic form, the problems above can be represented according to the principles of behavioural learning theory. The causes identified are psychological motivations. Empirically, this means that the phenomenon of being anxious and distressed affects the ability to empathise the viewpoints of others. This suggests that there are multifactorial aspects to being distressed because the increase in heart rate can correlate with the non-empathic refusal of the other's point of view as a valid one. This may explain why some issues in long-term relationships remain unresolved and why couples who argue can refuse the perspective of the other as a valid one. When it comes to extreme sensitivity to small impacts, Figure 5.1, below, notes some of the intentional implications in order across time.

When there are states of distress, defences that are ineffective, and crises, if distress is intense and persistent, people may drink to oblivion, take street drugs, and self-harm in order to calm themselves. While these defences are fast and effective, they have negative meanings to self and others because they are public objects also. Once known about, the social context often responds harshly to persons who cut themselves and make frequent suicide attempts, so they receive comments from the public and family that do not understand, sympathise with, or console them. Therefore, attempted solutions to the distress may exacerbate the problem and serve to lower self-esteem, enforce shame, and further disconnect self from others (Figure 5.2). If a high level of distress is maintained for long periods of time, any trivial problem, frustration, or upset is likely to be handled poorly because of the impairment of mood and functioning when distressed. When considering the events of any twenty-four-hour period, the following pattern can be seen in people who are exhausted and impaired in their functioning to the point of multiple crises.

126   ON ATTACHMENT

Triggers are interpreted by negative core
beliefs and habits of understanding and emotion
↓
High and persisting distress
↓
Through drastic and ineffective solutions, short-term solutions, restricted lifestyle,
unsoothed, out of balance distress is maintained through ineffective defences
↓
Temporary relief is gained and that negatively reinforces the problem by rewarding
the reduction of distress, which is why the defences used are ineffective
↓
There is an interpretation of self as bad, a shame-confirming reflection, for example,
"I am not in control", "My life is a mess", or "I am useless"

Figure 5.1. Specific instance of emotional dysregulation in borderline personality disorder.

Wake up distressed, their defences are ineffective in soothing distress
↓
Too distressed to empathise and rationalise emotions and employ
functional problem-solving. Defences are ineffective
↓
Drastic means to get to sleep. Defences are ineffective
↓
Poor sleep due to strong day residues of emotion that
cannot be processed during sleep. Defences are ineffective

Figure 5.2. A twenty-four-hour formulation of distress and ineffective defences.

Finally, and posed in the language of interpreting these problems as part of a control system for emotions that does not function correctly, in DBT the direction of the cure is to learn how to tolerate distress and uncertainty, and promote a problem-solving approach to reduce the habits of excessive sensitivity to distress. For instance, the types of interventions that DBT provides are of the following sorts and are achieved in a manner that teaches clients how to self-soothe, and move from defences that are ineffective to coping and eventual rebalancing, through knowing how to attend to one's own needs, and make necessary alterations as a result of accurate understanding of cause.

It is necessary to identify and lessen the usage of dysfunctional solutions, to reduce, accept, and substitute new behaviour and coping, and decrease the occurrence of defences that do not work. One way is analysing chains of events of thoughts, feelings, and attempts to manage distress, to understand what leads to problematic dysfunctional behaviours before self-harm or suicide attempts. For instance, creating a pact with clients to invent less risky forms of the expression of feelings is a better outcome than the drastic desire to escape. Therapy helps by looking for idiosyncratic reasoning about unbearable emotion and its consequences that might otherwise promote the use of defences that do not help.

The management of contingencies such as triggers, associations of meaning to social and physical contexts, habits, will decrease the frequency of defences. The use of exposure programmes in behaviour therapy is where clients learn to experience increasing amounts of distress, and find that with repetition, distress falls rather than increases if they stay in it for sufficiently long periods of time. There can be an increase in coping and toleration of distress by increasing the period of time in positive coping and rebalancing.

In response, the DBT approach teaches ways of learning self-validation of one's own emotions, needs, beliefs, and position-taking, and ways of protecting and increasing self-esteem. For example, the purposeful acceptance of what exists and how it feels is called "radical acceptance" and can increase the ability to return to balance (Linehan, 1993).

Another aim is to reinforce positive intentions and the use of skills. One strategy is decreasing punishing costs and increasing coping. This should decrease distress and defences that are ineffective. Overall, the process is managing the psychic economy for treating asthenia, an insufficiency of psychological force, by metaphorically, minimising psychological costs, increasing income, and removing debts as first noted by Pierre Janet (1903).

DBT is a model concerning the central role of tolerating distress and increasing adaptive coping, if the ego knows how to connect with others and look after its own needs whilst looking after the needs of others. For instance, in thinking of tomorrow and the next few days, what comes to mind is how to get some exercise and socialise, at the same time as allocating time for work, family, and activities with one's children and partner. There is the meeting of short-term needs for fun, time off, and relaxation, and setting limits to the work-oriented needs

128   ON ATTACHMENT

of the day, as opposed to also trying to meet medium and long-term needs. Everybody has rights for attention and a certain lightness of touch, no matter how pressured current events are. To aim to be happy and fulfilled is both optimistic and realistic. DBT therapists identify resistance to change and work on increasing motivation for attending sessions, and so keep highly distressed clients in therapy and motivated on learning how to deal with their distress and self-harm, despite them being initially reluctant to proceed.

Closing discussion

The idea of influence is wrapped up with associated ideas such as the ego and its choices in relation to the sum total of its passive and non-egoic intentional processes, for the meaning of control in the attachment context really concerns the ego's understanding and responsiveness to accurate empathy, emotions, and the felt understanding of its predicament. One aspect of distress is that when it erupts into consciousness, the ego is shocked and challenged into coping, and responding to that part of consciousness that constitutes emotion and mood. Immediately, the ego may not be able to respond at all. A theory of corrective action is similar to the decisions required to go on a journey. Minimally, an end-point needs to be known and sufficient provisions and time are required to get there. It is better to have a detailed itinerary with the overall means of getting to the journey's end. In this respect, recovery from distress is like any other action plan. Because therapy is tailored to individual needs, it is incapable of being standardised and the problems that it addresses are not uniform in nature. There are large numbers of views in contemporary therapy, with official brand names defining how to practice. But with greater attention to detail, there are very many individual preferences for practising. Furthermore, the proliferation of modalities of therapy raises the question of the self-understanding of the profession. Therapists deal with the private face of society: the taboo, what cannot be said elsewhere, the shameful, and the distressing are the daily bread of persons dedicated to exemplifying compassion and providing healing by finding ways of living in meaning. It is an occupational hazard to be contaminated by the topics that therapists hear about. This type of job stress is inescapable. Yet there is also the positive side of knowing that therapeutic processes can work and that it is possible to bring a sense of freedom and new life to people who

THE GOOD LIFE IS CORRECTING IMBALANCE   129

have been stuck in the same repeating problems of shame, unlovability, and senses of personal uselessness for decades.

Conclusion

One way of gaining clarity on what therapy tries to achieve is defining the good life that it aims for. Secure personality functioning expressed in therapy and mental health care as seeking a secure base means that collaboration is necessary to help clients move forward with their worker, through agreeing what needs to be discussed (Bowlby, 1988, p. 140). Two research questions are: what are the conditions of possibility for people to self-correct and *not* self-correct? However, the structure of the unconscious—what happens automatically at a remove from the ego's choices and strivings—is the work of the anonymous part of self that judges and values outside of the direct action of the ego. The major consequence is an argument to appreciate the influence of correcting distress and functioning in achieving the good life.

CHAPTER SIX

Achieving rebalance

This chapter extends the commentary on balance to provide a unifying way of understanding the recovery from distress as rebalancing through the emotional regulation of self by itself, and in relation to connections with others. Every life includes distress, illness, misfortune, and sheer bad luck, as well as the results of what any ego can be responsible for in terms of the community that it creates around it. Healthy emotional living co-exists with distress. Emotional intelligence shows itself when it takes rectifying action. The sections below begin with a theory of psychopathology and wellness that obeys control systems theory. It understands ineffective defences in relation to increasing problems of emotional overwhelm, poor functioning, and poor abilities to understand and select rationales that will provide the sought-after return to good mental health.

Cycles of balance and imbalance

Formulations of the key processes at work in secure attachment can be made through identifying repeating processes of overwhelm and recovery. This section introduces a way of understanding resilience and emotional dysregulation by looking at the treatment of excessive emotional sensitivity and of impulsive behaviour that may lead to the ego not coping and that, without corrective action, can be allowed to accumulate. Because these are cycles of repeating overwhelm, then each phase of the cycle needs comparison (Figure 6.1). The model that is put forward notes that there are five states that concern various choices for responding to stressors adequately, and returning to a relaxed state of psychological equilibrium. The first three states defined below occur in the functioning of the secure self-soothing process of responding to stress to move from the initial state, (i) balance, through (ii) distress, through (iii) restorative coping and recovering, then returning to balance. This is the good life. Distress is inevitable. Bouncing back through one's own efforts or through enlisting the help of others are functional ways of coping. In overview, one example of the positive use of awareness is shown in the case of healing negative feedback that understands distress and self-cares through seeking help; or the ego consults the personal set of resources about how to proceed, self-soothe, and problem-solve. This commences coping that leads to balance once more.

The first steady state is a balanced mood that needs no correction, a state of optimal functioning that features the positive self-constitution of self-esteem and proper contact with others. Challenges to the ability to cope are met positively. Persons who are in a secure process can focus on self-reflexively monitoring and coping when they are distressed by adjusting quickly.

Distress concerns being out of balance, emotionally hijacked, and in overwhelmed states that exist in various ways and include anxiety

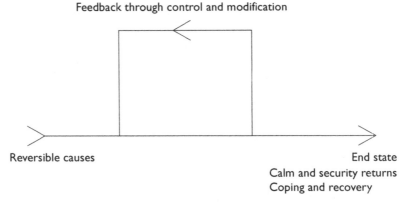

Figure 6.1. The type of emotionally regulated response in secure attachment and coping.

and self-doubt in reaction to various situations, and the interpreted meaning of them.

Positive coping uses negative feedback to close the gap through accurately understanding the meta-representational difference between distress and what could lead to coping, through a variety of means. It includes problem-solving to find and use inner resources, and connect with outer resources. Beliefs, values, behaviours, memories of previous experiences of coping and recovery are consulted including seeking help from others and accepting distress.

However, if coping and recovery do not happen, two more states ensue.

Defences are ineffective when they employ ineffective negative feedback or positive feedback that makes distress worse. If the defences employed cannot attenuate distress then it can remain and exacerbate the impairment in everyday functioning.

Finally, if defences are ineffective and exist for too long, there is crisis, the inability to function, and emotional and physical exhaustion, called a nervous breakdown, featuring anxiety, depression, and impairment of roles at work and home.

The five states defined above form a dynamic equilibrium. If the only parameters are movements between states of balance, distress, and positive coping, then the good life will be attained: if the distress is short-lived and coping is effective in returning the felt sense of balance, then good mental health is in evidence. Because disruption and distress are inevitable, the good life is coping with distress, overwhelm, and temporary poor functioning. The means of achieving this is through consulting personal resources and seeking out those of other persons, be it in the family or in the larger society. Secure emotional regulation is manifest.

Movement between balance and distress means that there is intermittent good functioning with occasional upsets. When distress is prolonged, faulty defences that are ineffective create a pre-overwhelm build-up that is at risk of producing a crisis of full impairment to roles at work and home. Both defences that are ineffective and crisis are dysfunctional because restorative coping has not yet begun.

When there are multiple repetitions of crisis, there will be a longer road of recovery back to balance. For example, if there are multiple trauma—such as rape, leading to drink and drug addiction as a means of overly defensive coping that include the unintended consequences of being unemployable and requiring treatment for the addiction—then

134   ON ATTACHMENT

years of the lifespan can be spent in trying to get back to balance, in coming to terms with the rape and the consequences of the methods of defending that did not work.

Movements from distress to defences that do not work, to out-of-balance defensive solutions, and movements to crisis, from being out of balance and highly defended, are both potentially damaging if the return to recovery does not occur sufficiently quickly. The movement is through defences that are lowered, on the way back to positive coping and then back to balance, and recovery. The meaning of distress is that it is the unconscious inviting the ego to lessen the distress and problem-solve. Distress is important information that should not be erased by repression and defences but properly responded to. Medication by itself will never be effective in the absence of real world changes.

The next section comments on the received wisdom of vulnerability called neuroticism and psychoticism, which can be mistaken for fixed aspects of personality. The remainder of the chapter discusses how to find corrective experiences that will support recovery.

Personality vulnerability and proneness to distress

The full range of the neuroticism of the emotional consciousness that provides long-standing distress for the ego can be introduced as follows, drawing on the stance of "five factor" personality theory. The mnemonic for remembering what the five factors are is "ocean": the five factors are openness, conscientiousness, extroversion, agreeableness, and neuroticism (McCrae & Costa, 2003). In order to connect with mainstream personality theory, six definitive aspects of the neurotic factor of personality are as follows.

1. Pre-reflexively produced emotions of various strengths and durations are neurotic when felt or expressed, when they are out of proportion to the amount of real threat. Emotional dysregulation generally includes histrionics, anxiety, disgust, and moods of negativity of all kinds. In meta-representational view, emotions can be understood according to what sort of evidence is being interpreted in what way. This thought applies to the emotional evaluations that support the defences in neuroticism and psychoticism.

ACHIEVING REBALANCE   135

2. Other strong and persistent emotions could be an angry mood, possibly due to monitoring fairness and justice, and interpreting that they are lacking when they might not be.
3. Feelings of depression, guilt, or loneliness, possibly even when there is no recent loss, wrongdoing, or within a loving social context of others, indicate the degree to which someone is distressed and the degree to which that impairs the ability to function in any role and context.
4. High levels of negative self-consciousness is a factor that exists in relation to shyness and social anxiety, with sensitivity that produces a potential towards feeling embarrassed, shamed, humiliated, rejected, and ridiculed. When such emotion suffuses self, it motivates gauche, standoffish, and non-harmonious inhibited social contact. The problems of self-consciousness tend towards the construction of inaccurate reified senses of self, of which there are many types. The core of self-consciousness in neuroticism is to believe that self is damaged and inadequate when it is not. Yet the emotions of anxiety and self-directed anger can be taken as evidence that self is inadequate.
5. When strongly swayed by emotion, the ego may only act with short-term satisfactions in sight: impulsive, immoderate, or excessive focus on the defensive use of pleasure can act as unhelpful protection from distress but not anticipate the long-term future consequences of repeated short-term actions. This is defensive when it is a long-term avoidance of actions and emotions that will bring benefit if the problematic object is dealt with.
6. Vulnerability, in the sense of being sensitive to the five items above, implies that the evidence of distress is not employed in the control system to show the ego how to balance itself.

Finally, trauma-induced psychoticism occurs when the past lingers on in the present. Because the damage has been so powerful, the trauma can become superimposed on everyday perceptual reality. The positive function of hypervigiliance to attack is to be aware of the possibility of future attack once more, but the wariness of repetition can put false frames of understanding around threat-free social reality. Social avoidance, complex PTSD, paranoia after attack, worry, and psychosis born of trauma share the conviction that risk is imminent and drastic means are required to avoid catastrophe. Dependent on the social contexts entered, they may be entirely safe in fact, but are felt to be

136   ON ATTACHMENT

untrustworthy. Vulnerability is open to change if it is understood correctly.

Problematic forms of responsiveness concern several versions of the following: starting with a state of balance, there can be intermittent good functioning, which means there is a cycling between balance and distress in such a way that coping is not continually achieved, as there is more distress than rebalancing. Over an extended period of time, this impacts negatively on the ego in such a manner that it begins to construe the world as a threatening place. The ego sees itself as insufficient because it cannot attenuate its distress. If distress is not mastered, the periods of being distressed have no end, and, accordingly, the self-reflexive sense of self becomes forced to accept that it is impaired due to emotional dysregulation because of its poor functioning. In this latter case, the constitution of the senses of world, self, and empathised other are representative of impairment and insecurity, not of balance and relaxed mental health.

However, if the occurrence and strength of distress and the cumulative effect of impairment in everyday and occupational functioning is high, and the forms of solution sought are ineffective, excessively defended, or have unintended negative consequences, then defences that do not work continue for long periods of time, and the road back to balance is delayed or not attained. When defences do not work and crisis remains, then acute episodes of distress and inability to function continue, so that there are movements from crisis back to ineffective defences. Crisis is where functioning in several domains of life is impaired.

If there are prolonged experiences of defences that do not work then crisis can become part of the core relational ability in personal development. Energy is expended in unnecessarily keeping the self safe in ways that prevent the potential of the self becoming fully manifest; these become long-standing parts of the personality functioning and the objectified sense of self is malignant. During long periods of being out of balance, conflict can happen because when under stress there can be an increased tendency to be angry. The ego knows that something major is wrong. When defensive solutions and crises become more frequent, the ego becomes more desperate, and then depression sets in. The ego inaccurately interprets itself out of its pre-reflexive experiences in a highly negative way. Self-harm, the valuing of suicide as an escape, and drastic actions including murder are motivated extreme attempts to escape from crisis. But such attempted solutions deliver a Pyrrhic victory, a form of respite with excessively high costs, or sometimes they deliver no relief at all.

On secure emotional self-regulation as the proper use of emotional awareness and feedback

In the phenomenon of secure attachment is the ability to understand accurately and pre-reflexively, and respond to the shared needs of others and self. Empirically, it is well-established that attachment is in part a biological drive but its manifestation occurs in a context of participatory sense-making of children about their carers (Waters & Cummings, 2000, p. 164). Indeed, the core definition of security for any age or culture is that an individual who manifests a secure process is one who can explore and return to their attachment figure. For adults, secure persons are those who can pass on such an experience to others, where their ability to self-regulate is both emotional and conceptual, and both externally and internally directed. Secure attachment produces a lifestyle that is responsive and shared with intimate others and strangers, that everyday language calls a co-operative win-win situation, an outcome of negotiation and collaboration. As a consequence, personal and shared values, preferences for long- and short-term goals are achieved, and mutual satisfactions are attained. For instance, Waters, Rodrigues, and Ridgeway (1998) found that children who are secure are more likely to be coherent in their speech, self-soothing, mature, and seek intimacy and support when required, and are good at problem-solving. These good habits are likely to support well-being in adulthood.

In the secure process, persons are more likely to speak with others to gain a fuller view. Security shows the phenomena of congruence between verbal and nonverbal bodily expressions. The role of the self-reflexive interpretation of self is important, for it is this composite act that is related to how selves understand and value themselves in their social context. Such a placing of self with others can be made according to IWM representations concerning how they value themselves in relation to others. One key for understanding is to grasp to what extent people feel entitled, and inhibited, to act within their attachments. The commonality with emotions and how they are managed is that for pre-reflexive immersion in life, at any point self-reflexivity can operate. However, IWM senses can become reified and valued in

138   ON ATTACHMENT

inaccurate ways. In addition, practising social skills concern how egos place themselves with respect to others to achieve a win-win situation, or not. Personality refers to specific details of how lifestyles are lived.

In attachment, there are different types of rebalancing required because the processes of care-seeking and receipt are set in various ways: the suboptimal types of self-correction are insecurity and disorganisation. However, empirically it is found that there are discreet types of action and reaction in this respect. And whilst there is the optimal case of secure process (leading to self-soothing and the self-governance of the emotions, functioning, and self-esteem), the forms of suboptimal insecure processes can occur temporarily for those who have secure processes most of the time. Disorganisation is the dysfunctional chaotic sort of attachment that offers a completely different type of solution altogether. These processes can become habituated to the degree that they become a tendency to react and express the relational part of the personality. Once they are engrained, they are taken between social contexts across the lifespan.

When there are insecure processes, clients' needs may not be met by the meetings, because they are more likely to be defended in a session, anxious or distressed, fearful in the moment, and alter their relational approach to the therapist, according to one of the insecure forms. On the other hand, if therapists can create a secure process in the meetings then the benefits are shared on both sides of the relationship. The guiding image is the secure base phenomenon that exists in responsive childcare, because attuned care-giving is provided. When children are soothed and relaxed, they regain confidence and trust, and explore and play once more. Similarly, when the care-seeking needs of clients are met they explore their material fully in an atmosphere of trust and safety, and share their interests in such a way that therapists are enabled in providing further care because its supply is well-received. However, the anxious process is likely to include more senses where the other is empathised as good but unworthy for self, neglectful of self, or attacking in relation to senses where self finds itself weak, needy or demanding, under attack, neglected or abandoned. The interactions between self and other have the tendency to remain out of balance in the anxious process.

The avoidant process has its own concomitants of the links between self and other. For the most part, others are empathised as unavailable (when they are not) and the self needs protection from intimacy, or others are too demanding and so self is repulsed. If the other is too close emotionally, and wanting to put too much pressure on self, then self feels invaded and persecuted. The secure and insecure sorts do not experience the sense of disparity and lack of harmony when the self breaks into pieces as it can in disorganisation and when surviving trauma.

Attachment security produces a basic sense of trust and connection experienced in empathising others are helpful, plus the belief that self has resources within itself, from its past experiences of having coped. Such senses can be accessible at moments of stress and can be carried forward into the future.

Discussion

In control system theory, the attachment thermostat operates at a pre-reflexive level but can be over-ridden by the ego. The qualities of emotions and the attachment involved are created by the events of the past in gaining an automatic and central tendency for being with others. The main medium for receiving the consequence of the influence of the past is empathy of the shared life; the emotions are nonverbal requests for others to respond to the self who expresses them. First, in a secure process, the psychodynamics of the emotional motivations are an attraction towards intimacy-seeking, and beneficial contact is anticipated to be achieved. In the insecure sorts, getting intimate contact and succour is uncertain, so threat and distress may have to be coped with, but in a new way. The control system way of looking at the relationship between consciousness and the world is one where the learned model of the world inherent to every individual is the individual difference taken to every context whereby persons work out how to understand and react to what is experienced. Being able to map the distress caused by the actual unavailability of others is part of the ability to understand the self (for instance, as lonely and anguished through disconnection) in comparison to the temporary or more permanent availability of others. The theoretical map used by researchers must have sufficient resolution to capture the qualitative nuances that are common in the territory of intimacy and its vicissitudes.

The ability of care-givers to be aware of what needs to happen in a session concerns managing the tipping point between various attractors and repellents in the interpersonal field. Pro-security is the

140   ON ATTACHMENT

direction away from dysregulation and towards pair-regulation and self-regulation that is explicit, and can be taught and replicated. It is not that some individuals in the community at large do not have these skills. There is nothing lacking if these skills are implicit to those who have them and they are brought out in the moment of need. The point of stating them explicitly is to make hypotheses capable of being tested, and for further refinement and discussion. The ethical responsibility of therapists is to be skilled in their duties when focusing on attachment needs. It concerns the ability to steer between opposing currents that may or may not be evident in the session itself. Mature emotional regulation as self-regulation, or as helping others regulate themselves in therapy sessions, requires understanding how the intensity of distress and the types of signal displayed are concurrent. Persons have their own unique pattern of communication and coping with the possible outcomes for both parties.

On the one hand, the fruit of secure social contact is satisfaction and the ability to connect and encounter others with openness. But if self rates itself persistently in its abilities and potential, due to inaccurate understanding, then the consequences can include beginning a habit of misinterpretation that believes self is incapable of acting sufficiently well at home, at work, or in a specific role. The emotions of self about self can be appropriate well-being, satisfaction, or guilt—or inappropriate shame, pride, or embarrassment with concomitant punishments of self by self for bad behaviour. On the other hand, the worst consequences of inaccurate interpretation can be self-harm, suicide, and murder. For what drives the desperate self on these occasions are motivations of self-criticism and negative comparison with others producing intolerable emotional anguish, a sense of overwhelm with continuing emotional dysregulation. Harsh interpretation is expressed in suicidal thought, feeling, and action. The motivating reasons for death in the case of suicide far exceed the reasons for continuing to live, within the emotional reasoning of the suicidal self. The task of helping the suicidal is to help them reverse the idea of death as blessed relief, and to reconnect them to those they care about.

What is learned can be unlearned

Across the lifespan, the object of the self accrues all manner of meanings. Some of these are reified from much earlier times and persist without challenge or self-critique. When the social conditions around a child are secure and responsive to her needs, the following can happen. Self learns implicit beliefs that it is capable, is not always easily overwhelmed, and has plenty of resources within and around itself, to deal with most stressors. It is, in the main, confident, unflappable, and self-soothing, even when presented with novel situations that are uncertain. It responds, adapts and is flexible. Furthermore, the secure self knows the warning signs of approaching hazards. It has within itself a non-egoic ability to identify automatically possible threats to the satisfactions of its own and others' needs: it has learned positively from prior experiences of non-optimal functioning. The ego and passive processes cue its own manoeuvrability in response to actual threat and is self-correcting even when merely recognising true potential threat. It is capable of self-managed self-care because knowledge that is accurate is used for responding when there is true threat. The connections between the emotions and mood, adequate planning and functioning, and the accurate understanding of itself and its limitations, form a whole. The ego's accurate appraisal of its situation leads to applying corrective skills and abilities of coping and looking after its own and others' needs. This is how it stays in optimal functioning as relaxed, confident in its abilities, and capable of making a thousand tiny changes on the way to being open in a new context, and dealing with unforeseen difficulties. The secure way of dealing with distress is a useful comparison for understanding how the insecure and disorganised processes are problematic and can be corrected.

Distress that remains unsoothed long after the initial trigger is like a burglar alarm that sounds when the threat has gone. The setting is very sensitive to the possibility of some meanings. When there is no resetting of the alarm and it remains sensitive, what occurs is called hyper-vigilance to the *possibility* of a specific meaning in the anticipated future, leading to the choice of avoiding a possibility. The defensive process is generalised and without the burglar alarm resetting itself, the misreading of threat extends long after the first event: after many repetitions for a decade, the imagined possibility of harm alters the life course. Thus, precious years are lost where opportunities to disprove the belief, that something bad is about to recur, never happens. As a result, and without proper evidence, the belief that the same meaning still might be present is repeated. Thus the problem is maintained.

Defence in attachment is a dynamic process that is centred on preventing distress through anticipatory pre-emptive means. Defences are

142   ON ATTACHMENT

part of a whole that maintains inaccurate low self-esteem by preventing catastrophes of risk and shame. In some cases the reverse can occur, where the self-esteem is set low and the habits of belief prevent good self-esteem, and maintain its poverty. Within abstract thinking about a controlling aspect of feedback, and the controlled supporting element, there are only a few possibilities that can occur. What needs to happen is an understanding both of the first constitutions of problems and of the way that people strive to help themselves before therapy, in preparation for understanding how to help people cope long-term with the problems they face.

Let us make a parallel: for instance, from a rational viewpoint it is worth the effort to persist in tackling panic attacks by persisting in going out of the home. The defence occurring is the decision to avoid being on the street, motivated by the benefit of staying away from panic attacks that are expected there. Yet when a full set of details of a person with panic attacks and agoraphobia is considered, it becomes clear that the balance between risks and gains, at time one, could become a new balance of risks and gains, at time two. Because of the decision to over-protect the self made at time one, the current occurrence of the problems is that the anxiety helps the self deal with an object that is felt to be dangerous. The very same distress acts as a motivator towards some meanings of the potential horror of the panic attack, and what others might think of self on the street, and away from the possibility that self could learn anew how to handle the anxiety encountered there. There is a whole of sense though, and that is the healing path of delayed gratification and increased conscientious self-control in the face of anxiety and distress. The use of rationality and problem-solving can tackle frustration, senses of overwhelm, anxiety, and distress, and look to provide short- and long-term behaviours and consequences that deliver carefully thought-through findings about restorative end-points, where there is less likelihood of negative consequences.

The corrective experience

In order to link the formulation of problems to potential solutions, let us take a familiar example of how persons in an insecure process can interpret possibilities as well as actualities. When the inaccurate belief that "others will let me down" is supported, the possibility of encountering corrective evidence and proper understanding remains incomplete. The belief that "others are letting me down just like they always do" can be repeated with no evidence and maintain the misinterpretation of evidence. Therefore, the problem of the commonalities of the mental processes at work in psychopathology and defensive processes are argued to be meaningful processes of the overuse of retained meaningful objects that operate at conscious and preconscious levels, where beliefs and understandings are maintained without proper evidence. In short, they are false beliefs. The way to interpret these processes is to make sense of them through the evidence of their occurrence, and create understanding and beliefs that represent the likelihood of risk more accurately.

The mainstream view of the nature of neuroticism in the personality does not grasp the different sorts of relationship between the ego and its unconscious passive processes. Control theory explains co-regulation that occurs between the motivation for using bigger signals to achieve closeness and prevent separation, and the direction towards deactivation and disorganisation where less optimal forms of defensive response are employed with their associated long-term risks. Co-regulation is most likely to be optimal in those who are securely attached in the negative feedback understanding of their relationships with others and in their own emotional involvement in them. However, there is yet another direction towards feeling overwhelmed that occurs when there is more imbalance felt because of anxiety and depression, or long-term despair felt as dysthymia, and a lack of vitality that supports the generalisation that "I've never been happy", or "There is something wrong with me". Such thoughts are beliefs that are often untrue because they do not refer to evidence. Good enough co-regulation between people generally works when it is possible for both the helpers and the public to go home at the end of the day with the felt sense that their mutual encounter was a positive and worthwhile experience. Any emotionally and bodily felt differences away from relaxed positivity are noteworthy as relevant information about how to surf the wave of negativity all the way into the beach. The role-model of secure process shows that what really counts is the connection between care-givers and care-seekers, and that there is accurate attunement between them.

The relation between the ego and its passive consciousness

In order to develop the practice of formulation with clients in a way that lends itself to knowing how to treat, then it is necessary to have

144   ON ATTACHMENT

ways of presenting and discussing how problems are maintained in the here and now, and further discuss how they have accrued across the years, developmentally. Non-egoic consciousness is a passively constituted sense of feeling something immediately. If all is well and emotions are positive, then there is a sense of unity and well-being. But if there is distress then the ego feels attacked by its distress over which it has no direct control: it cannot turn distress off (but it can influence it). In the latter case, the ego is decentred because its consciousness and automatic non-egoic emotions are at a distance from its egoic control. So while emotions can never be fully and permanently unconscious, they might be temporarily below the limen of consciousness in that they form a mood that is peripheral, rather than being the immediate centre of attention. Also, because emotions are constituted by anonymously functioning consciousness, they are non-egoic and related to mood, social contexts, the past and future, in ways that are not always immediately apparent to the person who feels them.

Within the self-understanding there are problems too. The ego (as the choosing, willing, determining, and interpreting aspect of self) is a small part of the whole. The greater part of self are those habits, emotions, and implicit beliefs that get expressed through anonymously functioning consciousness, sometimes called the "adaptive unconscious" in the sense that the ego sets a direction and the pre-reflexive passive abilities do the work of trying to achieve it (Cortina & Liotti, 2007; Osman, 2004; Wilson, 2002). The work that anonymous consciousness does is to make sense of current objects. It also has a type of inertia where habitual defensive and preferred meanings are overused and misapplied when they are projected on to the contemporary situation. This serves as a misrepresentation of the current object and has the consequence that potentially available true information is lost to the ego. This has consequences for decision-making and the lifestyle as a set of habits and beliefs. The following section discusses how the ego-consciousness balance in depression gets stuck and can become loosened through a more assertive practical approach to the doldrums of low mood.

The telling case of depression as an example of imbalance between the ego and parts of the world-whole around it

In order to focus on the specifics of one example of the connection between interpreting a psychological syndrome and using that understanding to support therapy, let us consider the example of the mood syndrome of major depression. The first point to make is that a state of imbalance is self-maintaining only because it has a purpose or function in the current moment (regardless of how the choice of a defensive action was initiated in the past). Despite the many causes of depression, when a sense of loss occurs through a contribution from the most important intimate relationships, it is necessary to understand that the relationship between the ego and its consciousness is like a rider and horse: each are part of a greater whole. The psychology of the processes of depression shows that the unconscious speaks loss to the ego. Low mood is a meaningful communication that demands the ego to work with an accurate understanding of its relation to itself and others. The easiest way of working against low mood is to refuse to be swallowed up by the demotivating consequences of melancholy. The depressed ego needs to challenge itself and not accept what it feels, as necessitating mourning without end, in order to restore balance. In this way, the rider helps the horse rather than letting the melancholy horse go its own way.

In the case of low mood, the contemporary research into the thinking, acting, relating, choosing, and the general living of people with depression supports the view that it is the mood that acts as a motivating cause on the interpretative stance of the specific form of depressive rationalising at work. The manner of interpreting the evidence that depression values is one of avoiding difficulties and identifying with the low mood itself, where the ego in a non-self-aware way begins the processes of ruminating, selecting painful memories of loss and alienation, and anticipatorily imagining the future as a desolate place where more catastrophes will occur. Research shows that mood is causative of thinking biases that occur when depressed persons make sense of themselves, the world and the future in a specific way (Garland, Harrington, House, & Scott, 2000; Garland & Scott, 2008; Moore & Garland, 2003). Research findings show that depression becomes all-consuming when the ego permits extended melancholy and mourning to influence it. For instance, there is a specific type of identification of the ego with melancholic states. This type of emotional reasoning disconnects the ego from its usual ability to move between perspectives and stay in contact with the inherent changeability of experience. A similar detachment from a previous ability to rationalise and act occurs when the ego becomes aware of how it is with respect to its own ego ideal of how it believes

146　ON ATTACHMENT

it should be, where the latter is used as a measure of how it interprets itself as insufficient and inadequate. In depression, the emotional evidence comes to be understood in a way that maintains and deepens depression without acting as a catalyst for restorative action.

In the example of depression as one form of imbalance, emotions motivate the ego so that it generates a manner of defensive reasoning that maintains the problem. What should really happen is that the ego could understand how it feels depressed, truly acknowledge that, and then do things that will bring about satisfying its needs, recovering from the felt loss, and righting the lifestyle to bring about repair. For what also occurs in depression are memory biases that repress the reception of contemporary positive meanings (Dalgleish & Watts, 1990; Sprock, Braff, Saccuzzo, & Atkinson, 1983) and produce problems in mental processes of generalisation. So, not only does the mood syndrome dictate the form of the ego's activity that comprises impaired functioning, but there are also problems with daily living and making sense of self negatively, so problems accrue (Marx & Schulze, 1991). Depressed persons are generally restricted in taking practical action because their low mood impacts on their functioning (Blankstein, Flett, & Johnston, 1992). Also their self-understanding is impaired because they misinterpret themselves (Dixon, Heppner, Burnett, Anderson, & Wood, 1993; Maes, Schotte, Maes, & Cosyns, 1990). The specific type of memory problem in depression is staying at a level of generality and having difficulty in being able to be specific. The developmental origin of this type of memory has been linked to early trauma and neglect (Spasojevic & Alloy, 2002) possibly resulting in an avoidant attachment and rumination in adults. Depression as a meaningful whole makes sense because the meaning that is supplied comprises a general narrative of what it is to feel loss that seems irrevocable, while the ego can tell itself it is without resources in itself and in its social context.

Although there are different varieties of depression that arise in different contexts, research shows that behavioural activation is the most effective treatment to overcome severe depression (Martell, Addis, & Jacobson, 2001). Whatever the means of the current maintenance, past accrual, and the future prognosis, being as physically active as possible and taking an interest in meaningful activities, moves depressed persons out of their low mood and raises their sense of well-being, possibly through changes that occur at a physiological level, as well as at the level of reflection after they have achieved a thing that they set out to do. When the understanding attained is believed but inaccurate, it is frequently tied to anxious or other distressed mood states that may prevent openness to the experience of what is actually present coming into consciousness. Given the discussion above, the helpfulness of interpreting how various types of awareness fit together, to create the mood of chronic depression, makes it simpler to state what is helpful.

Using the psychology of depression means that the following list of ten helpful interventions could be explained and then enacted by depressed persons, because they want to help themselves and alter the balance between their mood, their choices, and activity levels, and because they are committed to persist until they achieve them. How to work with depression interpersonally is that, once clients have invested positively in the therapeutic relationship, they can be asked to create a morning practice where they choose an activity on waking up that has the sole aim of helping them start their day well, by having the high possibility of raising their mood and pleasing them for a few minutes. The way to present the task is to ask them to structure their week with enjoyable activities on getting up to help commence their days through having something positive to look forward to. It requires commitment because of the realisation that staying in bed for four hours after waking up, ruminating, and worrying, only works to create a mood of profound pessimism and despair.

1. Given that depression is connected with generalisation, going in the opposite direction can be practised, such as having precise achievable goals for the next week. For instance, creating the personal aim of going for a walk each day for twenty minutes and helping persons to set a concrete goal for themselves, such as "I will get up and dressed by seven. I will take the children to school every day, no matter how I feel", is a way of getting started on recovery.
2. When I engage in some activity that works to improve mood, I will write it down and do it again.
3. As a remedy to ruminating on past upsets and worrying on upsetting future subjects, I will think of something positive and safe for five minutes. I will practice doing this whenever I find that I have got stuck on a problem. With practice it gets easier to change the focus of thinking to more positive objects.
4. Alternatively, if clients are facing decisions and real problems, it helps to encourage them to be specific about what these are. Encourage them to ask themselves "What is it that I don't like

148 ON ATTACHMENT

doing and why? Why do I doubt that I can do it?" These pour gentle scepticism on to their negative certainty.

5. When clients begin to realise that they have got fixed on regrets, or some event from the past, ask them to be aware of that, and bring that to a close and stay in the present moment.

6. The use of a diary to record achieving small tasks, and the amount of pleasure felt for each hour of the day, shows how a person's mood varies, and what works to improve it.

7. Having psycho-education information sheets on depression helps by explaining how depression commences and how it lifts.

8. Making a list of what helps improve mood at the end of each week is useful and can be achieved by looking back at the diary and thinking constructively.

9. Asking the depressed person simple practical questions such as "What does not help your mood?" is a way of beginning reflection on how the pieces of their low mood fit together. Asking them to write down what helps and what does not help on stickers and put the answers where they will be seen, for instance, on a bedside table or similar place, make a reminder for what has been discovered.

10. When a person has discovered what improves her mood, she can be very specific about what that is. For instance, "I went to ____ with ____ and did ____ for __ minutes and felt ____ and thought ____". This helps to overcome negative generalisation also.

Conclusion

One research question is: "What are the conditions of possibility for individuals *not* to be able to self-correct on their own problematic emotions, beliefs, and behaviours that constitute their distress and affect others?" If the understanding employed decreases distress then there is problem-solving. Understanding works because it is accurate. The question of finding understanding and beliefs that work devolves to finding correct understandings that deliver the goods of being able to communicate how to decrease distress and cope with inevitable difficulties. This means that it is necessary to know what an answer looks like in order to be able to work towards it and recognise it when it occurs. The good life is having accurate understanding plus the important ability to be self-correcting when it comes to knowing where the self is on its territory and map of the world, even when that map is inaccurate. The skill of orienteering is the skill of knowing where one is in the territory and on the map. It is the case that the ego and its world-constitution, seen with respect to what is and what could be, are the first topics of understanding maps of the world.

On the other hand, when there is imbalance and distress, automatic passive constitutions of senses of loss, hopelessness, and despair, give the ego the bodily and emotional sense of distress and danger (with respect to the past learnings and future expectations) that are dictated by the map of the world held within consciousness. The source of the problem in self, and its answer, operate outside of the usual reach of the ego. The ego can neither turn off a problem, nor turn on an answer, without help.

It is argued that the example of the secure process, self-soothing, and problem-solving indicate that one of the fundamental processes that therapy must provide is a basic sense of trust and safety in the therapist, sometimes called holding, the secure frame, or the secure base, in order for sufficient self-disclosure by clients to occur. Specifically, the research findings noted above emphasise the importance of safety, closeness, and the ability to be separate in a mature way. When the ego is able to access secure feelings and memories at times of distress, this is one way of soothing self. The sense of being cared for by mental health professionals gets communicated through the totality of verbal and nonverbal social acts. What it feels like for clients leads to the thought that, despite the risk of self-disclosure, it is anticipated, at an emotional level, that they will be accepted and the alienation they feel will decrease. A thought that expresses this emotion with anticipatory focus is that "my therapist is interested in me and has designed with me a tailored package of care entirely addressed to my needs". The sense of safety and being cared for can be communicated through such actions as involving clients in the discussion of their needs and the order of topics to be covered in the meetings. When this is provided, the effect is that clients get improvements quicker during the important first six sessions. The early success experienced in a secure process includes clients valuing the help they receive because they have been involved in it from the start. What helps is the basic provision of caring that makes persons with the anxious process more relaxed and the avoidant process more expressive. The making of shared goals with clients and sharing the responsibility of advancing with them is a good means of providing informed consent at the beginning of the series of meetings and across their course.

PART III

INCREASING SECURITY AS A
CONDITION OF SUCCESSFUL THERAPY

Introduction to Part III

The definitions of attachment and its links to emotional regulation are now applied to meetings with the public. It is difficult to provide sufficient detail in a book or lecture series concerning how to engage the public in a therapeutic process when there are so many variations in the content and relational process between two persons. Working with attachment translates practically into asserting simple statements that reduce levels of hyperactivation and decrease levels of deactivation, so that both persons in individual therapy feel more comfortable with each other. In the light of attachment, Freud's understanding of unconscious communication translates into knowing how to understand emotions, sensations, and imagery and make statements that save the frame, promote a sense of safety, and enable a secure process to begin, if that is possible. If that is not possible, then insecure and disorganised processes will ensue and even then good quality work can still take place.

In this introductory guide, what follows below is a rough map for practice. This final part of the work uses the interpretations of mental processes for understanding attachment to shape individual therapy with adults. When attachment ideas interpret intimate, caring relationships, it becomes possible to provide care that works with the needs

154   ON ATTACHMENT

of the public. There is difficulty in specifying general principles for working with adults from the adult attachment literature. It is easier to comment on a real specific case than to theorise and state general principles. However, it is the aim of this part to state hypotheses about how attachment appears in the public's relating. These hypotheses need corroboration. They are shared here as the initial stages of circulating them for the responses of colleagues. The unifying theme below is to be aware of secure process as a model for successful care, and that despite the presence of insecure and disorganised processes, there are changes in process between the persons involved (Davila, Burge, & Hammen, 1997). The many forms of therapy and mental health care provision share the characteristic that they are about the felt sense of the care provided. It follows that when clients and therapists meet it makes most sense to create services that can be secure, or tend towards being secure, even if they start in another way. Focusing on the processes of the provision and receipt of care engages the public in something meaningful. What helps is being clear about what will help and explaining why this is the case. Thus, theoretically as well as practically, there is a need to grasp what the characteristics of therapeutic services should be according to attachment theory.

A return to Freud is made in seeking continuity with his original psycho-analysis and connecting with the hypotheses about caring shown in the SSP, AAI, and other forms of trustworthy empirical enquiry that demonstrate adult attachment in individual therapy. But Bowlby abandoned the transference and counter-transference way of interpreting relating in preference for thinking about IWMs, because control theory is the better image to explain the central phenomenon of the perseverance of IWM settings and their inertia to change. Once again, it is a mistake to think that attachment is a fixed part of the personality. Freud advised colleagues to "become aware of the 'counter-transference', which arises as a result of the patient's influence on the therapist's 'unconscious feelings'" (1910d, p. 144), but this is not itself a definition of counter-transference in relation to transference. Because Bowlby advised therapists to help clients know their IWM in order to help them alter them (1977, p. 421), an attachment-oriented therapy prefers to focus on the qualities of past and present attachment dynamics. It interprets in terms of the self-other caring at work when clients describe their impressions of the greater social world, specific other people, and themselves in these contexts.

What is presented below is a brief overview of topics that could be presented in far greater detail. However, the connection between Freud's work and the contemporary empirical psychology of attachment in adults is specifying repetitive mental processes that create emotional, relational, and psychological problems, shaped by a number of co-existent causes, operating within different levels of the human being considered as a biological, social, and psychological whole. To a degree, emotions connected with trauma, and other topics that need to be discussed, are inevitably re-experienced in the telling. Thus, re-experiencing is inevitably a part of presenting oneself for mental health care of any sort and it requires careful and sensitive handling. The presenting problems of having received poor parenting, violence from any source, and the myriad other problems that people want help with, are problems to be expressed through the medium of relating. The therapist's role is to enable rather than enforce. So, understanding attachment shows the inherent contours and necessities of these experiences. The connection between accurate understanding, and good quality practice and research is that hypotheses can be made and tested to highlight and explain observable phenomena. If there is sufficient security, the felt senses on both sides of the relationship are likely to be more relaxed. In this atmosphere it is easier to bring up questions and comment on what occurs between the two persons.

Chapter Seven states the case for continuity of theory between Freud and contemporary attachment-oriented practice as validated by empirical psychology. Chapter Eight makes hypotheses about how attachment appears in assessment. Chapter Nine provides details of how to work with specific attachment processes through some cases. Chapter Ten concludes by discussing the guiding role of the secure process in relation to the frame, the intersection between a number of interests. Specifically, the practical endpoint being argued for is a view of practice, theory, and research focused on the therapeutic relationship. The holding environment or frame of clarity about what is being offered is fundamental for the provision of quality care. Collaborative working and informed consent connect when professionals work with attachment forces rather than against them. One benefit of helping the public understand what is being offered them is to pre-empt mis-understanding and disappointment at assessment, and during the course of meetings.

CHAPTER SEVEN

Psychodynamics of attaching

This chapter makes a clarification by a return to Freud to understand the psychodynamics of mental processes, mentalization, empathy, insight or reflective function—call it what you will—in detail. A specific reading of the original senses of Freud's terminology, within his original practice, are argued for to define a contemporary attachment-oriented psychodynamic practice and restate the basics of good basic practice across all brand name types of therapy. The central dynamic in any therapy is to monitor and decrease resistance and its accompanying anxieties and increase openness to the public's concerns, so that their material becomes public to both people in the therapy relationship. The movement towards openness of self-disclosure by clients is a statement of the obvious and a direct consequence of Freud's legacy to mental health care. Openness as basic awareness is a contemporary rendition of the Freudian motto *"Wo Es war, soll Ich werden"* (1933a, p. 80) which is translatable as "Where It was, the I must be", in the sense of being able to understand one's own biases and blindspots. The sense of Freud's intent can be understood as the necessity for openness in mindfulness practice and in attending to the repressed and distressing aspects of experience, including attempts at owning what has been disowned, to include it and work with it. But as with all aims, the devil

157

158 ON ATTACHMENT

is in the detail. Just how should it be understood? The secure base and its secure process in individual therapy exist as one possibility alongside other reactions. It is argued that a secure process needs to occur for a sufficient amount of the time in meetings in order for a sufficient amount of self-disclosure to occur, and for distress and trauma to be explained.

This chapter summarises the key psychodynamic processes at the heart of attachment theory. The sequence below begins with a return to psychodynamics to express the temporally and intersubjectively changing set of motivational forces that exists in any social field. Therapists and mental health workers who offer secure relationships offer care and take responsibility for their own well-being. Secure persons can calm themselves and this enables both autonomy and connection to occur, it feels good and provides a sense of confidence, on the way to producing the beliefs and habits of good living. The secure IWM is a map of relating at an emotional level of understanding, according to how secure co-operation is possible. The secure self-balancing ego and its consciousness is the result of supportive social contexts. A flexible responsiveness in the selection of various aims for satisfaction in everyday life, in any twenty-four-hour period (or over much longer expanses of future time), is a sign that the ego can choose how to react and not be impaired in its choices because of defensive barriers, and excessive distress. A relaxed ego can prioritise between competing desirable aims, and can change priorities to act and achieve with comparative ease. It is good mental health when persons can deal with ambiguity and lack of certainty.

A return to Freud

The discussion of therapeutic relating below concerns a return to basic Freudian terms, properly understood in the context of his practice. The aim is to link them with defence and attachment, and show how to interpret conscious material by connecting it to contemporary qualitative research into what happens, moment-to-moment between the two parties who form the relationship in individual therapy. It is necessary to acknowledge the contributions of Sigmund Freud, whose terms are still in use in attachment research and contemporary practice.

When learning about psycho-analysis, psychodynamic therapy, and how to make an attachment-oriented psychodynamic practice, there are incorrect readings of Freud that have instigated unhelpful

PSYCHODYNAMICS OF ATTACHING   159

understandings about how to relate and speak. For instance, Freud's mention in passing that the therapist "should be opaque to his patients, and like a mirror should show them nothing but what is shown to him" (1912e, p. 118) has been wrongly understood to be a mandate to be silent and unresponsive. The more accurate reading of this phrase is to understand when to introduce a pregnant pause into a conversation, so other persons can finish their own thoughts rather than leave something half-said. What Freud actually urged was for therapists to avoid indifference and aloofness. For Freud, there was never neutrality in the sense of appearing unconcerned when faced with another's suffering. Furthermore, Freud argued that there should never be rigid technique (Lohser & Newton, 1996, p. 14, p. 180, p. 183, p. 185, p. 193). Consequently, an excessive focus on boundaries is not Freudian. Nor did he believe therapists should hide behind silence and a blank face; rather they should be restrained and disciplined in how they pay attention. For Freud, one key to therapeutic work is managing resistance in order to get clients to present their narratives and stay in the relationship, because they are being properly heard. What Freud's clients said of him was that he was kind, responsive, and compassionate (Lohser & Newton, 1996, p. 175, p. 180, pp. 189–193, p. 204). His advice to be silent and reflect back what has been understood has been taken out of context by those who have urged therapists to be excessively formal and unresponsive.

A therapeutic strategy of Freud's was to ask people to change their behaviour, to bear distress, and practice a skill if doing so made them anxious. In his treatment of the composer Gustav Mahler, who was anxious about returning to conducting, Freud encouraged him to do so in order to regain his confidence. Psycho-analysis in its original form was not opposed to behavioural change and the promotion of more satisfying habits. Perhaps in the light of Freud curing himself of his own phobias, he understood well that, for example, for people with agoraphobia, therapists should "induce them by the influence of the analysis … to go into the street and to struggle with their anxiety while they make the attempt" (Freud, 1919a, p. 166; cf. Ellenberger, 1970, pp. 444–450). In providing help, this can be taken as an encouragement to think about how relating needs to change also.

Discussed below is an exploration of the consistencies between Freud's terminology and current empirical research on attachment in therapy. When bringing both together by expressing them as mental

160   ON ATTACHMENT

processes, it helps to make clear that the commonality across the years is that mental processes make mental senses conscious. It has been shown abundantly in experimental psychology that priming produces unconscious presences; these are motivations within and between people that connect them in various ways. Priming is a term that is used in experimental psychology, where objects that have meaningful associations for participants, can be shown to make measurable differences in experiments where one group is primed and another is not. When priming people to be aware, the experiments show biases in thinking, choosing, and feeling that are demonstrable, but not open to conscious inspection (Schachter, Dobbins, & Schnyer, 2004). Even when this is not in full awareness but is merely an influential presence, priming can still be a force to motivate action, relating, understanding, and belief.

Sigmund Freud's legacy is neither one of empty historical interest nor is it a bench-mark to show how far therapy has progressed. Despite his haste to theorise, he observed some major aspects of human beings that are universal for all therapy brands and have been part of mainstream therapy since its inception, that is, his concepts of interpretation, motivation, drive, economics and dynamics, resistance, and the unconscious. I have previously explained how these can be identified through intentionality (Owen, 2006b, 2007, 2015). However, his concepts and practices have sometimes been misrepresented. Historical explanation is required in order to grasp what Freud really meant, by studying how he deployed his ideas in his sessions. However, the understanding of the human condition has changed considerably since Freud's day, and many who now use his terms are likely to do so in ways that would not be recognisable by Freud himself. Freud worked by empathising and interpreting his feelings and actions, but many of his theoretical writings obscure the phenomena that he was treating and the reasons why he practised as he did. On closer inspection, credence needs to be given to what Freud practised in order to offset those understandings that are contrary to the spirit, and the letter, of what he actually did, which was not always what he requested his readers to do in his writings on technique (1904a, 1911e, 1912b, 1912e, 1913c, 1914g, 1915a, 1937c, 1940a).

Understanding resistance

In his work Freud promoted the quality of the therapeutic relationship. He monitored the amount of resistance occurring and aimed to reduce

PSYCHODYNAMICS OF ATTACHING 161

it to enable clients to self-disclose sufficiently to get help (Freud, 1914g, p. 155; 1940a, p. 179). What Freud did with resistance was to uncover it, lower it and identify what might motivate it, aiming to encourage clients in the task of speaking freely. He did not analyse resistance but worked with it (Lohser & Newton, 1996, p. 165, p. 168, p. 172, p. 176). Resistance is cessation of speech because of what is felt. There needs to be a way of talking around the inhibiting concern. Such a discussion starts with the origin of the inhibition and should make explicit the anticipation that the therapist will be unsympathetic, in order for that to be set aside. An absence of speech hides another part of the story that is not being told, because distress chokes speech. What is refused to be said is connected to that which is most painful. So resistance is a type of unassertiveness as part of social anxiety and ambivalence. Previously free expression comes to a grinding halt because the negative motivation of social anxiety inhibits expression because of the futurally imagined repercussions of a topic. What the ego ambivalently wants to discuss produces emotions about the possibility of disapproval, criticism, and rejection, and other negative consequences. Regardless of what happens next, receiving help in itself contains the possibility of a cure, through finding new meaning and less distress, through discussion in the therapeutic relationship, which acts as a reframing atmosphere of trust and care, brought about by the withholding of value-laden criticism, and the upholding of the desire to empathise clients' views of the world and of themselves in it.

Some of the most basic of Freud's terms can be defined as follows. When people speak freely, they "free associate". They express understandable cultural senses of the cultural object that they are talking about. Most often, they are telling the truth about their experiences. Free association refers to the soliloquies of clients in psycho-analysis where clients speak into a receptive silence. Free association occurs to a lesser extent in all relationships. In the moment when the ego chooses what to say, any abrupt changes in its narrative may show that an internal taboo has been encountered, which Freud called *Widerstand*, "resistance", as in the sense of there being a resistance to free associate or, more generally, to speak the truth and to speak at all (Ellenberger, 1970, p. 490, p. 566). *Widerstand* is "resistance to association" (Breuer & Freud, 1895d, p. 270). For example, "there was something attaching to the idea of 'love' which there was a strong resistance to her telling me" (Breuer & Freud, 1895d, p. 273; cf. Ellenberger, 1970, p. 518, pp. 542–543). Resistance is

162   ON ATTACHMENT

caused by repression and is heard as the slowing down of free speech and even its cessation, as was noted by "Anna O" (Breuer's client, Bertha Pappenheim) who called what Breuer was doing with her the "'talking cure', which she referred to jokingly as 'chimney-sweeping'" (Breuer & Freud, 1895d, p. 30).

The link between the need for openness and decreasing resistance originally came to light in Josef Breuer's work with "Anna O". The learning experienced as a result of speaking with women with hysteria was that the relation of problems located in the body to memories and speech was such that *"each individual hysterical symptom immediately and permanently disappeared when we had succeeded in bringing clearly to light the memory of the event by which it was provoked and in arousing its accompanying affect, and when the patient had described that event in the greatest possible detail and had put the affect into words"* (Breuer & Freud, 1895d, p. 6, original italics). Not only was there expression, there was relief, and symptoms disappeared through a change in meaning. At the end of his life, Freud stated that the "overcoming of resistances is the part of our work which requires the greatest time and the greatest trouble" so giving some indication about its importance in practice (1940a, p. 179). Freud's boon to therapy practice still serves a function in understanding the basics of the provision of care and the difficulties of its receipt, when understood in the context of attachment. Freud's client Elisabeth von R gladly accepted being permitted to talk freely and this became the technique of free association (Breuer & Freud, 1895d, p. 56; Ellenberger, 1970, p. 543). Freud's interpretation of the causes of repression, or in the later terminology, the repression and resistance to the free flow of client's speech, became central to practice and provided a definitive context for understanding how to work with the therapeutic relationship.

Resistance is an inhibiting social anxiety in the therapeutic relationship specifically about the possibility of not being understood but judged negatively, and is linked to how the ego dislikes itself for being the way it is. The motivated cause of the inhibition of speech is what Freud wanted to identify in order to restore its free flow, and permit treatment. Resistance might be related to the sum total of anticipated comparisons that have a connection to the past. Resistance could exist in relation to any potential object of speech, the anticipated empathised response of the therapist, and the anticipated emotional states of client and therapist. For instance, items about self that are felt to be shameful, disgusting, and weird are expected to be met with horror and revulsion from others rather than compassion. Resistance occurs when clients refuse to self-disclose, self-disclose selectively, or self-disclose with great difficulty. However, self-disclosure is necessary in order to get help through rationalising the objects of private experience, and bringing them into the public domain, and the relationship with the therapist, or with persons in the home.

If one party is anxious or fearful in any meeting, then she might be inhibited in speaking her mind, or be unable to think rationally and assert herself and her viewpoint in the moment. When clients falter and put the brakes on self-disclosure in this way, it is because of the resistance to speak what comes to mind. When resistance occurs clients are unassertive and do not present the material they need to speak about, or explain how come they feel bad in their own valuing of themselves, because of the expected consequences of disapproval from the therapist. The anxiety felt could be associated with the topics being discussed, or with respect to being in the therapeutic relationship. If an insecure process is triggered for any reason in the session, then the likely consequence, if it remains unnoticed and unaddressed, is that the session may be the last one to be attended, or the course of the meetings become not what they should be, because there is avoidance of truth and its accompanying distress. There are many felt responses to attempted care-giving interventions made in the sessions, and to the material being expressed, and in the manner of accepting the therapist's influence. In an extended consequence, resistance also occurs in the egoic refusal of change and experimenting with a new lifestyle, and the abandoning, of restorative experiences. This is problematic because refusing to adapt to new challenges across the lifespan, means not going with the flow of life. A fundamental event in any form of therapy is when clients verbally present and reflect. If their narrative comes to a halt in a telling way, or is suffused with anxiety for an unknown reason, or there are problems of attending the assessment, then resistance is present. However, it should also be noticed that therapists too can become resistant. Heinrich Racker introduced "counter-resistance" into the lexicon to refer to therapists' own resistance to interpretation (1958, p. 215). Counter-resistance is born of a fear to interpret because the interpretation itself is incomplete and indicates links to important material.

164 ON ATTACHMENT

The importance of openness

The major teaching point of this brief review of Freud for any type of practice is as follows: listening to any conversation requires being genuinely open to what is being said, its full sense, and not prejudging what the speaker means. Responding to the personal resonances and implications it provokes is like listening to music. The listener's perspective may catch what is being genuinely communicated if the message is adequately expressed and the listener is open to its receipt. In psychoanalysis the purpose of the free-flowing soliloquy from clients, and the agenda-less meetings, is to follow this fundamental rule. Open attention encourages thoughts and feelings to enter into consciousness and be spoken so that therapists can understand truthfully how clients think, feel, and behave. For therapists, trying to understand accurately what is being said, there is the aim of listening without jumping to conclusions by keeping open to the perspective being expressed. Freud called it *"gleichschwebende Aufmerksamkeit"*, free-floating attention (1900a, pp. 528–529; 1912e, pp. 115–116; 1913i, 1915e, p. 194). Being maximally open to clients is a guiding ideal though. As Wilhelm Reich noted in his first-ever definition of psycho-analytic practice, there are opposed forces in self-disclosure: the "basic rule of psycho-analysis, which requires that the censor be abolished and one's thoughts allowed to 'associate freely,' is the strictest, most indispensible measure of analytic technique. It finds a powerful support in the force of the unconscious impulses and desires pressing towards action and consciousness; however, it is opposed by another force, which is also unconscious, namely the 'counter-cathexis' of the ego. This force makes it difficult and sometimes impossible for the patient to follow this basic rule" (Reich, 1950, p. 4). What can be drawn from this observation is that what is already known and well-practised tends to be experienced in moving into the present moment in a relationship. Trying to know any topic is limited by prior understanding. In philosophy, it is called the hermeneutic circle. "The whole must be understood in terms of its individual parts, individual parts in terms of the whole. To understand the whole of a work we must refer to its author and to related literature. Such a comparative procedure allows one to understand every individual work ... more profoundly ... So understanding of the whole and of the individual parts are interdependent" (Dilthey, 1976, p. 262). The word interpretation, a translation of Freud's *Deutung*, never referred to anything other than the quality of the experiences of the people he treated, and Freud was open because he permitted himself to be corrected by empirical research (1925d). However, following Dilthey, interpretation is a self-consciously making explicit the conditions for something to have meaning and requires specifying the relationship between the part and the whole. Grounding is drawing rational justifications for further research and therapeutic practice that always includes some uncertainty due to the fact that human meanings and intentions have multiple ways of being contextualised: the part always appears differently according to the background that encircles it.

The study of interpreting is called hermeneutics. A formal psychological hermeneutics dares to specify motivating meanings in the attachment sphere. If clarity is achieved and the college of the academic community agree, then theory can move forward even when it has some of its cherished ideas disproved. When it comes to comparing meanings across time, working out which option to take demands meta-representation across time, now and then. Put simply, the present and the future are understandable on the basis of past learnings, conscious and unconscious. What comes to mind for therapists are the possible understandings of attachment aspects of clients' developmental histories, how they interact with the present, and appear dynamically from moment to moment.

Between Freud's directive for both persons in the relationship to be open to the resonances of meaning that come to mind about what clients say and how they represent themselves, and Reich indicating that such an attempt is forever limited if not impossible, there lies the skill of how to engage clients in a constructive piece of work. The great majority of therapists have abandoned Freud's model of sitting behind clients and requesting them to free associate. Yet the dynamics that permit a sufficiently self-disclosing client require there to be enough spontaneity for both persons to speak if what they feel needs to be said and enquired about. The secure process is a fine example for therapy because it attends to the important dynamic that happens. Therapists are the more enlightened persons and leaders who take responsibility for providing therapeutic conditions such that the public get to feel sufficiently safe to self-disclose, agree their aims for the meetings, are supported in reflecting sufficiently on what they express, and find relief and spontaneous reframing of the meanings they discuss: the very meanings that have been wrapped up in shame and secrecy, and kept to themselves. When these become public in the therapeutic relationship, the meanings and experiences clients suffer are stated aloud, which gives them the chance to hear themselves and feel the full extent of what they have repressed. On speaking for the first time, their self-disclosure often brings with it spontaneous catharsis, and this leads to further re-evaluation of their experience. Any brand of therapy necessitates adequate self-disclosure, and, once in the relationship, the verbal and nonverbal responses by therapists are interpreted by clients, and the therapeutic response becomes further food for reflection to sustain change. The take-home message after self-disclosure, plus the context of the relationship with the worker, should provide a series of new events that shape and mould new meaning. So the fundamental rule from Freud in the context of attachment is that openness is required from both persons to the shameful and distressing objects of old.

On therapists' side of hearing and spontaneously emotionally responding to what is said and felt, there exists the working life of helping distressed persons by being sufficiently open to that distress. Willingness to engage with it is a necessary and inevitable part of mental health workers doing their job properly and helping the public get the service that they need. The pitfalls to be avoided are many. Members of the public who suddenly feel over-exposed by what they have said and felt, and therapists who regret that they did not respond adequately in that moment, are two factors in promoting drop-out and preventing adequate self-disclosure. If clients reckon that their worker cannot handle what they truly want help with, then there will be unmet need. So the balance to be made is one of helping people express themselves in ways such that the possibility of dropping out are minimised through agreeing clear aims for the meetings, with both parties asserting themselves to create a shared direction.

The relations between the conscious, unconscious presence, and the biological substrate

From the perspective of looking back into history, the multiple ways in which therapists can be urged to hone their attention, their responding skills and be more psychologically minded, emotionally intelligent, empathic, and insightful, are central to attachment-oriented psychodynamic practice. When looking at the broad span of Freud's writings, it is clear to see that he vacillated in his comments. But to provide an

PSYCHODYNAMICS OF ATTACHING   167

overview, and to sketch the complexity that lies therein, it is possible to select some passages that are concordant with contemporary attachment research. Freud commented that "psycho-analysis is part of the mental science of psychology. It is also described as 'depth psychology' … If someone asks what 'the psychical' really means, it is easy to reply by enumerating its constituents: our perceptions, ideas, memories, feelings and acts of volition—all of these form part of what is psychical" (1940b, p. 282). When he was explaining the psychical he meant the full extent of conscious and unconscious processing. However, the relation between (i) the psychical, (ii) unconscious presences that register at some level, though subliminally (literally below the line of consciousness), and (iii) the biological substrate, are woven into a complicated cloth. "Our reply is that it would be unjustifiable and inexpedient to make a breach in the unity of mental life for the sake of propping up a definition, since it is clear in any case that consciousness can offer us an incomplete and broken chain of phenomena" (Freud, 1940b, p. 286). The commonality between Freud's position and the woven aspects of being human is that there are most certainly observable conscious thoughts, feelings and intentions. Yet these are powered by the neurological and biochemical substrate in relation with others, which only science can study. Mental processes for Freud and for contemporary psychology involve pattern-matching and the encoding and decoding of brute conscious impressions, that presents finished meanings for the ego to inspect. The primary processes of automatic meaning-creation of all kinds are done without inference by the ego. The ego can only deliberate and infer how it understands someone else's experiences or its own *after the fact*. The qualitative bedrock of theorising in psychology comes about through bringing together findings and perspectives from attachment research, for instance, to interpret, to make sense of what qualitatively exists for anyone—even those experiences that make no sense to the persons who have them: that is the challenge at hand.

Freud held the view that emotions and representations in perception or memory form a whole, as he noted in *On Aphasia* (1891b). The phenomena that Freud was theorising in his ideas of repression and splitting are the breaking of a previously whole object that occurs in defensive forgetting, or through the socially motivated suppression of distress, desires, and actions (Lane, Groisman, & Ferreira, 2006). For instance, in sexual abuse, there can be pervasive anxiety, dissociation, and non-egoic but purposeful defensive forgetting, alongside clear

168   ON ATTACHMENT

memories and ongoing effects of the abuse in creating semi-permanent amnesia. Repression, the splitting of emotions away from representations, is variable because the split-off aspects re-enter consciousness as imagination (Bernet, 2003), for instance, or as the replaying of retained experiences that re-enter current experience, such as trauma-induced psychosis, and the return of learning associated with trauma and PTSD. Such a return of the disavowed object into consciousness and its emotions can occur with the triggering of a syndrome after a sufficient time of stress where the subclinical vulnerability in a person flares up. And, similarly, the process of openness and listening provides an expanded context to make sense of material that is threatening and distressing, and needs to be reassembled in a secure context. However, defences are knowingly employed by the ego *and* unknowingly employed by passive consciousness. Despite well-known drawbacks, short-term gain is a defensive choice that is seen, in the light that values short-term fixes, as a positive one. This type of choice is where it is clear that short-term fixes are not the best option, but they bring a reward that is sufficiently valued. The term "meta-representation of choice" is a way of unpacking what happens in choosing defensive strategies when under the threat of risk, and being able to compare them to long-term benefit.

Promoting understanding: the case of intuition

This section discusses some of the fundamental aspects about being aware to be found in mainstream psychological literature. The commonality between reflection, mindfulness, psycho-analysis, and therapy meetings is remaining open to what exists, in the spirit of Freud's fundamental rule. When consciousness stays open to what exists in a relaxed way, then qualitative experience, and the basic self-presence of self to self, is available to awareness. This means that important information is capable of being registered so that the ego can become aware of links between processes and mental senses as they happen. Freud's original psychodynamic interpretation explained the aims, teleologies, and functions that the ego wants to create, in order to help clients understand themselves. For instance, beliefs and decision-making about how to manage emotions from childhood will be out of place if they are still being used thirty years later. The phenomena that Freud wanted to explain are irrational; for example, how persons who had survived murder attempts have taken their own lives later on. Or, for instance, how receiving another's sadism in childhood can turn that child into a masochist as an adult (Wyss, 1966, p. 123). With this in mind, it becomes possible to spot what is common in the interpretative features under consideration, without getting lost in Freud's rules for interpreting that took him away from the phenomena and sent him into speculation about unconscious communication.

Freud's *Deutung*, the interpretation of unconscious causes, is sharing a hypothesis with someone about the causes of their here-and-now behaviour and experiencing. The purpose of interpreting why, for instance, it is difficult to speak is to help clients understand themselves better, and enable them to speak. This is important because the route to them receiving help is by reducing their resistance and repression, so enabling them to speak and self-disclose (Breuer & Freud, 1895d, p. 157). Concomitantly, a block to truthfulness guarantees failure of understanding and change. The speaker may have spoken well but the listener's attention might have wandered off on to some topic of his own, which in turn, may or may not be related to what is being said. For *"whatever interrupts the progress of analytic work is a resistance"* in a more general sense (Freud, 1900a, p. 517, original italics). All the while, despite the definitions of attachment made so far, it is urged that those who apply them are tentative when thinking through how to help the public and be ready to reconsider the evidence they are referring to when making their comments. In order to provide a quality of care that deals with the possibility that the meetings might unfold in an insecure direction, it is best to explain one's own thinking to the public clearly. Mental health care must gain informed consent in a way that the public understands: it necessitates making decisions with them about what sort of care they need, and stating how it works is part of creating care with them.

The most basic phenomenon is that there can be a dynamic awareness of what is actually in consciousness, in the most basic aspect of merely being aware of an object that presents itself for the ego's attention. But whether it is called "living consciously", "insight", "intuition", or grasping the gestalt of what something means (Boston Change Process Study Group, 2010), what is being discussed is the degree to which the pre-reflexive presences of emotion, belief, thought, and awareness of objects in the world appear in consciousness. Awareness may happen without full, reasoned evidence to support understanding. So therapists have their hunch, voice it, and get it confirmed or denied.

170   ON ATTACHMENT

One example of fast, accurate, primary understanding is emotion that functions automatically as part of the living set of sensations of the personal body in relationship with others. Meanings and communications of all kinds have implied senses. Automatic implicit attitudes and learnings from the past get attributed to behaviour, relating, and emoting about what there is felt to exist. A gut feeling can promote instant snap decision-making, which is often felt as the lived sense that something complex will work or not, without a thought-through set of rationalisations. It just *feels* likely that something will work (or not). The pattern-match that occurs, and promotes the emotion, is the result of identifying something accurately for what it is, while the degree of accuracy is established retrospectively.

But this is not to say that all emotions, immediate understandings, and spontaneous behaviours, are accurate. Extra proven factors may need to be included because some identities are counter-intuitive, and sometimes rationality and experiments are required, to demonstrate something. Paranoia and extreme depression are two situations that show inaccurate understandings most easily. However, the receipt of wisdom is shown at automatic levels of behaviour and relating, in knowing immediately what to say, and how to maintain balance in a relationship through applying attachment theory, and being able to spot patterns due to the learning provided by years of practice. Self-confidence in one's abilities is gained through the explicit checking of one's aims against one's actual achievements. Skilled practice is the result of understanding a set of similar situations so many times that complex matters for rational analysis become an unconscious ability, in that understanding and decision-making become fast and accurate.

The general process of listening is to be aware of what is being communicated by the other and what is felt by self. The most basic process of understanding any phenomenon starts with merely being aware, focusing on what it is and how we are aware of it. For in contemplation, there arise the many forms of awareness that consciousness possesses. How the object appears depends on what forms of awareness are involved in its appearance in consciousness. First impressions can be subtle, flimsy, short-lasting experiences that are easily ignored or swept away in a rush to attend to something else. Two cases arise. Case A: in the view of hindsight, what is realised is that the brief thoughts and feelings of intuition did turn out to be accurate predictions and they were given credence at the time. But there is case B: something did not feel right and there was a short piece of internal dialogue where an understanding arose immediately, and came to consciousness as a prediction or worry. This was ignored, yet later it was shown to be true. In case A, intuition occurs when consciousness identifies an objective pattern that it already knows. The pattern registers at a conscious level and becomes an object of attention for a brief moment. In case B, there is also the correct recognition of the identity of the object, its meaning, but it was hastily ignored. So intuition is only proved to be truthful sometime after its first occurrence. Accurate insight can be consigned to the rubbish bin of irrelevance rather than spotted as a genuine concern that could have been further enquired into, and dealt with properly.

The self can also make predictions about future consequences, which it ignores, and then finds that they occur at a later date. One way to improve the accuracy of intuition is to check fleeting experiences, particularly where they concern other people, so that these thoughts and feelings can be verified or discarded. This is a way of developing accurate intuition through training oneself in becoming aware, and then checking to see if there is proper evidence for the hunch. What this training produces is the ability to trust self and the abilities that consciousness has in spotting patterns that are already known: they are part of the pre-reflexive immersion in the total set of presences that comprise being in a cultural world. The procedure of checking intuition enhances the overall skill of differentiating accurate understanding from inaccurate (as opposed to anxiety-driven anticipations that obscure an encounter with someone). In the context of everyday living, one example of this would be:

- Becoming aware of one's emotions in connection with specific other people.
- Naming these emotions and attempting to state what they are about, what causes, motivates, or conditions them to be as they are, and hypothesising what they are about.
- Empathising and becoming aware of the emotions that others seem to be feeling (when sometimes these emotions or intentions to act are poorly expressed, verbally and nonverbally, they hardly appear visually or auditorially).
- Naming the emotions and intentions of the others involves asking them to discuss how they think and feel, when interpreting their meanings with them, as a shared activity.

172   ON ATTACHMENT

- Helping others take action, or taking action on oneself to regulate oneself, emotionally, and discussing what is happening between self and others. This is part of helping both parties work out how to act for the best, and be together in a calm and secure way.

In the context of commenting on associations and the retaining of dim presences that are connected to conscious objects, the first necessity is an increase in awareness. So the commonality between psychology and attachment psychodynamics is a focus on the process and the form of emotional processing that might be context-bound or the result of self-conditioning during the personal history. Literally, if a presence is unconscious it does not register for conscious attention, but registers subliminally; there is still a referent that is interpreted as acting as evidence (Gillath, Giesbrecht, & Shaver, 2009). Objects that are fully and completely unconscious is an oxymoron and that is unacceptable. If something is a subliminal presence, it is a motivator and descriptively unconscious. It is preconscious in the sense that its influence can be worked out after it has passed. For anyone who wishes to understand unconscious processes, it is necessary to establish knowledge of the conscious first, before beginning to theorise or experiment on what does not appear, but is argued to be present through interpretation. This is because psychological interpretation is based on observed evidence. When therapists make interpretations of possible cause they should also be open to the possibility of being corrected according to clients' views. The early spirit of psycho-analysis was to use clinical cases and experimental procedures to indicate that there was something causative that was affecting what could be experienced in self, and heard or, interpreted in another. This was demonstrated in Carl Jung's experiment with a stop-watch and a list of words, which he read out. The speed of the response to the stimulus word was recorded (Ellenberger, 1970, p. 692). Jung was able to deduce that the words with the longest time before a response were related to a trauma and its accompanying complex. At least on one occasion this was confirmed by the person concerned. But causes cannot appear by themselves (Bernet, 2003, p. 217). The unconscious is a necessary dependent moment of the conscious and shows itself in spontaneous non-egoic solutions to problems at any moment in the day, and in dreams. For instance, paranoia is thinking that people who the ego has never met actively dislike self and harbour bad intentions. If evidence is presented to the effect that others have good intentions, that evidence might be rejected. The work of the unconscious in the clinical setting is equivalent to the other ways of looking at passive processes in priming, association, and developmental learning in experimental psychology and attachment research. In the case of paranoia, approximately half of all persons who have been physically attacked experience it, and when the trauma of the past is included in the explanation, then paranoia makes sense. The sense of anxiety about the possibility of being attacked again are easily understood.

One piece of reasoning that results from Freud can be expressed as the hypothesis that distress can be experienced as ego-dystonic and irrational, not under the control of the ego. Distress is caused, literally made, by implicit intersubjective and intrapsychic associations, motives and conflicts. Freud emphasised sexual and aggressive drives at a non-personal level within the self and in connection to others: these processes are the felt interpersonal fields of immediate sense in the emotions and the lived body (1905d, p. 168). These are important meanings and intuitions, some of which are fleeting and flimsy, and quickly pass away if they are not caught by the ego. There are connections between experiencing meaningful conscious objects and relating them to the mental forces that operate through interpreting conscious experience as comprised of primary and secondary processes of sense-making— another connection between psycho-analysis and contemporary psychology (Freud, 1900a; Osman, 2004). The original focus in Freud was dreaming, where the unconscious expresses itself in emotions, implicit meaning, and nonverbal associations, learnings about all kinds of nonperceptual sense. Secondary processes refer to the deliberate following of explicit rules for making sense in language, using logical reasoning and meanings derived from conceptual interpretation and representation, belonging to two apparatuses or systems of word-presentation and object-association (Freud, 1891b). When the focus is on empathising and understanding other persons and their perspectives, this means that there is a felt sense about the other, even if it is vague. The ability to empathise another person by looking at them visually or hearing their speech is a primary process of immediately being able to empathise, without egoic effort, the states of others that cause their actions. Such states are their beliefs, purposes, empathising of others, emotions, hallucinations, or memories that occur immediately, at some level in oneself, prior to and in the absence of, rational thought. Secondary

174   ON ATTACHMENT

processes are all those higher ones required in expressing what is felt and intuited about others in the primary process way. What appears implicitly in empathising another is given over to higher-order intellectual beliefs and habits of mind, in how to make sense in language.

Relationships as wholes

There is a wholism concerning any psychological event or process: any whole makes sense in such a way that the ego may or may not be aware of its own contributions. In ambivalent situations it can be the case that the ego prefers avoidance when it also wants to engage with a problem or an unmet need. When there are positive adaptive choices, it is possible to engage with the world because there is a clear positive intention that what is enacted will lead to a positive shared outcome for all concerned: a win-win solution. When there is ambivalence with respect to what is being chosen by the ego, there can be a defensive action even though it is clearly understood that it is not healthy and not the best one for self and others. A good example is recommencing smoking when under stress even though it is known that it is unhealthy. It is clearly a bad habit and although this concerns physical health and decision-making, it is also emblematic of mental health choices: something is chosen which is clearly known from the outset to be detrimental and contravenes the application of logical understanding to maintaining safety.

The rationale for the emphasis on both individuals' tendencies and the mutual process enacted is that the phenomena themselves, when reflected on, become properly recognisable when the processes are presented in a strong way. So it needs to be noted that these phenomena exist in continua of more subtle and diffuse forms between people over and above one person's tendency. There is negotiation and refusal before agreement of mutuality on both sides of the relationship. What is of interest are the attachment dynamics of the interaction between care-givers and receivers that can alter from moment to moment (Heard & Lake, 1986, 1997). The lead given by Una McCluskey is to focus on the moment-to-moment qualitative differences that can be studied to provide information about the patterns that appear in individual and group therapy (Heard, Lake, & McCluskey, 2009). This can be called the relational process view of the interactive quality of what can be identified between any two persons qualitatively. Once an IWM is achieved, it can frequently be automatically selected. The default achieved is somewhat open to change and further influence, yet it has an inertia to change, for in some cases the IWM maintains itself across decades of the lifespan. Yet there can be the momentary presence of changes between attachment processes. For example, the contemporary picture of the attachment dynamic post-Bowlby is that there is moment-to-moment relating with another human being, where each pattern can change into another according to changes among the here-and-now influences (McCluskey, 2005, pp. 196–225). When McCluskey analysed video tapes that used a well-positioned mirror to record both sides of the same conversation, it showed that clients want to make five types of bid towards their therapist. These include three types of resistance plus a secure process and disorganised attempts to present themselves for help. On the therapist side of the relationship, the professional offers of care being made, fell into five types of quality of care provision including secure offers, counter-resistance, avoidance, and inability to empathise clients' emotions, and they too become disorganised when they feel strong distress themselves, or go blank. However, research indicates that childhood attachment is almost entirely reflective of the caring received, in a way that reflects the overall quality of the relationship and the roles of the persons involved. (Other researchers claim that attachment is, in part, transmissible genetically, which suggests that to a degree it is trait-like and part of the biologically inherited personality not open to change). However, the soft cause that is attachment can best be regarded as a tendency or sensitivity to form a specific type of connection with another that is semi-fixed. There are the influences in the current series of events, with further influences from the distant past of childhood, the more recent past of the last few hours and days, including the influence of the immediate future of the next few hours and days, plus the current intention to achieve something or defend against something (even if that possibility is not itself factually present).

In therapy meetings, attachment processes and nonverbal sharing form two halves of a whole. The meetings are influenced by the desire of therapists to give care and the desire of clients to receive it. The contributions of clients are various forms of attempts to seek care and their responses to therapists' attempts to provide it. The contributions of therapists are various attempts to provide care and their responses to clients' receipt of it. Both parties empathise the other person and respond to their contribution to the exchange. Carl Rogers was

176   ON ATTACHMENT

right that feelings need to be reflected (1986) but it certainly is not the whole of the story to say that only the clarification of emotions is helpful. Properly functioning wholes gets broken into pieces when specific skills are identified in such a way that it might cause competent persons to fall flat on their faces when a video recorder is pointed at them, or they have to demonstrate skills in front of a group of colleagues, or trainees. The most basic therapeutic skill is to work collaboratively with clients on agreed topics, in an order that is agreed with them, so that what happens in the meetings has informed consent. The degree to which there is accuracy between intuition and the transcendent presence of the other is governed by discussion and expression, although the senses made can be accurate or inaccurate. If accurate understanding can be distinguished then it can be put to good use. When therapists focus on clients, accurate empathy of the emotions, intentions, and the meaning of what clients say is only gained by checking what has been understood with them. Properly understood, empathy is seeing persons in a balanced way, with their strengths and shortcomings. In this way therapists ensure that their understanding is accurate and listening is honed by their clinical experience. Therapists also have imaginative and anticipatory empathy of what might happen, and what their clients might feel, say and do. These anticipations need to be checked with clients to find if they are accurate.

Clients contribute to the current relationship through nonverbal presence and speech. It is necessary to pay attention to the type of relating concerning how they are nonverbally present, knowing that there can be a place for lightness in the meetings and, at times, even laughter. Therapists work to help clients understand, soothe and care for themselves, and work through what is happening for them. Therapists use their emotional reactions and intuitions to select a key issue on which to comment, focusing on it in sufficient detail to meet the client's needs, an emic openness to others' points of view, where there are degrees of access to it. Emic means a type of understanding of others that expresses their motivations and understanding of their map of the world in their own terms, of what counts for them. An understanding that has been gathered together by oneself is always checked out with others in order to verify the sense made. There is a major difference between emic openness to the other, and the etic closed process, which is a jumping to conclusions and gaining a distorted understanding of the other's point of view. It is the therapist's responsibility to lead, and make a secure series of meetings, where most of the insecure public will be able to enter. The emotions felt on both sides of the meetings occur when clients push or pull one way or another, and when trying to deliver care. The basics of practice need to be done well and what is being asserted below is a way to support the relational aspects. One way to promote how two or more consciousnesses can be together in the world of meaning, the motivations for psychological intimacy, is through the use of standardised procedures.

The feelings of practice

In the light of the empirical psychology of attachment, the conditions of possibility of successful therapy, and mental health services of any sort, require an understanding of the difficulties of presenting oneself to a stranger to get help. For a healing narrative to emerge, sufficient attachment security in the meetings has to be made through the skills of the practitioners involved. Successful therapies can be made without attachment knowledge. However post-Bowlby, a much more precise understanding becomes possible. Freud's psycho-analysis was not about the care-giving and care-seeking dynamic, but a submission to the fundamental rule for both parties involved. The point of clients speaking what comes to mind, and the analyst's free-floating attention on it, is to speak truthfully about the events held in memory and their sensual living. Relief from distress can be gained through making the original event and its accompanying emotions public in the therapeutic relationship, in order for the stored distress to be discharged, and for the traumatic and distressing event to be validated in the "talking cure". Employing the findings of empirical research into child and adult attachment, provides further guidance to support complex and challenging tasks, specifically how to provide caring and a tangible sense of being held to members of the public. When clients are taken seriously they feel safe, so they should be seen to relax and speak more fully because their attachment needs concerning attending appointments are being met.

Clients can evoke in their workers a number of emotional states that are usually referred to as counter-transference enactment. However, the best way to understand emotion is in the context of trying to provide help, often to persons who have difficulty in presenting themselves for it. Therapists, in this respect, are like sewerage workers or refuse

178   ON ATTACHMENT

collectors. They take away the rubbish that is perpetrated on others, particularly when treating the traumata left by violence of various sorts. The emotions that some clients evoke in their therapists are hard to bear yet it is utterly necessary to be sufficiently open to these reactions and understand them to provide help. In this regard, there is an interesting difference between those clients who are hard to help because they have little to say, cannot express their emotions, and do not want to self-disclose for the shame it brings them, and those clients who evoke overwhelm in their workers. In the latter, it is possible, and necessary, to feel a little of what clients feel, yet what they arouse needs to be handled maturely when workers seek their own comfort in social interactions with family, colleagues and supervision.

But when working with the great majority of the population not in extreme distress, therapists creating a secure process are likely to feel comfortable in themselves, despite the distress of clients who tend to be embarrassed and ashamed about what they are bringing to the meetings. Frequently there can be a sense of movement despite difficulties for the public in saying what they need to. A good connection with the public is one of responsiveness that feels comfortable and relaxed, and shows acceptance. Conversation in therapy flows and it is possible for both parties to speak freely. For therapists, this means being focussed on the meaning of what clients are saying and being capable of attending to what is being said in the moment. When listening to anyone speak, it minimally requires being aware that there are emotional and internal resonances of thought, feeling, empathic imagination, and memory.

In the attachment view of therapy presented below, the dynamic between the participants concerns the amount to which clients feel cared for, on the one side, and the degree to which therapists are able to provide the sense of caring for, on the other. Of course, these topics must be discussed because they are the medium for change. So to make it clear, the therapeutic relationship is an object for awareness and discussion on both sides of the relationship, to ensure that clients express themselves and get the help they need. Therapeutic relationships involve turn-taking in speech and small segments of the dialogue have verbal and nonverbal aspects, where the nonverbal aspects are very influential.

Opening oneself to the other person's perspective, emotions, and understanding means being able to see that inaccurate understanding has pragmatic consequences. Pragmatically, inaccurate understanding leads to ineffectiveness and dysfunction, argument with others, and failed collaboration. Accurate understanding proves itself in social relationships because it leads through negotiation and authentic communication to win-win outcomes for the parties concerned. Similarly, accurate understanding shows itself scientifically in well-designed experiments, sound methodologies, and success in everyday life. And that which is understood well leads to the confirmation of accurate expectations. The falsification of inaccurate belief in everyday life is also demonstrable. Explicit beliefs can be tested in therapy too. Edward Hocking's negative pragmatism concerning "that which works bad effects is not true" (1926, p. 442) means that incorrect understanding creates unsuitable outcomes. For therapy and everyday living, Hocking is read as meaning that inaccurate understanding leads to unhelpful actions. On the other hand, accurate understanding provides information about the direction of the cure.

According to pragmatic epistemic rationality, accurate understanding is manifest as efficacy in the world. In the pragmatic view, inaccurate understanding of the needs of self in relation to the needs of others is what generates distress. Yet to make the simple distinction between rationality and irrationality is not the way to understand. For the ego to be rational, it needs to use its emotions to run away from what is actually dangerous or a threat, but not to be frightened by shadows, mere appearances, when there is no likelihood of damage. Whether it is irrational to run away from something that is feared is dependent on meta-representing a real threat, as opposed to merely being incorrectly frightened because of something that is no real threat. The worth of the formulation of intentional processes is to see the functioning of distress in a value-free way between a short-term time frame and a longer-term one. What transpires is that those situations with the greatest distress exist because the most inaccurate understanding is applied. Therefore, how to make and manage the self in social exchange with its others, partner, children, family, and associates goes wrong. The understanding taken to the real situation is proven not to fit. When it comes to understanding others, people from time to time, mis-empathise each other despite paying full attention to them. This is why it is so important to get accurate understanding. All those who use inaccurate theoretical beliefs can only misinterpret what they hear and see before them. A good attention to detail entails checking and explaining reasoning and distinctions. Through this means it is possible to engage clients in

180   ON ATTACHMENT

understanding and check the sense that therapists make of them. This means that suboptimal attachment and disorganisation are able to be discussed with the people who have them, although this is not a technical discussion but rather a personal one in the sense that what needs to be said can be said for both people in the room.

However, there is a further problem when concluding on Freud's position because his theoretical writings do not coalesce into a single cohesive position and it would be unacceptable to portray them as cohesive when they show him continually rethinking his position. In this discussion of a specific portion of his legacy, only the briefest of accounts is provided. One key issue is how to understand the relation between the conscious and the unconscious. On the one hand, at times Freud did attend to conscious phenomena (1915e, p. 166, p. 177, pp. 201–202), but in other places he rejected phenomena in preference for theory (1900a, p. 562, p. 600, p. 615; 1915e, p. 193; 1940a, 196–197; 1950a, p. 308). When therapists attend to conscious phenomena that are evident to both parties in the therapeutic relationship, the following corrections are required to understand Freud's basic terminology. He made it clear that in proper science "any portion" of a theory "can be abandoned or changed without loss or regret the moment its inadequacy has been proved" (1925d, pp. 32–33), so putting himself in agreement with philosophy of science positions such as Popper's falsificationism that limits the scope of genuinely scientific claims to only those that are capable of being shown to be false. Freud's aim for psycho-analysis was also that hypotheses could be falsified in any of its founding principles.

But Freud introduced a number of contradictory instructions concerning whether to attend to phenomena or not, and at times he argued strongly against paying attention to phenomena in favour of finding the biological and neurological substrate for human behaviour (1915e, p. 193). Freud commented that the "unconscious proper" of "mental processes or mental material" can only ever be inferred and could not be known because they are fundamentally unknowable, which leaves his audience with a riddle (1940a, p. 160). However, the intellectual inheritance for psychodynamic therapies is that meaning is not to be merely read off the signifiers of conscious experience. Rather, discussion is required to contextualise the parts and wholes of what is being discussed, and the understanding gained needs to be checked. The core area of agreement between psychology and therapy is the interpretation of mental forces within individuals, to explain their emotions, choices, observable behaviour, and speech.

Conclusion

The fundamental task of therapy is to enable clients to put their own lives to rights. However, the history of how self-management has been achieved is a diverse one indeed. Freud's practice of open listening requires the monitoring of resistance, a type of social anxiety that inhibits speech, to enable clients to attend sessions and explain their viewpoints in sufficient detail (Breuer & Freud, 1895d, pp. 278–279; Freud, 1920g, p. 19; 1950a, p. 165).

Freud was distrustful of phenomena, contrary to the need to understand the unconscious that starts from a fine attention to conscious evidence. In this light, the unconscious sources of conscious meaning, emotions, and imagined representations, show themselves as the ability to provide habits (good and bad, functional and dysfunctional), and make instant emotional readings of interpersonal dynamics (whether this turns out to be accurate or not). The dynamic unconscious has both problem-solving and problem-making capabilities. Freud's original focus on the dynamics of the unconscious means that there is a psychodynamic interplay between opposing dualities of mental processes (1915c, 1915d, 1915e, 1920g, 1940a; Wakefield, 1990, 1992). If there is a lack of safety and trust for any reason then for those who suffer distress currently, due to a set of causative damaging experiences, there is a lack of exploration in life and narrowness of lifestyle.

It also has to be noted that despite Freud making scientific pronouncements in his papers, it is also the case that confusions can be found within the course of adjacent sentences: "We seek not merely to describe and classify phenomena, but to understand them as signs of an interplay of forces in the mind, as a manifestation of purposeful intentions working concurrently or in mutual opposition. We are concerned with a *dynamic view* of mental phenomenon. On our view the phenomena that are perceived must yield in importance to trends which are only hypothetical" (1916, p. 67, original italics). The last sentence is a non sequitur. It makes no sense at all for an instance to be altered in its meaning by hypothetical general understanding that is unrelated to the phenomena. In fact, if the phenomena are ignored in favour of theoretical assumptions then the position is anti-scientific.

182 ON ATTACHMENT

The theory of therapeutic corrective action and working with the therapeutic relationship in attachment psychodynamics can be clearly formulated. When therapists remain as care-givers then the aim is to make attendance at sessions safe and trustworthy for the public. "Unconscious communication", following Freud's original use of this term (1915e, p. 166, p. 177; 1923b, p. 21), is now understood as the moment-to-moment emotional and relational interactions between care-seeking and care-giving. This attachment dynamic in the therapeutic encounter concerns the meeting and how the participants feel, primarily, and how the emotions are interpreted to mean something attachment-wise, secondarily, by both parties. So that even if no word is spoken, if both parties are sufficiently intuitive then they might be able to empathise the emotions that are relevant to the other person's perspective. Both conceptually interpreted thinking and emotional senses of the current connection occur on both sides of the relationship.

CHAPTER EIGHT

Attachment processes in assessment

This chapter addresses the problems of assessment for any brand of therapy from the perspective of attachment. The following remarks discuss what can be experienced on both sides of the therapeutic relationship in individual therapy. The previous definitions of processes are applied below. Assessment meetings are the first contact between therapists and the public and are a golden opportunity to see, hear, and feel the elicited responses when help is being asked for. Some aspects of attachment as it appears in assessment, which are stated below, have not been empirically tested and would benefit from experimental support. Several topics will need to be discussed and agreed whilst triaging clients, starting always with the risk of harm to self and others, and then working through a set of priorities with them in a manner called "collaborative empiricism" by Aaron Beck (Beck, Schotte, Maes, & Cosyns, 1979, p. 6), but begun by Freud whose "attitude towards the work helped establish the formation of a strong therapeutic alliance and made the pursuit of the task a collaborative effort" (Lohser & Newton, 1996, p. 161). Collaboration includes, if nothing else, being able to provide psychological explanations about repeating mental processes that constitute psychological problems and personality tendencies. Being collaborative with clients involves explaining to them

184   ON ATTACHMENT

during the assessment phase what the process of working with them will entail. In this way, transparency is created to pre-empt potential disappointment and complaints that something has not been delivered when it should have been. There is plenty of scope for clients to be disappointed that arises from an incorrect understanding of assessment and therapy. The general tendency is for one attachment process to get overused and there can be a number of representations of the self as inadequate, unlovable, irreparably damaged and shameful.

It is usually assumed that through discussion clients will become action-oriented and make changes on their own without prompting, but there are those times when people understand their problems well, but no change is begun. If it is assumed that the purpose of therapy is self-initiated change, then if change does not occur, the meetings become an impasse. But two levels of treatment are available. There are those treatments that are formulation only and those that use formulation to orient both parties on the agreed problem. While therapists can offer encouragement, there is a very great deal they cannot do for the public: for clients to do particularly well, changes usually begin when they take responsibility for what they want in their lives, and push hard and persistently against an uphill gradient towards it. Self-managed changes in lifestyle, like other types of aims that are difficult to achieve, require persistence and flexibility. Satisfying attachment relationships require the ongoing maintenance and valuing of an outcome in the face of adversity. It is possible to formulate the material gathered to draw a representation of the causes and effects and check the accuracy of it with clients. Only achievable outcomes for the meetings should be agreed. If the aim is overly optimistic, failure to achieve something that was unachievable from the start will lead to disappointment that may further demotivate.

The remarks assembled below are made with the explicit understanding that there can be contrary aspects within one person's attachment processes as manifested in her life history. People can express one or more attachment processes, and be involved in attachment processes of momentarily different sorts, in successive phases of the same meeting. If they are under acute stress or when their general functioning in life is low, for instance, they may feel unable to work, go shopping, and struggle with childcare. Or perhaps there are major problems with their relationships with their partners. If people are close to emotional exhaustion they will often appear as depressed, or anxious and depressed.

The importance of assessment

Assessment has a number of aims. One is that, when defined in the negative, assessment seeks to prevent further harm being done to people who are already injured. If clients say after the therapy is over "I failed in therapy and now there is nothing that can help me", and its cousin, "Therapy opened me up then did nothing to put me back together again", then an iatrogenic problem ensues. Having therapy is stressful enough without the sense of overload that, in a visceral way, expresses the feeling that the type of help received is not right. The matters to be discussed can be very distressing and shame-inducing, and for some who seek help there are no solutions. The leadership role of being a secure carer means understanding the likely consequences of actions and, when it is possible to mention the likelihood of distress, then disappointment can be limited and poorly motivated clients can become better motivated through knowing in advance what they are letting themselves in for. The limit of tolerable distress may need to be discussed in relation to clients' triggers for self-harm and suicide, or other means for preventing the collapse of their basic functioning. It is an expectation that risk of suicide and self-harm should decrease during the sessions. The assessment phase should make some estimations of how well a person will fair in basic self-disclosure and whether that can be maintained across the meetings. Specific comments are made below concerning how to tackle the particular types of problem that are likely with insecure processes.

The assessment phase exists because a recommendation is going to be made and discussed before collaborative work starts. Either some form of help is suitable now, suitable later, or currently there is no form of psychological help that is suitable for stated reasons. Assessment concludes in stating that specific clients will benefit from what can be offered. Assessment recommends what will help the public best according to the attachment-in-therapy evidence base, regardless of who can offer the service, and entails telling people who cannot be helped why that is the case and making further recommendations that will help them. The following are a few comments to tackle repeating problematic relationship types that can be ascertained at a first meeting, or the first few meetings. The main point of making interpersonal problems clear is to avoid, minimise, or handle them in the current meetings. While there are protocols for interviewing and assessment, as well as self-report

186   ON ATTACHMENT

questionnaires, the point of focusing on assessment is to emphasise the need for persons to be aware of the attachment process that occurs with their therapists. From the client's perspective, having to meet a stranger, to speak truthfully about personal matters, is frequently felt to be anxiety provoking. It is a sad fact that some people deteriorate in therapy, and if that possibility cannot be ascertained during the assessment phase, it cannot always be pre-empted. If clients have expectations that are unrealistic, these need to be ascertained during assessment in preference to midway through the therapy. What this prevents is the setting up of unrealistic, unachievable goals for the therapy.

Making a thorough assessment during the first six sessions is the way forward in getting an accurate picture of a person's motivations to change and the impediments that are involved. Distressing things will, out of necessity, have to be discussed. When offering extended assessments it should be made explicit why this is the case. The possibility of not going forward into therapy needs to be mentioned, with explanations such as "This may not be for you, given that you …" or "Because you found … distressing, perhaps talking about it in detail may be too much for you." Nonverbals of looking sullen, distrustful, resentful, or reluctant to speak about deep emotional topics—and then suddenly speaking of deep matters that have never been discussed with anyone else—are indicators that clients are ambivalent about self-disclosure and may be experiencing resistance and shame. The focus of the meetings and the order of working through issues will need to be discussed and agreed after initial triage, starting always with the risk of harm, then working through a set of priorities where therapists need to provide structure to the treatment, particularly in the first few meetings. But if there is no risk and depression, then the decision about what to work on can be given over for further agreement about where to start the work.

How to assess

When clients first sit in the chair they need to be told about the existence of the limits of confidentiality. One opening explanation, after having asked for permission to assess, is "Let's see what will help you best, whatever that is". Another explanation to a new person is "I want you to understand that if having therapy is going to be of benefit to you, it may bring on some effects that you do not like. For most people, talking about their problems helps them understand them better and feel less distress. However, for some people this does not happen and they feel overwhelmed during the process of getting help. If this happened and someone were too distressed to go to work, go shopping, or look after children, then I would not want to offer a form of help that would make the person feel worse rather than better." Being collaborative around extended assessments means discussing complex repeating attachment problems, personality and other problems prior to starting work. Setting an explicit agenda with clients at each assessment session, and working on that as agreed, gives the meetings value because it becomes obvious that client issues are being taken seriously. Making explicit the number of sessions being provided, and agreeing what will be discussed, and working to a number of meetings before recontracting for another set of meetings, provides a sense of control and collaboration. Any complaints, conflict, or disagreement about the care provided needs to be included in the sessions as clients have the right not to participate if they do not want to, and therapists have the right not to offer something they think would be triggering and harmful. It has to be noted that those who get as far as asking for help are already likely to feel distressed and disappointed, angry and beyond help.

The role of therapist is to promote security ethically by explicitly obtaining informed consent before interviewing, taking a history, and in clearly committing to a technique, or manner of therapeutic work (Department of Health, 2001). The lead role for therapists includes reviewing the quality of the meetings, say at the sixth one, and establishing ground rules to promote a secure process in the remainder. Therapists use their prior clinical experience, guiding concepts, and feelings, to direct treatment and understand what is necessary to help this particular person. However, when talking is not working then the sessions have to be stopped and there needs to be collaborative discussions about how to proceed. On both sides of the relationship, attention and action apply to self and other simultaneously when providing a calm and mature corrective response. There is mutuality of action and reaction between both persons in the manner of not jumping to conclusions and permitting flashes of insight into the client's life to be checked with them. Difficulties in the therapeutic relationship can be handled maturely by asking for feedback and so pre-empting drop-out, containing complaints, and managing any lack of understanding pre-emptively, before it makes a mess of the therapeutic relationship,

188   ON ATTACHMENT

despite the whole endeavour being based on the quality of relating. Effective and assertive verbal communications come from therapists to clients. Therapists lead where appropriate and create informed consent for interventions through discussion. The leadership role means seeing possible impasses in advance and moving away from them during the meetings.

If therapists have doubts about whether clients are able to look after themselves when they are distressed in the times outside of the meetings, this can be addressed collaboratively. "I'm not sure about how ... will help you ... . What can we do about that?" And asking for feedback: "How was it to talk about ... today with me?" Some more general questions in asking for feedback that are helpful at early meetings are: "How do you feel about our meetings so far?", "What do you want to change in your life?", and when there are difficulties with acceptance, "What is it about that event that you can accept?" It is possible to elicit some idea of what clients hope for and fear, by asking: "What are your expectations about having therapy?", where the latter is useful to pre-empt disappointment. Complaints need to be voiced during the therapy for them to be answered. In addition, what has been grasped thus far needs to be checked and large amounts of qualitative information need to be summed up. One way of ending assessment is to ask if it is okay to go ahead with therapy. "If you have questions you want to ask about the therapy then please do so. If there are things that we do or say here that you don't like or understand, then please tell me in the first instance and we can discuss them." What follows are three sections on what specifically can be expected with the anxious, avoidant, and disorganised processes as they appear and are felt during the assessment phase of the first six sessions.

Anxious process is related to short-term frustration and remaining distressed

Before the meetings begin, clients are thrown into imagining how it will be to meet the therapist, and in the first few meetings they fear the reactions they will get to self disclosure, and are thrown into imagining how it will be to meet the new person, while considering this in an anxious state of mind, alongside needing to say something true about some of the deepest hurts in their lives. Because of this sense of trepidation on the part of the public during the first few minutes of meeting with them, how they arrive at the clinic and are met by the receptionist, can make an important contribution in putting people at ease. The problems that most often co-exist with an anxious attachment are those where there is an alternating ability, with attempts to grasp and bind others to self but with a reversal that pushes them away, often driven by doubt and criticism. When high standards for one's own behaviour are held and when such standards are not achieved, and are followed by vicious self-hatred and shame, for those who are most self-critical, a path towards self-harm and suicide is formed. When people are clearly anxious, paranoid, or wary of being interviewed, there is a delicate balance to be struck between the need to get close enough to make the enquiries necessary to make decisions with them, and the need to bear witness to their concerns.

The two phases of the anxious process are a pull to be close followed by a push away to reject the helper. This creates its own resistance. In the strongest cases, the pull to be close is over-intimate and the push back can be shocking in its vehemence. It is galling indeed to be working hard on other peoples' needs yet to be accused of being insufficient. Clients who are anxious also may have poor empathy about what is being presented to them nonverbally and may have poor verbal recall because they are stressed during the meetings. Making a problem list with them is a good way of getting started. The presence of long-lasting moods, and states of fear and anxiety, may indicate that anxious attachment is the major quality of a person's relational life.

It is interesting to think about what specific clients would find soothing and safe because people who overuse the anxious process are likely to upset themselves and have mildly paranoid beliefs, in the sense that they do not know how to contain themselves and are likely to let their anxieties run away with them. What can start out as seductiveness from clients can end up in verbal aggression, delusional beliefs, or threats of violence. If previous therapies have triggered delusions, paranoia, or threats of violence, then more therapy should not be offered. Some clients have the strongly felt need to express themselves all at once to their therapist, but are likely to benefit from a slower easing in to self-disclosure. The motto for helping them is "slow and steady". Agreeing a fixed number of topics for a fixed number of sessions, and working through them to get some practical improvement on each one, sets an achievable pace for persistence, and has an explicitly agreed direction at the outset.

190 ON ATTACHMENT

An anxious process is likely to be in play when there is a strong desire for help followed by strongly critical comments about the type of help given. This two-way movement occurs in an attempt to provide help that gets tangled, in that there is always found to be something wrong with the help provided. What is demanded is too slow, insufficient, insufficiently special, too short, and such like. When therapists notice what is coming to them, and the manner in which it comes, it becomes obvious that despite the urgency of demand, there is still the necessity of reflecting properly on the anxiety and what it is about. This is particularly obvious in family therapy, and in contact with families where there is an identified patient but where the members of the family are resolute in pointing the finger at the one identified person, while taking none of their own contributions into account.

What arrives with people in an anxious process is anxiety in general. Anxiety about the process of therapy exists because there may well have been a number of complaints about any previous therapists who were allegedly ineffective and did not live up to expectations, even if the quality of what has been provided was objectively excellent. If there is anger and anxiety, they need to be handled carefully and fairly. The preferred defences are to demand or to control in such ways that the attempt is made to control the meetings themselves, because there are expected dangers and negativities. Even before the first appointment, phone calls and letters from third parties state that it is impossible for a client, who has not attended yet, to discuss something (such as childhood) and they can only attend if this can be promised in advance. Or special needs are expressed such as demanding that the client can only be seen in the company of someone else for the duration of the meetings. Anxious process is expressed in excessive self-disclosure and in a pressure to speak about difficult issues. For instance, even before attending, it is requested that assurances "must be given" so that explicit worries about rejection, abandonment, or other topics, get added to the already long list of distressing occurrences. When there is much anxiety expressed in speaking, then the verbal expression of worry, and the communication of what is possible, get confused with what is actual, in the sense that worry creates new shame and then promotes avoiding such experiences. In this way anxiety maintains the felt senses of negative self-esteem in relation to positive others. People who are visibly nervous in the meetings might ask permission to stop attending. Or they might not talk about topics that they had previously said they wanted help with. Or they agree to talk about something, but, when attempting to do so, they go off at a tangent.

There is always the possibility that if the shame of clients is not reduced or begun to be accepted by them, then they may not return, and they will not get the service they came for. So, what is required is tactful directness in a manner that is non-threatening and invites clients to express themselves, despite them purposefully inhibiting their emotions as part of resistance and defence. Thus, setting aside all other matters, and not getting completely lost in what is being said, it is possible to practice increased awareness and sensitivity to others and their meanings, and model for them the skill and attitude of commenting on their meanings, emotion, and intentions with compassion, even with the most sensitive and disturbing of topics, and the most subtle forms of expressions. This sensitivity and responsiveness is central to the role of therapist or mental health worker. It includes being free to improvise, because it is impossible to know every twist and nuance of what will play out in advance.

Furthermore, indicators of insecure processes include clients who come late, have nothing to work on, are nonverbally angry, flat, sullen, awkward, and refuse to speak about how they feel. What needs to be added to this are those occasions where clients have voice tones of criticism, annoyance, defensiveness and make rejecting or critical remarks about the therapist or the process of getting help, and they persistently change the topic away from that agreed for the therapy. When the therapist feels as if he is working really hard, guessing how clients feel, and repeating that back to them, it is time to take a pause from working that hard and to mention it out loud.

If a person is continually nervous during the first twelve sessions, say, and only gets small improvements with little decrease in distress or increase in understanding and wellbeing, then they are not receiving the benefits of therapy. It is likely that they may cease to attend. People who might find self-disclosure upsetting, and do not find any lessening of distress, may ask to be seen less frequently or introduce cancellations into the scheduled appointments. If they are highly reluctant to self-disclose and highly anxious in the meetings, then they may find no value in them. This possibility should be pre-empted by further explicit discussion about how to handle it. In order to maintain proper attendance, the best way to tackle such matters is head-on. Yet doing the basics well is not just about someone attending. The opportunity offered to

192   ON ATTACHMENT

clients is one of learning to tolerate and reduce distress by addressing it and finding themselves sufficiently strong to survive it. In order to preempt occurrences of poor attendance, the possibility of non-attendance needs to be considered at assessment, and explicitly discussed in order to get commitment, or a pre-therapy plan should be implemented to enable clients to improve their attendance prior to starting.

There is also the possibility that what began as an attempt to get help ends up in clients seeking to get away from assessment, because beginning to talk about problems has brought out unexpected distress, and they want to leave the meeting after twenty minutes. These people are surprised by what speaking about their lives makes them feel. So, in addition to relaxed therapists being able to empathise accurately, the other benefit of a keen attention to the emotional communications of clients is that the basics are attended to. For example, large negative reactions to the meetings by clients may well indicate that an insecure process is underway, leading to holding back of the material that needs to be assessed, and with that comes the possibility of sudden drop-out: people just do not come any more and do not answer correspondence, even though no complaints have been raised, and no worries or misgivings have been stated.

Avoidance is the attempt to build self-containment and deal with absence of connection

When there is an avoidant process, then there are various degrees of unreadiness for the work of naming and feeling what is distressing. Clients may not be ready to begin therapy, and may have low trust in the person of the therapist. Clients need to go slowly because they dislike feeling distress, which in itself may feel dangerous and out of control. If people tell themselves that they must not feel a specific sort of distress, and they enter triggering situations because of various factors in their working week, and they begin to feel what they dread, then this might be experienced as overwhelm. When there are barriers to feeling, it becomes a major impediment in having therapy because self-disclosure is necessary in order to get help. If other problems remain unvoiced then the persons will not get help and therapists are ignorant of the bigger picture. The therapeutic alliance is a major test of the ability of clients to drop their defences and let someone in. For avoidant process, people may continue attending sessions at the rate of one meeting a

ATTACHMENT PROCESSES IN ASSESSMENT   193

week, and may ask to be seen less frequently, and experience distress during treatment so that they receive no improvement when talking through painful topics. From the start it is obvious that clients will have to be self-disclosing and this is where the trouble can begin. To walk the therapy path requires restrictions. People who have been sent by well-intentioned others experience relief when the sessions cease, as it is too daunting to bear that much distress.

Because the phenomena of repression and its undoing concern the absence of communication and the interpretation of meaningful distress (when there is good cause for it), the problems of avoidance are manifest as relative absences with respect to the other types of attachment dynamic. In the strongest cases, repression shows as not paying attention to conscious bodily and emotional senses that are the unconscious's way of calling for help. Repression happens in those situations where something weakly surfaces but gets swept aside through other concerns. There may be other times when the repression is lifted, and shocking and intense distress is expressed in outbursts and tantrums that are contrary to the same person's views of how to be and act politely. These are all part of the overall phenomenon of repression that may include the denial of bodily sensation and emotional feelings when they are present and asked about directly. The problem this makes for interviewers is that false impressions are provided such that a brief and mild expression of a large negative impact in a person's life gets expressed as some minor event barely worthy of interest. Expressions such as "Dad beat me but he has mellowed a lot now" are typical of the denial of maltreatment. The concomitants of repression are alexithymia, the inability to name emotions, a dislike of discussing them, and people experiencing themselves passively. Because they do not explicitly state their dislike of psychological discussion, they can feel forced to contribute, but are strongly resistant to psychologically minded discussion. This is because any meaningful disclosure about psychological topics is seen as weak, foolish, and dangerous. Sometimes there is the explicit declaration from clients that "talking will not help" (to which the most direct response would be to ask "What did you expect to happen?)." But when the ability for recognition of the representations of the self is faulty, so too is the ability to empathise accurately.

Another aspect of self-disclosure is covered by the term assertiveness, the ability to self-disclose and have proper influence in one's relationships. Insecure and disorganised processes include forms

194   ON ATTACHMENT

of unassertiveness. One consequence is that the tendency to low assertiveness means that central problems may not get addressed. For clients, the assumptions at work are that anything emotional is potentially shameful. Sometimes the avoidant process is manifest in a general reluctance to discuss anything psychological or personal and in attempts to prevent distress. But often there is nonverbal leakage because the living body is continually nonverbally expressive. When shameful topics are discussed, as they will be, the consequence is to feel exposed and uncomfortable because self-esteem is threatened and disturbed. Other nonverbal clues during the meetings can be that clients look as though they are wearing masks, in that they are blank, or that they are wearing an angry mask, which seems like a protective shield to hide their vulnerability. Vulnerability in this sense is a part of the personality that is latent and brought out under conditions of stress where there is a flare-up in syndromes, a decrease in personality-functioning, and changes in attachment, for instance, so that clients cannot work or leave home to do basic shopping. However, a reluctance to self-disclose is a general part of therapy and of intimate relationships for that matter, yet when it is an aspect of avoidant process, the reluctance to express what must be spoken about becomes motivation to cease attending suddenly, attend less frequently, come late, or attend but have nothing to talk about at sessions, despite numerous problems being present. Another indicator of an avoidant process is someone who has experienced horrible assaults but is notably blank when talking about them. It is as though no emotion is expressed or felt. There is nothing to work on in sessions despite the abundant horror of their childhood and current living. The psychological causes, the felt motivations for therapists, are interpreted according to the here-and-now influence of clients. This could be the result from having received responsive caring, or it can be achieved through personal therapy and self-management, and be the sign of one's own good understanding in action.

Because persons who deactivate their attachment needs in therapy sessions do not want to open up and discuss their distress, it is possible for therapists to discharge them prematurely but any tendency to ignore needy people or mistreat them is cause for concern. The primary attitude towards clients is one of caring, responsiveness, and verbal acts that regulate emotions and monitor the therapeutic relationship. If therapists are actually dismissed, or they *feel* dismissed at the end of a session, or the client has rejected or criticised something the therapist has said or done, then this needs to be made explicit in order to talk about it openly. "How does your dismissiveness of ... help you?", would be a good way to open up the topic. There is another possibility that the therapist could be dismissed at the end of the meetings, even when much positive work has been done, and therapists feel close to their clients. If clients get up hurriedly at the end of the last session and look blank or dismissive on the way out of the room without a word of thanks or goodbye, then the explanation is that they never felt that what had been happening in the sessions was a positive force for them, but rather it was something to be endured.

One way to help people in an avoidant process is to praise them for self-disclosing and ask how they feel about it and whether they are comfortable with it. This should be done at the end of each of the first six sessions regardless of how relaxed and at peace they seem to be with what has been said. Asking if they feel excessively exposed after talking about something that they may feel shameful about, serves the purpose of defusing further distress that is not apparent nonverbally. If an avoidant person feels something strongly then it may be verbally and nonverbally expressed in a very mild way. When it is obvious that people are resistant to self-disclosure, suffer inhibition, and fear negative judgement, the pace of the work needs to be slowed to fit in with their capacity to process the distress. Clearly, the need is to reduce any pressuring effects that the work has for them and it needs to proceed slowly. There is a myriad of possibilities of how people can present and how third parties, such as other family members, might be putting pressure on those who are reluctant to attend. It is necessary to help avoidant persons express themselves, communicate, and tolerate what overwhelms them. This can be achieved by mentioning that the sessions to come will require clients to self-disclose and that in speaking about their material, they will feel the distress of the original event but that the process of making sense of it should provide new understandings and a sense of emotional resolution in the letting go of tightly held distress that should become more relaxed and at ease. In the avoidant process there is the practical limit to which some people are able to self-disclose at all. Perhaps specific topics might be delayed during the therapy, and sufficient time to discuss them might run out, and they may not have enough to speak about something dreaded. Even when distress seems nonverbally absent, it is still best to prepare well for endings in case clients feel a bond has been made that is hidden from view in verbal

Disorganisation in adults

A formulation-only treatment is the contemporary version of psycho-analytic interpretation. The manner of interpreting the repetitive patterns of distress and their resolution can be made explicit verbally and may include the creation of formulation diagrams of major influences on the mood and self-esteem, which can be done in front of clients in the session with their involvement. The definitive aspect of disorganisation in adults is that despite them having a partner or children, they remain distressed when talking about their problems and find it hard to receive the benefit of a decrease in distress, and increase in self-esteem and mood. People who exhibit the broad category of problems that disorganised attachment entails may be unable to benefit from the improvement that talking about problems in therapy could bring, nor might they continue attending. Persons who bring the disorganised process have behaviours that are harmful yet continue for decades, such as gambling, drug taking, binge drinking, smoking, comfort eating, and unsafe sex. These can be understood as the co-occurrence of different aspects of the self that are seeking some form of expression, although there is a felt tension between desiring them and those aspects of self that are regarded as being most central. The man who is a bus driver and drives sensibly all day, and drives recklessly while wanting to kill himself at night, has two radically different senses of himself. The woman who calls herself "pig", "brain", and "dirty girl" has three disparate representations of herself that make little sense to her. Many individuals share the problem of lack of integration between parts of themselves. Disorganised clients can change the subject of a discussion on to heavier matters, and the answer provided to a question might be an answer to another question altogether. This may show poor listening skills or indicate that the person's attention has gone elsewhere. Conversations that move on to radically different topics need to be investigated. If some things that are mentioned cannot be spoken about then that is a theatrical wink to indicate that the full story is being omitted.

Problems occur in getting overwhelmed easily, dissociating, and having a variety of means of coping that might include physically leaving home, abandoning others, and thinking of suicide as an idealised escape, and the ultimate answer to disconnection, distress, and shame. The problem is one of integrated parts of the personality pulling in different directions in a dynamic way so that shame, pride, and self-hate follow as a result of the different relations that the ego has with itself. If there are large quantities of dissociation, hallucinations, and paranoia during the ordinary week, then sleep quality will be poor, and worry about possible attack is also a possibility. The worry might be grounded in the fact that death threats have been made, or some other harsh attack has been promised by abusers. These problems will benefit from explicit statements of therapists' policies for helping clients feel safe, which might be aided by techniques such as the safe place, compassionate imagery, and other personal experiences where kindness and care have been offered. Such techniques would also benefit from being practised in the meetings to make sure that they can be carried out in the right manner. Other topics for techniques might be ways of beginning to reflect on the current processes of flashbacks, nightmares, rumination, and worry that becomes uncontrollable. Being able to begin attending to problems and respond positively, rather than being fully *in* the experiences unreflectively and driving them along, is a way of learning to set limits on the current mental habits of getting carried away with feeling intense distress.

If the topics coming back in flashbacks, nightmares, and trauma-induced psychosis are rape or physical attack, then interventions in the following modalities may help to increase clients' abilities to feel safe and show them that they have some influence over what they feel. In this situation, persons feel disconnected from current perceptual reality because past reality keeps intruding, because its impact is too large to process emotionally. What can help are the following:

- Vision—a photograph on a phone that marks a happy event, secure attachment figure, or personal achievement.
- Audition—inspiring uplifting music.
- Kinaesthetic—pleasing and calming touch, various types of breathing, movement, and relaxation exercises in order to work with the living sensuous body.
- Olfactory—favourite smells, fresh coffee, fresh bread.
- Gustatory—vanilla custard or the taste of tea.
- Conceptual—short positive statements and mottos for future attainment.

198   ON ATTACHMENT

- Memory—personal bests can act as a marker for self-esteem.
- Anticipation—reaffirming what the person wants in life as a means of stating what he feels he lives for.

Sometimes techniques are carried out in the sessions themselves, although other techniques are agreed homework tasks to be carried out between the meetings. These are made at the invitation of therapists, and can include activities such as writing something down or practising some identified skill. Homework might be for the purpose of gathering more information, asking clients to practice being more assertive, or taking part in an exposure programme.

There may be a lack of personal resources, so techniques that ask for a five-year plan for recovery, and encourage sustained effort towards desired goals, are helpful as are any means of creating some experience of compassion towards others and self. If there has been some positive comment that can be made into a motto, this will rally efforts to affirm long-lasting desires to create a positive lifestyle. Simple questions can be asked, such as "What do you need to make things a bit better for you?" Or if a deceased loved one wanted something positive for the client, this can be used as a positive resource. For the dispirited it can become easy to think that there never have been any positive events in their lives.

If there has been multiple rape during childhood and the adult presents with a lack of emotions in the session, and has low mood and a poor ability to feel something positive, then it can be assumed that what seems to be an absence in what they express verbally and show on their faces, is a means of coping in past family and educational contexts. The blanking out of what would be explicit justifiable shame and rage, is the loss of what would be a confident and extroverted set of communications. When trauma has occurred, and there is a lack of nonverbal and verbal communications about it, the lack of shame and rage can be notably absent. The absence of emotional material may need to be supplemented by drawings or some other means of expressing the past such as drama or writing. This could include the following:

- Written individualised crisis plans made with persons who are suicidal and self-harming show clients that therapists take the possibility of their deaths as being worthy of attention. The simple act of taking people seriously can help decrease their distress.

ATTACHMENT PROCESSES IN ASSESSMENT   199

- If persons hear the voices of their rapists telling them to shut up or telling them to kill themselves, then getting answers to the hallucinated voices will benefit and increase their sense of self-esteem.
- Having a structured week with positive mood and activities serves to enhance self-esteem, and improves mood and functioning, and serves as protection.

When there have been large amounts of loss and trauma in the person's life this leads to the higher likelihood of aimlessness, multiple overdoses, and a disconnection from the needs of self. In suicidality, there can be a type of overdosing that is about playing with the person's ability to stay alive, as opposed to a determined and sustained attempt to thrive and recover as fully as possible. If this is the case, clients may have abandoned responsibility for themselves and be playing Russian roulette with their existence. Such problems contra-indicate therapy and need to be addressed before beginning intense work that has no guarantee of success. Looking after one's own most important asset, the basic desire to stay alive and enjoy life, is far from reach for them.

Problematic requests for help

This section deals with those situations where the road towards making an offer of therapy is not straightforward. What these comments hope to achieve is to sketch some of the contours of what it means to look at any form of care provision through the lens of attachment. During the first few meetings, clients who have more anxiety, more depression, new symptoms, or run into the same previous problems that led to multiple ineffective therapies, require a thorough analysis of what has happened during assessment about past therapies, in order to minimise the likelihood of recurring ineffectiveness. What comes into focus are those cases where what has been provided has been insufficient, and complaints could have been expressed on either side of the therapeutic relationship. Because what is being complained about is the process of providing mental health care in individual therapy, or in some other type of mental health work more generically, this section indicates another dimension to support attachment interpretations. Clients' experiential evidence is entirely their own material, which they take with them into every relationship of intimacy, so there is no such thing as an unbiased perspective. And just because one person is an expert with thirty years

200   ON ATTACHMENT

of practice, while the other has thirty years of chronic mental health problems, this does not mean that the public is always wrong in what they think and feel about the intentions of their worker. This is particularly evident when clients empathise the helper's momentary nonverbal communications of disgust, surprise, and shock as negative comments on themselves, but neither does this mean that every impression they have is the truth of what the worker intends and feels. The truth of the matter lies somewhere in-between the two in a way that cannot be specified in general. For the moment, the following comments are made with respect to the evidence of repeating patterns of seeking care from previous therapists and mental health services, where different workers have had precisely the same complaints made about them by the same clients. First, what is recommended for clients should work despite the uncertainty of what the outcome will be. Second, if it can be spotted that persons will deteriorate in mood, self-esteem, and functioning during the sessions, then therapy cannot be recommended. Even when there is a consensually agreed evidence base for a brand of therapy, clients may refuse to take part in it because they see it as a way of losing control of the content and the manner of contact that it demands. (It is an open question as to what is genuinely effective in real clinical settings).

There is, however, a small number of people who have great difficulties entering therapy and have difficulty in using what it offers. The overall quality of the therapeutic relationship is most significant because any techniques used are only able to be carried out because of the strength and support that the relationship offers. Some people who have had multiple therapists and psychiatric services for decades, with little or no improvement and who refuse to be discharged, fall into two groups: either they complain in order to be kept in the service or they ask for some special treatment. However, even if the contact does continue, it might never be felt good enough, or supportive or motivating enough, to make the sought-after improvements. This would seem to have features of both anxious and avoidant strategies because mental health workers are kept at a distance, but sufficiently close, to maintain the minimal ongoing contact to be satisfying for clients. It becomes the easiest option for workers to agree to see the person, yet it is not a proper use of their help. If an intervention is not of noticeable benefit to clients, the worker feels a sense of reluctance and grievance at "having to" help someone when they know that no positive change will occur, which can make the worker feel frustrated.

What can be seen across the years is that every episode of offering care can promote criticism, irrespective of the brand of therapy being practised. If critical comments made during assessment are taken personally, therapists can believe that they are lacking in technical ability (or indeed that they are just poor therapists). But an aspect of an extreme anxious process could go unnoticed. There can be short-lived improvement because of the sadistic expression of harsh and excessive criticism. For clients, it can feel really good to criticise and know that the target has to be there next week and has to take some more. In some cases, objective improvements made during a phase of the overall cycle can be lost, which means that clients return to their initial position on psychometric measures of mood, functioning, self-esteem, etc., so that, objectively speaking, the meetings have had no positive effect. On further questioning what transpires is that clients are ambivalently motivated into this state of affairs through fear of being without help, and that is why therapists are motivated to keep them close although they are attacking. Such behaviour has the added benefit for clients of preventing there being time for effective self-disclosure about their genuinely motivating problems. Parallel to the anxious pushing and pulling is the inability to tolerate uncertainty that gets transformed into anger and verbal sadism. For instance, if people in an anxious process gain pleasure from criticising and verbally attacking others, they can be anxious, critical, and verbally attacking in their therapies. If this is the case then it is best to acknowledge the positive intent in the behaviour: they are trying to get their needs met by this manner of asking for help although it withers relationships rather than permits them to bloom.

Contrary to the belief that any expression is helpful in therapy, if there is insufficient protection and encouragement of the secure process, then those who are very angry, sadistic, or paranoid could be permitted to ruin the therapeutic relationship. In their own best interests it is necessary to cut short tirades and unjustified outbursts against the therapist in order to rescue the overall process of having therapy, and prepare the ground for a higher incidence of genuine self-disclosure. Restating the roles of client and therapists is one way of increasing security rather than decreasing it. While false hopes and justified dissatisfactions need to be exposed, and brought to a close, it is also the case that the secure process meets and contains dissatisfaction and promotes moving on together. Similarly in note-taking, notes should never be written that you would not show to the person whom it is about. Therapy meetings

202   ON ATTACHMENT

do not have the purpose of venting anger and paranoia without end. Threats of violence to therapists are unacceptable and may need to be reported to the police if they involve genuine intent.

The purpose of detailed examination of previous attendance and episodes of care is to find out what the repeating attachment processes have been and enquire into how these things have happened, in order to help them not to happen in any forthcoming meetings. When people have had multiple ineffective therapies, or have proceeded on some topics whilst keeping others hidden, then each therapy needs to be enquired into. "What did you get out of your last therapy?" "Was it useful?" "If not, why not?" Getting clients to express their negativity about current meetings is a way of helping them get their needs met. To make a request at the first meeting such as "Can you let me know if I am doing things and saying things that you don't like?" can help fearful and unassertive persons talk about impediments in the therapeutic relationship, and pre-empt rupture, misunderstanding, and non-attendance.

On the one hand, if therapy of any brand is clearly going to be beneficial at assessment then it should be offered. And on the other, if it is not going to be beneficial then it must not be offered. There are situations where persons who have substantive sets of problems find the process of getting help itself to be destabilising. Those who made very little progress for a number of reasons can keep on asking for more help. Some of the following patterns can be seen in situations where complaints are made about the help being offered.

- Those who demand further help but criticise it when it is offered may be showing the anxious process. The evidence to support the observation is that there have been multiple workers, all of whom are kind, well experienced, and capable of delivering help, yet what was provided was seen as unwanted and unhelpful.
- Another problematic process is that of clients who demand care when they do not need it, and there are those who ask for care that is not recommended, as it would have little or no effect on their central problems.
- A specifically negative set of events can occur in paranoia, narcissism, and those situations where expert sources of information are sought from third parties. Care can be repeatedly sought and then rejected in an anxious process. Help is sought and then tangled up so that it

gets criticised publicly outside of the sessions (after attempts to deal with it during the meetings have broken down). The process of making complaints can satisfy a need for conflict, but it has drawbacks for clients and clinicians. From the perspective of clients themselves, help is gained very slowly and painfully, if this is what therapy meetings have become.

If it is found that people are unable to change themselves and cannot change with the assistance of therapy, then there has to be a rethink concerning what the meetings are for. Whilst it is implied that therapy is about helping clients change their relationships, emotions, and behaviour. It might also be the case that if clients cannot make changes or get plateaued during a treatment, then the work has gone as far as it can and the sessions may need to stop. Psycho-education is useful in helping people understand their problems. However, if people refuse to take responsibility to stay safe, in the case of multiple self-harm and overdoses, then there is a question as to whether they have the capacity to be self-caring at all, because they are enacting self-destruction in their defensiveness and jeopardising their physical body. To see people who make weekly suicide attempts, without looking after their distress and modulating it, makes one feel as though one has full responsibility for their lives without the power to help them for the better.

There is an unfortunate assumption that therapy suits everyone and that it can cure every psychological ill. This assumption is a profound disservice to the public and the profession, and it needs to be debunked. Whilst approximately eighty per cent of those people with complex psychological problems can be helped by thorough assessment that prepares them for what is to come, there remains twenty per cent who cannot get going that quickly. Furthermore, there are a number of problematic events that can cause even thoroughly assessed and prepared persons to falter on their way towards what they would like to attain. As the purpose of this work is to focus on the quality of attachment that can and should be created with a stranger who is in need of psychological help, assessing a personal history includes listening for what has been the quality of relationships with parents, siblings, and other close family members, and ascertain the current quality of relationships with partners and children. If clients lose hope and feel beyond the help of any services, then they might keep their negativity to themselves. A further aspect that might be part of the overall clinical picture is self-harm

204   ON ATTACHMENT

in order to begin once more, the cycle of getting cared for by others. If the cycle is not identified, it self-maintains without end. The phase of not getting a service is merely a prelude to no improvement in self-care, social life, mood, self-esteem, or attachment process. If this is maintained then it is a lose-lose situation for both parties.

The IWMs that appear are interpretable from interpersonal events in assessment meetings that can be understood as a motivating set of pictures of the inter-relationship between self and other, according to some already significant relationship with someone who has been an influential figure. The picture of self can be inaccurate in a variety of ways though. The sense of self may not be an accurate appraisal of objective abilities nor will the value of itself to itself be accurate with respect to how others value the person. Most often, the good news is that the abilities, and potential abilities, of the majority of the population are greater than they believe. The picture the self has of itself as efficacious is small, when in truth abilities are large. This is the problem of lack of confidence in the self as effective. When it comes to considering its cousin, the worth of the self as felt and believed by self, self-esteem can be damaged, and this sets a rule for the social inclusiveness of the ego. This is a different type of self-imposed limitation based on the felt emotions about the picture presented of the self to itself.

Conclusion: security as feeling held and clarity about the treatment

Nowhere is the creation of the sense of basic safety as necessary as when meeting the needs of those with high levels of distress and who have ongoing self-harm and suicidal thoughts and feelings. If persons are able to learn to refocus their attention on external or internal objects, learn grounding and breathing techniques, and go on courses about recovery and mindfulness meditation, then they increase their ability to regulate themselves emotionally rather than going into overload. Complete personality change and the eradication of symptoms forever are not possible. On occasion, it is possible to make changes to the ability to be neurotic and psychotic, and increase functioning, although some psychological syndromes and mood problems may return in specific circumstances. Attending to the public demands being sensitive to their speech and manner, moment to moment, and being properly responsive to what they say and imply. The most basic aspects of the therapist role are making comments on the local laws around confidentiality, and what to do in the case of risk to clients, and the people they know. However, the overall administrative process of setting up the meetings and providing details about them aims to help clients understand what to expect. The methods used in the sessions, how to cancel meetings, the importance of regular attendance at a standing appointment each week, and such like, are administrative in the sense that such conditions are necessary to promote secure relating in a holding frame. Deviations from these conditions only exacerbate tendencies to drop out and promote worry about what clients are letting themselves in for. How to handle boundary issues, confidentiality and its limits, and the possibility of complaints are all topics that need to be addressed as a standard part of assessment. One way, particularly early on, is to enquire at the end of every session how the meeting has been and not to take "okay" as an adequate answer. Both liking or disliking the meetings are topics to be explored. The secure process includes the desire to connect, co-operate, become satisfied, and decrease frustration, and distress.

A major responsibility is to make clinical judgments in knowing when to say "no" to someone who will not be helped by therapy. This raises the issue of knowing how to say so in a way that does not provoke a sense of rejection and disconnection from hope. It is part of the responsibility of therapists to become skilled at helping assessment feel like the beginning of something difficult but achievable in that both the focus and the means of achieving it can be agreed. The central problem of doing the work is finding ways of judging between being too optimistic in accepting someone (when they should have only had preparatory work and a self-care plan) and too pessimistic in rejecting people who can be helped. It is problematic when therapists have been overly pessimistic and rejected someone that could have been helped. It is a responsibility to check that the first few sessions are able to provide a sense of being helped, even in those instances where people get little or no decrease in distress for as yet unknown reasons. If they find the process of self-disclosure too upsetting then therapy promotes more distress. Another key question concerns being able to agree on achievable aims for the meetings because there might need to be some preparatory work to enable self-disclosure when there is a strong dislike of distress. It is inevitable that when a topic is vocalised by a client, it generates an inherent sense of aversion and is a stressor for the therapist as an occupational hazard of becoming tired at the end of

206   ON ATTACHMENT

the working day. It is important to bear in mind four categories when assessing:

- *Suited* for therapy and *motivated* to bear its requirements, including those who are just able to use therapy despite several impediments that need to be overcome.
- *Unsuited for therapy* but *motivated to ask for it* but they cannot be accepted because they are unable to use it for a variety of reasons. They need to be turned away at assessment with a careful explanation and a plan for their well-being. The explanation might state plainly that they currently have too many problems and become too distressed during their discussion to make the meetings useful.
- Those who have been wrongly offered therapy also include those who are unsuited but who have over-optimistically been given the benefit of the doubt. They find that they cannot tolerate the unexpected side-effects of self-disclosure and intimacy. This includes clients who drop out suddenly with no explanation, so it is impossible to ascertain what the reason was for their non-attendance. There remains the question as to what made them leave.
- Finally, there are those who are *suited* for therapy but *unmotivated* to ask for it. They can be given psycho-educational material or hear the stories of those who have gone on to recover and achieve earned security in their lives. They need a plan for accessing motivating and supportive experiences that will give them the knowledge and confidence to access services when the time is the right time for them. They should not be pressurised into having a therapy. To have an ineffective therapy can become part of a failure to access future help at all.

The tricky path to follow is not to be overly optimistic in accepting people who cannot bear the necessities of therapy. Sometimes, rather than accepting all comers, therapists should refuse some and create with them a plan for their well-being to improve their mood and self-esteem. The danger of accepting people who are later found to be unable to achieve their goals is that they lose hope and feel beyond help from any source. Whilst techniques such as exposure programmes, behavioural experiments, and behavioural activation can have large and lasting positive effects, if people are unwilling or unable to tolerate the distress involved, then that consequence may add to their distress and negative self-esteem. Also at assessment, major avoidances, such as sleeping during the day and being awake at night, or fear of going to sleep because of nightmares and panic attacks during sleep, are generally indicators that the level of emotional reasoning and avoidance of distress are well-engrained.

If previous assessments and therapies have been detrimental, or provided too little benefit for too much cost, then no more should be supplied. This is a clinical judgement and the reasoning involved in it is public property. The rationales required to make such decisions are the specifics of the individual's history of seeking help and what happened during it. The way to make such conclusions is to ask previous therapists what they advise would help the person. This might include community-based organisations for social support and other sources for making positive lives. In a private health-care system, it would be unethical to take money from people who cannot benefit from what is being offered. In a public system, there is a limited resource, and it then becomes a tough decision to work out when a returnee can be helped by the scarce resource, or if it is more equitable to those who are waiting to decline the referral, and ask the person involved to accept the idea that the current services are insufficient for their needs on clinical grounds. Contrary to the assumption that therapy suits all, it is untrue to claim that everyone can benefit from it. There are those who would be destabilised by therapy and may need less formal interventions such as a face-to-face drop-in, community support, occupational therapy, befriending schemes, or an internet-accessible virtual meeting point via a chat room or similar, to gain adhoc support.

CHAPTER NINE

Some complex cases

A large variety of unforeseeable problems can arise in practice with clients who have complex psychological problems and earn the diagnostic categorisation of personality disorder. This chapter provides detail about working with the therapeutic relationship by providing a collection of complex cases that exemplify the different emphases expressed above. Meetings between adults are seen as dynamic time-variable attachment processes. When it comes to considering which aspects of people with complex psychological problems indicate that therapy is suitable and which contra-indicate it, then the mere appearance of sexual abuse in childhood, current self-harm, suicidal intent, psychosis or domestic violence are not by themselves reasons to refuse treatment. Rather, what suggests that therapy is not indicated is when self-disclosure makes some people feel more anxious, depressed, and worthless, so that their defences are initiated, to produce an overall deterioration in functioning and increase in their self-harm, suicidality, and psychosis. What contra-indicates therapy are those situations where the track record to date is one of self-disclosure producing intense distress without actual improvements of understanding or current functioning. If one aspect of an attachment process seems to be present, its associated aspects predicted by theory can be asked about,

210 ON ATTACHMENT

to see if they are occurring in conjunction, to test the impression that a specific process is being employed. This is how attachment theory predictions can be tested with clients in therapy meetings. The sequence below defines the idea of complexity with respect to expert opinion in psychopathology and then moves towards some exemplary cases where attachment processes are highlighted. Mary Main has recorded some introductory conclusions on the verbal styles of people who gain different attachment classifications, which is useful in promoting identification of attachment as it is experienced (1991, pp. 143–144).

The received wisdom on complexity

The syndromes defined in psychiatric textbooks are decontextualised in that standard definitions are given. The term "syndrome" is used in preference to "disorder" because syndrome entails the idea that there can be several forms or variations of a problem whereas disorder refers to ticking five out of nine boxes to receive a diagnosis. The relation to the psychodynamics of what motivates people to act in meaningful ways shows that specific types of rationality and emotionality form defensive wholes. But a personal limitation is that even across the course of a working life and seeing people at a steady rate, year in, year out, unique client presentations are met that will never be repeated. There are many significant combinations of personality syndrome, clinical syndrome, lifestyle choices, sub-syndromal vulnerabilities, personal abilities, and valued preferences. Standardised formulations and treatments cannot be applied yet what is required is theory that is sufficiently complex to capture the idiosyncrasy of individuals' presentations. Formulation maps the problems of specific clients in individual therapy through interpreting the repeating mental processes that constitute them, in written or verbal formulations. Therapists can educate their clients concerning the nature of the meaning-making processes in which they are stuck in their lives. It is possible to tailor interventions precisely to the needs of clients, so they understand and can find new ways to provide themselves with hope, and that provides value to the meetings. It is also the case that the formative role of storytelling in general is being broached. Heuristics, rules of thumb, proceed in this area of uncertainty, understanding that complexity is empirically found only in attempting relating and treatment. When people have more than one contextually bound syndrome, it becomes difficult to know where to first intervene.

SOME COMPLEX CASES 211

This section discusses the increasing levels of complexity found across the full range of psychological distress.

A syndrome is judged to be extant when, for any frequency of occurrence, there is a consequent inability to do something necessary for the minimum performance of a role at work, home, or in free time. The meaning of dysfunction is the inability to work, for instance, or being too distressed to do childcare because the distress is so strong as to impair the ability to concentrate and remember, or other aspects of social contact are avoided or impaired. Also, because of inaccurate belief and understanding about how to respond to the distress, persons remain distressed while they try to perform their roles in life. This in itself has consequences that may maintain the distress. If the distress is high it becomes impossible to function in the factual sense of being able to do things that could normally be achieved.

In the received wisdom, the lowest level of complexity starts with one standard contextual syndrome where there are well-known standard formulations and interventions (www.nice.org.uk), and the number of sessions required to treat the problem and its level of severity can be estimated in advance. If a standard treatment is provided, most clients should receive permanent benefit.

The first level of having a tendency towards being distressed, and being unable to soothe it, when it occurs forms a sub-syndromal vulnerability, a sub-clinical level of problems in personality-functioning or in relation to social contexts. Having vulnerability means that a person has some of the features of agoraphobia, for instance, but that the strength of the problem is insufficient for it to qualify as a syndrome. The lowest level of impairment features sub-syndromal occasional episodes of mild negative experiences at the rate of, say, one a month to one a week. This indicates that there is a persistence of vulnerability to distress due to an initial episode and the felt consequences for how the ego manages itself. The following set of levels of treatment difficulty start with assuming that persons are motivated to attend, have no risk, and believe that they can be helped.

In the simple case of a once-in-a-lifetime occurrence, of moderate to mild severity, of a psychological syndrome that appears in one context, empirical research predicts therapy outcomes that are well-known in advance of starting the work. The simplest problems are once-in-a-lifetime occurrences, merely one episode, or a single occurrence for less than a year, of mild to moderate severity. Simple psychological problems

212   ON ATTACHMENT

include the following: only depression by itself, similarly only panic, phobia, social phobia, social anxiety, agoraphobia, performance anxiety, post-traumatic stress disorder, generalised anxiety disorder, and mild to medium severity obsessive compulsive disorder. Simple psychological problems also include relationship-distress, mood and role-change problems, pervasive anger, and adjustment reactions to stressors. There is an empirical body of knowledge that supports the view in these pages that personality and contextual syndromes can be understood together. Bruce Pfohl (1999) argues for recognising that the onset and maintenance of psychological syndromes is intermittent. When both contextual and personality syndromes are present they can co-occur with a flare up of personality functioning, which means that both contextual and relationship-oriented events and personality functioning problems are reactive and not constant. And the converse occurs—the cessation of psychological syndromes co-occurs with the cessation of syndromes of personality functioning. The same phenomenon of the variability in personality and standalone syndromes is noted by Tracie Shea and Shirley Yen (2003), who add that sub-syndromal levels of distress can occur such that the syndromes are officially absent diagnostically, but they remain as latent vulnerability or continue to exist at a residual, low strength of influence. For instance, a person who is very conscientious about how she deals with other people, and has high inflexible standards for herself, falls in love with a colleague. Despite both persons being single, she has difficulties expressing herself because of the taboo against relationships in the workplace. The sense of tension triggers social anxiety because the desire to initiate intimacy and love meets with the force to obey the taboo. In this circumstance, she feels socially anxious and uncertain of herself in meetings at work. The social anxiety is similarly overwhelming and distressing as the last time she felt like this, which was seventeen years previously.

At the commencement of a triggering event, and when such distress may be prolonged, the next step up in complexity is when a psychological syndrome recurs and persists, even though the initial stressor might have been absent for a year or more when seeking help. What is being identified is something belonging to the individual that means that a part of the personality itself is vulnerable on an ongoing basis.

The next higher step in complexity is when one syndrome is established, but the amount of impairment in the performance of roles increases due to the same motivations of inaccurate understanding of how the self defends itself and responds to its distress. The attempts at defending currently used may or may not work but are still persisted with. These can include the frequent occurrence of unbidden thoughts, urges, images, or memories that are disturbing or distressing in what they are taken to mean. The key to understanding why the distress is maintained is to find out how people look after themselves and attempt solutions that actually maintain the problem: for example, through avoidance, drinking, and worrying but not through problem-solving or discussing the worries.

The next higher level of complexity is when there are two or more syndromes that require tailor-made interventions and a sufficient length of treatment with relapse prevention to make sure that the gains received during therapy remain after the meetings have ended. The final phase of ensuring that the positive changes made remain is called relapse prevention and requires foresight about what could go wrong after the therapy is over and how clients can be supported in rectifying it. This level of complexity is a middle ground, a grey area. One middle case is people who have had psychiatric admissions in the past for psychosis or who have been suicidally depressed, but now want to focus on something else after having recovered from the more serious problem. The middle area of difficulty also includes cases where there have been two or more episodes of the same syndromes, indicating there might be some vulnerability in the personality because the recurrence suggests there are maintaining factors in how the person responds to their needs. People with relationship-oriented problems such as ongoing difficulties with their partners, work colleagues, children, or parents also comprise this middle ground. This is an area of moderate psychological difficulties that may benefit from couple or family therapy as opposed to individual work.

The next higher level of complexity is when there are difficult-to-treat syndromes that require multiple, tailor-made interventions. There is a struggle to find the central focus of where to intervene, which reflects an actual lack of clarity that exists (and does not reflect the level of expertise of the therapist). Not only are there two or more syndromes, the difficulty lies in knowing how to find the most causative problem and work on that, to establish change and become self-caring of their needs, mood, self-esteem, and relationships with others. Some egos try to protect themselves through explicitly choosing narcissistic self-esteem to bolster the valued sense of self (Baumeister, Campbell,

214   ON ATTACHMENT

Krueger, & Vohs, 2003). Real complexity arises when people do not respond to standard intervention or refuse to do obvious things that would remedy the situation. Such observations might be obvious to someone who was relaxed and psychologically minded perhaps. The key here is to find out how the problem is maintained for each individual through basic interviewing and formulation (Owen, 2015).

Finally, the highest level of complexity is the co-morbidity of contextual on-off syndromes and personality syndromes, where the latter also vary in strength. Contextual syndromes might be lifelong or persistently recurrent if they are anxiety-related, or there is shame and low self-esteem about personal identity. Research shows that contrary to the clarity of the personality versus contextual problems, contextually recurring anxiety problems that are currently categorised as context-related, might be better understood as belonging to the personality and indicate ongoing neuroticism and vulnerability. Shea and Yen (2003, p. 378) have found empirically that anxiety syndromes are more persistent than personality syndromes. What this means is that contextual syndromes of anxiety are better understood as the neuroticism personality factor because they show a tendency to be lifelong. Low self-esteem in itself is not a syndrome, possibly because huge sections of society would be seen as having a mental health problem. However, the personality characteristics that define personality disorder co-occur, so it is confusing when specifying which personality features are the major ones, such as someone who is both paranoid and obsessive compulsive in being controlling, pedantic, and demanding, for instance.

Complexity of contextual and personality syndromes

A fully complex case is where there are multiple context-related and personality syndromes, where it becomes extremely difficult to formulate, get an agreed focus with clients themselves, and sustain work on that focus. In long-standing complexity, there may be numerous ongoing crises in these persons' lives. And because their level of functioning is low, their personality factors forever prevent steady progress, and their lives are chaotic, preventing weekly attendance: this is likely to prevent a sense of ongoing progression and improvement across the meetings. When there are recurrent, severe, and enduring syndromes with decreasing functioning across the lifespan, where there have been multiple interventions of ineffective therapy, hospitalisation, and medication, which have not brought sustained improvement, this may indicate that there are biological causes at work. But it might also be the case that the ego has not been able to understand and manage its triggers, its contexts, and its reactions to them. Complex problems are treatment resistant because clients who have never responded to therapy or medication indicate a riddle as to how the distress is maintained and how the help previously offered has been unsuccessful. The problems of full complexity may include the presence of resistance to change, of therapy-interfering behaviours, ineffective relating, and difficulties in naming thoughts and feelings, and low motivation to engage in therapy. Or clients may believe they are beyond help and incapable of change. Complexity includes those who have previously had psychiatric admissions or long-term experiences of post-traumatic stress, trauma-induced psychosis, depression, schizophrenia, or difficulties in the management of bipolar mood.

The list of what constitutes complexity can include the following: multiple lifelong problems, lifelong suicidal thoughts and feelings without intent, but perhaps with a recent, potentially fatal attempt at suicide during the last year. There is a group of people who ask for help but reject it once it is offered: treatment resistance may often be an expression of anxious attachment process where the problem is that therapists get too close to the person or to topics that are distressing and overwhelming. But the difficulty in helping clients might be for a number of reasons, which need to be asked about, where the first task is to help them engage and understand themselves, before going any further. Perhaps it is because of their inaccurate empathising of other people, or what they feel and tell themselves, that makes relating with them difficult. The problem in working with the hard-to-help is that frequently at assessment, on the client side, there is uncertainty and an estimation taking place about the therapist's ability to help. If therapists are over-cautious, then people who could be helped are turned away with the implied message that they are beyond help; therapists are over-ambitious when accepting clients who then have crises and current stressors that make them feel overwhelmed and unable to continue with what was agreed at assessment. If persons are easily distressed by discussing their problems then what follows are impasses, setbacks, and difficulties that should have been found out at assessment and pre-emptively planned for. (Sometimes it is impossible to foresee problems in providing treatment so these need to be dealt with as they occur).

216   ON ATTACHMENT

Complexity can be recognised post hoc on starting treatment when therapists make their usual opening remarks—and usually the majority of clients respond positively. Yet people with complex problems may not engage with their necessary tasks and may have a poor sense of their own needs, abilities, and those of others. Instead, therapists can feel frustrated, impatient, rejecting, dismissed, overwhelmed, ignored, or become aggrieved. Similarly, clients feel despondent, untrusting, unable to progress, and fearful about their own abilities if they are not supported. Or they become blaming and angry because of some slight that they mis-empathise in the therapist's manner or way of speaking, which the majority of clients do not. Whilst it is impossible to eradicate the lack of responsiveness in others, it is possible by reflection on it, to minimise its influences and work on handling it when it does occur.

There are potentially helpful treatments for psychosis, auditory and visual hallucinations, and for delusional beliefs that are often part of the clinical picture of trauma and abuse, including how to work with dissociation (Boon, Steele, & van der Hart, 2011) which automatically qualify as complex psychological problems. There are further complexities when a person is involved in substance abuse or is addicted to alcohol or street drugs because self-medication masks the full extent of the emotions and difficulties and provides an easy, defensive escape at times of distress. This is why it is often best to encourage clients to be abstinent twenty-four hours before and after attending, or to ask them to minimise their usage during treatment, with a view to lessening it long-term. The remainder of the chapter is a focus on working with attachment processes.

Interpreting attachment

The legacy from Freud's *Deutung*, interpretation, is sharing hypotheses with clients about what causes their emotions and behaviour. One way of working with attachment is to make explicit hypotheses about the type of dynamic for clients in the past and current relationships they describe, and to ask them to comment on the hypothesis, to falsify or verify it. There are ways of hypothesis making and testing that can be participated in easily. Once the four attachment processes are understood it is possible to identify a hypothesis that may fit the situation clients are referring to. For instance, if clients mention scenarios that are related to an attachment relationship, then the understanding made

SOME COMPLEX CASES   217

needs to be checked to make sure that the senses identified in the client's narrative are actually present. If therapists suspect that they are hearing an anxious process being described, for instance, then that impression is tested through raising questions. Statements such as "You felt a strong need for your friend's attention so you sent her texts every day to show her that you cared" should elicit confirmation or denial of this hypothesis. Because an attachment process has a number of predictable features, the formulation of a relationship event is a likely aspect of an attachment relationship that can be tested by inviting clients to confirm or disprove hypotheses concerning allied attachment features that the theory predicts and the therapist's intuition can feel. Similarly, if an avoidant process is suspected to be present, it can be tested through comments such as "It seems as though it was all too much for you and you just wanted to get some distance from those demands. Is that right?" This is another way of inviting comment on the felt sense of what clients are referring to.

The psychodynamic heritage is to name attachment-related thoughts and feelings in a tentative way. "I wonder if you felt you had to be self-contained when you were growing up?" is a way of testing a hypothesis that the client's attachment pattern in childhood was an avoidant one. The point of the exercise is to check impressions of what the major attachment effects have been for clients with them, in such a way as to invite them to be curious about themselves and make sense of themselves. Such invitations forge ways to help them feel understood and provide an opportunity for professionals to be corrected if their impressions are not substantiated. The way that hypotheses are made is through listening to accounts of a person's childhood and allowing oneself to make an impression of what the attachment pattern was. The hypothesis can be voiced as follows: if a process is secure then a wording such as "It seems to me that you felt loved and cared for and if you had a problem with something, you could easily talk about it with your parents" can be used. If a process is anxious, it might be phrased as "It seems like you can trust people and feel warm about them until you become doubtful about them, when you feel let down and then want to reject them". The types of hypotheses stated for avoidant persons are most useful in checking impressions that clients find it difficult to express negative feelings in relationships, that it is frightening to get close, and that the preferred means are to stay away from demanding, intrusive others. The general unwillingness to talk about relational

218   ON ATTACHMENT

difficulties and express emotions blends into separate difficulties in being unable to identify emotions (alexithymia), and feeling exposed and vulnerable after talking about personal matters. People with a dis-organised process may need careful explanation as to how the sessions are structured and how therapy works. If they trust the process and attend, they may want the sessions to continue even when the process stirs up strong feelings of vulnerability in persons who can be free with their anger and intimidating. The next four sections address the attach-ment processes specifically.

Anxious process

The clearest indicators of the anxious process are attempts to contact therapists to control assessment and therapy, through requests from third parties or the clients themselves, to limit the process of self-disclosure to safe areas in order to help clients feel more at ease. While trying to limit the scope of therapy or focussing excessively on confiden-tiality and making explicit criticisms of therapists, are more apparent in paranoia, there is something similar happening in requests to remain silent about something. For instance, a request to omit all mention of childhood indicates that there is anxiety about receiving care and that talking about childhood is expected to be overwhelming. The general process of resistance has previously been commented on as resistance to self-disclosure, a type of social anxiety in the situation of attempt-ing to get help. However, the process of anxious attachment between adults in therapy meetings is present in varying ways and degrees, in a strong desire for help that co-exists with a strong desire to resist the process of being helped, and to be critical of the help supplied. If it is possible to identify such possibilities and check the hypothesis that it is an anxious pull from clients, then it is possible to pre-empt clients who are demanding or critical, and help them attend, and participate more fully in receiving care. For the anxious process four possibilities are:

- One phase of action is to move towards others in such a way as to demand their attention and quickly make a connection with them.
- Another phase is to be quickly disappointed or frustrated that others are insufficiently supportive of self and this leads to rejecting them, an angry huff or other sulking behaviour, and criticisms, because others do not want to be sufficiently intimate.

SOME COMPLEX CASES 219

- The purpose of a hyperactivated attachment system is to ensure positive responses from others in the first phase and minimise distress in the second.
- Criticism of others frequently weakens the bond with them and indicates an emotional investment so that criticism produces distance not intimacy; whereas dealing with feelings of anger, disappointment, clinging and despair in a more mature way, would deliver increased security.

In speech and relating, the two phases of the anxious process are identifiable in intense, worried, tangled, and vague comments that express preoccupation with attachment. If discussing attachment relations, the discussion will be long and is likely to be overly detailed and contain two senses of the objects, self and other. The manner of speaking is liable to be loud and might include demands and rejections, and be confusing to speaker and listener.

One aspect of clients who bring anxious attachment to the therapy relationship is that they can misread the facial expressions of therapists, for instance, in being sensitive to the idea of having their meetings suddenly terminated. One case is that of Marcia, who heard the attempt of her therapist to clarify the reasons for meeting and make an agreed focus of the meetings as being dismissed, and that no further meetings would be possible. There was mention that the sessions needed to be focused around specific agreed outcomes, in order to help her. But the explicit intention to discuss and agree a principle with Marcia, was not heard in the way that it was expressed. What Marcia heard was that her therapist, Jane, who mentioned that the reason for meeting "should be based on clinical need", believed that the meetings were being concluded and Marcia was being summarily discharged. This produced a sense of panic for Marcia who said she felt faint and that the room was beginning to spin. If Jane had not been attentive and voiced some questions about what Marcia thought and felt in the moment, when Marcia misheard herself as being discharged, that alone would have been sufficient for her to cease attending. However, once the misunderstanding had been ascertained, a further restatement of what Jane was trying to communicate was made to good effect. At this point, Jane understood how brittle Marcia's positive feelings were about the quality of help from others: it was easy for her to assume she would be dismissed when attempting to get help, and that could occur right at the start of

220 ON ATTACHMENT

their meetings. Jane was able to restate the principle that she was trying to explain: for her to help Marcia most easily, it would be best to agree the focus for their meetings, and for them both to apply themselves to work on specific agreed problems until Marcia was satisfied that she understood them better, or that something could be done about how it made her feel, even if was impossible to stop her distress altogether.

Avoidance

The avoidant process in therapy is most often noted in those clients who have many needs but are reluctant or unwilling to work on them because the mere mention of the problems evokes distress that clients do not want to feel. In this way the habit of avoiding care from any intimate outside of sessions, gets used in dealing with helpers of all kinds. In the specific situation of avoiding care from a therapist, because it brings on emotions of inadequacy and the strong expectation that having problems implies criticism and weakness, then the most frequent problem is that the desire for help gets outweighed by the desire not to self-disclose. The fear of negative emotions, and topics that are too embarrassing, is concurrent with the dislike of asking for help that makes clients feel excessively exposed and distraught by the current upset and humiliation they experience. This is parallel to when their parental carers were not there for them. Asking for help provokes a current expectation that intimates will not be there for them, parallel to when their parental carers were likewise absent. This anticipated negative scenario is avoided through the avoidance of self-disclosure. The general therapeutic response is helping clients understand more of what they discuss through educating them about how therapy proceeds. There is a need to go at their pace and be clear in other matters that provide a sense of basic trustworthiness, such as written details of the confidentiality agreement, or indicating early on, that it is possible to go slowly through their material, so making it feel safer for them. However, there are different versions of avoidant process and the following phenomena can occur:

- If the deactivation phase is current it may be associated with emotions of abandonment, hopelessness, and inability to connect with persons who avoid psychological contact, increasing the likelihood of excessive psychological distance in the relationship.

SOME COMPLEX CASES 221

- People who grew up in a family where it was unacceptable to talk about emotions may also have had parents who did not know how to soothe distress in themselves or their children.
- It was seen as unacceptable in the family to be distressed or over-whelmed as a child. Being distressed was met with disapproval when wanting help from one's parents or family when growing up.
- Clients who have never learned what to do with the repressed topics of conversations, that are distressing yet cannot be voiced, are led into more general difficulties in terms of how to rationalise emotions and problem-solve.

Given that the psychodynamics of avoidance are centred around the avoidance of attachment issues in order to avoid distress, workers can expect there to be difficulties with clients asking for help, attending, and being present in the sessions in such a way as to be able to explain clearly what has happened, and what they want help with. They have plenty of need for tender and supportive invitations to take part in something constructive but are often unreflective, terse, or unable to speak and think psychologically, and are unable to participate in the opportunities that therapy offers. They may not be able to remember their personal histories, but if they are, then there may be a superficial gloss about the details that it has been too distressing to voice to anyone previously. For instance, parents can be described in idealised ways yet other stories told about them paint them as negligent, cold, and aloof.

The following example between Paul, the therapist, and Anne, the client, shows more about how the avoidant process feels for therapists. Paul had started to see Anne, a young middle-class professional woman, but as the meetings unfolded he began to be surprised by her. At the first session Anne came with her mother who fully expected to accompany her daughter into the appointment. When Paul tactfully declined and saw Anne alone, the story of her suicide attempt came out. It became apparent that it had definitely been the right thing to do to ask Anne to explain her story herself, because Anne had a good deal to say about her mother that was negative, and potentially, Anne may not have been able to tell her side of her story at all had her mother been present. Anne spoke over the next few weeks of her mother's indifference to her distress. Distress and illness were seen as signs of personal inadequacy to the extent that Anne learned to keep all that she felt under a cloak of secrecy for fear of being told off or told to pull herself together. Anne had been very depressed the previous year, in part because her self-esteem was very low. For instance, whenever she had a problem with her partner with whom she lived, she could not bring herself to mention how she felt to him or anyone else. She had attempted suicide during the previous year because she had fallen out with a close friend after a prolonged period of stress at work. While intellectually, Anne accepted that she wanted help, she admitted freely to Paul that she did not understand emotions and frequently found it difficult to say how she felt. Her difficulty in attending therapy was that at assessment she did not know what she wanted to work on and asked Paul to suggest to her what he thought was for the best. But Paul liked to start every session with a request to his clients to tell him what they would like to work on in that meeting. Anne's repeated answer across the first few meetings was that she did not know and she genuinely looked at a loss for words.

Anne was very hesitant in speaking, and at some of the meetings Anne was almost mute. Paul would ask a question after which there would be a long pause that he did not fill. For him, the sessions were hard work. Instead of waiting for Anne to speak, Paul realised that an alternative was speaking on her behalf, as it were, and voicing what he intuited she might be feeling. Paul realised that he could easily fill the silences because it was easier for him to put to her how he thought Anne was feeling and to voice that for her. The problem with this strategy was that it meant that he was doing all the work, in terms of naming her feelings and making sense of them, and Anne was then commenting on the sense that Paul was making of her. Paul described the difficulties that Anne had in presenting her thoughts and feelings to his supervisor, Julie, who quickly saw what might be going on. Julie commented that Paul could not do the work for Anne, and as soon as she said this, he knew that he had omitted one of the basics that even a trainee should have recognised. It wasn't helpful for Paul to take an easy short cut to hurrying Anne and make excessive usage of his empathic insight into how she felt through exercising his ability to discuss her empathised thoughts and feelings.

At the next meeting Paul strove to reset their roles and described the process by which he thought the sessions would work best. He requested that Anne be prepared before coming to sessions and have something to talk about. As a result of the restatement of the purpose of the meetings, and the explanation of and discussion about how best to help her, Anne was enabled to feel more at ease and be more active in asserting herself. Paul was relieved that he had mentioned the topics discussed at supervision. He made an explicit commitment to Anne, to be more patient with her and more understanding of her difficulties in speaking. Thus he was able to recover the aim of the meetings and help Anne be more present in them. Paul also spent time exploring what had been said at the time of the referral and invited Anne to speak about her feelings about being helped. He was successfully able to bring together the need to be tactful, to proceed at a pace Anne needed, and monitor the impact of how it felt to be cared for. Anne also admitted that she disliked receiving any sort of help because, for her, being distressed and needing help meant she was a failure.

Disorganisation

Disorganised attachment in adults is likely to co-occur with complex PTSD, diagnoses of personality disorder, and dissociative phenomena such as DDNOS, DID, or trauma-induced bipolar disorder or psychosis. A few brief comments are made about the key aspects of disorganised attachment in adults first, by reference to its core aspects in children. One problem with this type of process is that it is a stronger force, which increases with the severity of the damage produced by previous traumata and leads to the possibility of highly inaccurate understanding on the part of the therapist, even when clear and transparent co-thinking is done with clients. This is not a reason to abandon co-thinking though. Rather, it has to be expected that therapeutic actions can be completely mis-understood in their intent, or are triggering of deep distress, merely through recalling a memory, for instance. What can be expected is the possibility of the expression of high emotion that draws the therapist in, and the possibility of silence, of having nothing to talk about, despite having received abuse. Unusual events can occur, such as clients arriving at the clinic but refusing to come into the room, and problems with planned absences of the therapist when taking holidays or time off sick. On starting therapy, and when, according to therapists, it is going well, clients may want to cease attending because of what they see ahead. Any brand name attempts to help psychologically with trauma, though modalities such as eye movement desensitisation and reprocessing (EMDR) can be experienced as re-traumatising in the

224 ON ATTACHMENT

session itself and, after any intervention, including assessment, can lead clients into high arousal and distress, dissociation, and sometimes be a motivator for suicidal feelings. Mindfulness as an adjunct to therapy can be used as a way of increasing awareness of persons' own thoughts and feelings, to help them become more aware of themselves, and find where they habitually go in their minds. But gaining such new, more accurate awareness, might be distressing.

Bowlby's original idea was that there can be "segregated systems" at work in the personalities of people who have suffered violence and abuse, sufficient for them to be incoherent and incongruent in their speech and manner of speaking when describing their trauma. If there has been gross abuse, it can be the case that the personality gets broken into dissociated fragments that mimic the behaviour of the perpetrators, an introjection of relationships in to the self. The problem with these forms of personal relating is that cognitive dissociation, and hyperactivation and deactivation, fail when under stress of any sort, or under attachment stress in particular. One source of problems of emotional regulation and of the difficulty in being able to self-soothe and calm the self when distressed, is that there might be a lack of agency felt in relation to others, alongside, strong unresolved attachment issues with previous carers and the family of origin. In addition, there are likely to be problems with the long-term sequelae of early abuse and violence that can structure the mood and personality, and produce reliving the violence when talking about it. Three things are likely:

- In children, there is sequential or simultaneous contradictory relating with anger and avoidance, approach and rejection, proximity-seeking and resistance, with emotional intimacy.
- For adults, there are likely to be similar confused, unclear and contradictory approaches to attachment figures such as the therapist or intimates in the person's life.
- Clients might appear angrily defensive *and* frightened. As a consequence, time needs to be spent at assessment in creating a set of clear ground rules about how therapy works in order to make its aims clear, even when such explanation does not make clients feel safer immediately.

Let us consider an example where an adult client has a disorganised process. Steve, a powerfully built man in his early thirties, appeared as macho and slightly intimidating because of the certainty of his manner of speech and casual asides made about the violence he had received as a child. But his worker Patibha, for a reason she could not explain, did not feel intimated by him. In fact she felt that he needed a mother and wanted, on several occasions, to hug him although she did not act on the feeling. Steve had received sufficient violence, in the form of unfair beatings, to make him almost continually traumatised throughout his childhood. Steve went into care aged three, followed by a catalogue of broken attachments in fostering and adoption, followed by custodial sentences in young offenders' institutions, and jail for violence. When stressed, Steve had trauma-induced psychosis, hearing the voice of an angry woman criticising him and telling him to do absurd things. He might hear voices and see hallucinations that were associated with the beatings he had suffered. Steve also had an extremely negative view of himself and felt guilty because he had been violent towards others in his youth. He had had a secure relationship with his mother's parents whom he had adored. However, Steve had high standards for the behaviour of other people as well as for himself, and if his expectations about what might occur were disappointed, he would be intensely angry. He took an electric drill to his arm when he was angry with himself and he had the scars to prove it. Yet he was very unassertive. The problem in helping Steve was that he was strangely obedient in the meetings and clearly valued Patibha's comments, which were quietly spoken yet straight to the point, but the number of difficulties that Steve currently had, and his chaotic lifestyle, marked him out as unusual. He had previously lived in squats and had been a multi-drug user and binge drinker until he met a much younger woman whom he eventually married. In recent weeks Steve had become very stressed in his home life about things that he would not discuss. He did admit that he could see in this recent occurrence a repeating pattern where he began to feel overwhelmed, which would reach such intensity that he would want to murder someone or kill himself. When this occurred, he resolved it by leaving whoever he was living with and going to live elsewhere. Patibha praised him for his decision and acting in the best interests of others and himself. However, it was at this point that she wondered how to help Steve get a proper hold on his problems and motivate him towards making some changes. It then came out that Steve also dissociated a good deal of the time, especially when he felt overloaded. Steve appeared to her as both

226　ON ATTACHMENT

frightened and frightening in how he had learned to protect himself from extreme levels of violence.

Patibha found herself repeatedly asking for more precise details of what he was describing, and while she was patient with Steve, and felt proud that she could help him, when it came to helping Steve do something specific for himself and make changes in his life, it felt to her as though Steve could not move forward. Patibha recommended that he seek a psychiatric opinion as to whether medication might help him with the psychosis. Steve attended appointments with a psychiatrist and did accept that form of help. Patibha provided Steve with written formulations of his difficulties, which he found interesting, but when it came to him acting according to these understandings, nothing was forthcoming. Patibha felt responsible for Steve and although she felt that he could be intimidating in his manner, she found that she liked meeting him and felt protective towards him and was confident that she could help him. After hearing about his dramatic childhood it was clear to her that Steve's struggle to be loved and respected by others had repeatedly run aground until he was sick of trying hard and not getting anywhere.

When Patibha took her work with Steve to supervision, she was advised to provide a formulation-only treatment to Steve. What her supervisor meant was that, given the problems Steve had, then maybe he was unable to make any changes in his lifestyle. When Patibha tried to get Steve to select a specific focus for the meetings and help him be clear about his own strengths, Steve made criticisms of the time-limited treatment being offered and ceased to attend. Patibha offered him a chance to spend time closing down their work together, but he missed the last three sessions, after saying he would attend them. So at the end of the meetings, Patibha felt abandoned and was left to ponder the unknowns of what had happened.

The consequences for practice

Therapy practice in the light of attachment theory means that there needs to be a strong emphasis on providing and encouraging a sense of safety and trust through transparency and collaboration in therapeutic work. There is a wide range in the backgrounds of people who show the secure process in therapy. Despite trepidations to the contrary, when handled in a pro-secure way, those who are distressed but functional

SOME COMPLEX CASES   227

in their communicative manner show themselves by running with the opportunities that are offered them. Just as a quick reminder, here is a brief recap of the major aspect of a secure process: having received good enough parenting and having made meaningful connections between distress and past experiences of being helped through it, persons can believe that, having been helped before, they can be helped again. This is the reason why it makes sense to seek the help of others or consult one's own memories of being helped. Such an ability promotes problem-solving because one has representations in memory of being helped. A relaxed and confident approach to life involves thinking through a few options and considering them. This develops the ability to reduce distress, and manage and tolerate frustration, so that there is the likelihood, for the most part, of being calm and achieving well-being and self-soothing.

Therapy works through the provision of basic ground rules and the setting of boundaries, which once agreed, are kept. The conditions required to promote secure process include being kind, fair, sympathetic and understanding. Visibly frightened persons with high voices and uncertain speech can be seen to relax during a meeting, and as they slow down, they look visibly more present and sit upright. There is a need for minimal standards of pragmatic effectiveness and these include persons turning up once a week, to receive the promise of caring. However, when attachment needs have not been satisfied, there may accrue the sense that negative distress and its consequences cannot be avoided. Clinical reasoning in attachment terms is particularly relevant in designing assessment procedures and making collaborative decision-making about how to help distressed persons. Collaboration occurs in working with people to help them decide whether to commit to a formal therapy. Or if not, the minimum that the public can expect is a formulation and a plan for their well-being, such as helping them to decide on some other type of self-managed treatment plan, occupational support, and lifestyle management. When attachment processes are taken seriously, the consequences are a qualitative acuity to the forces that individuals bring to mental health work (Degnan, Seymour-Hyde, Harris, & Berry, 2014). These forces need to be worked with; as opposed to working against them in an unaware way.

If it becomes necessary to work on the sense of self to make it more accurate with respect to the evidence that shows its worth in society, then the form of non-integration of parts of the self, according to how they

228   ON ATTACHMENT

have been repressed and denied, becomes the topic of attention. This is a dimension sketched by Otto Fenichel (1945, p. 39) and by Theodore Reik (1952). Let us take the lead from Reik who refers to the sense of self as being a key motivator in understanding defensive behaviour. The number of senses that the ego can have for itself vary between shame and narcissistic hubris. Because the sense of self is socially created and enacted, Reik notes that motivations to defend the self vary between the prideful "ego-ideal" of a wished-for idealised sense of self as potent and capable; and a shameful "ego-horror" of repressed, denied, and feared shadow aspects of the self that must be avoided at all costs (Reik, 1952, pp. 173–174). But the fact of the matter is that both possibilities exist. The direction of the cure is always to own and incorporate the repressed and denied aspects of the self, even if these are aspects of DDNOS, DID, and other unintegrated types of needs. The direction of the cure has been called radical self-acceptance by Marsha Linehan (1993) in order to include all that was previously felt as shameful, disgusting, and weird, so as to increase the felt-experiences of "I am comfortable about aspects of myself", and expand the sense of self to include and alter the relationship with the previously feared and avoided aspects, to become genuinely acknowledged and safely expressed in pro-social ways. (Clearly, anti-social aspects and the desire to do violence to others, need further investigation).

Conclusion

Therapy is primarily about relating and not about techniques. The power of therapeutic relating includes and shares responsibilities for working together and is a way towards lower stress on both sides of care-giving and care-receipt, which brings rewards for both. Well-being can be the result of social contact. When working with people with severe and enduring complex problems, what succeeds is engaging them in a therapeutic relationship in which they want to participate. This chapter has stated a dynamic view of attachment processes in the moment-to-moment aspects of the therapeutic relationship. The most fundamental model for practice is that its conditions of possibility are to know how to interpret and understand, before knowing how to act. Psychologists and therapists are interpreters of the human condition. Attachment provides basic theory for an applied psychology that understands the human condition overall. The aim is to understand the set of everyday lived experiences that people have when they are distressed, to help them regain hope and cope with what life throws at them, so that they can begin to alter their meanings and meaning-constituting processes. The theoretical task is to synthesise knowledge from the disparate areas of the biological, psychological, and the social, and reconcile the differences. Despite occupying different stances for interpreting that which appears, the starting point is the same: accurate understanding. Indeed, this is the same starting point for the biological, neuro-cognitive, and neurological explorations of the human territory.

As far as knowing how to work with the relationship, the message is always the same regardless of whether it is the first meeting or the last. Because relationships are subtle, fluid, and dynamic, it might be possible to have a usually secure relationship but momentarily, it might dip into one of the insecure forms, but because of the overall shared history between the two people, there is the possibility of a return to the functional status quo of secure process. In insecure processes however, there is the occurrence of rejecting, demanding, and refusing secure connections. The overall tendency is to maintain specific types of conflict, tension and dis-harmony. Between any two dynamic states, however, there is a "tipping point" (Owen, 2009, p. 103). When one party in a pair promotes the recreation of pro-secure patterns of behaviour that decrease differences of perspective between persons, there is likely to be improvement in the quality of friendship, respect and liking that is expressed and received. Of course, the corollary occurs in the other direction, a once-secure relationship can become insecure. So the tipping point is two-way. In some conditions there can be a connection that gets broken, in divorce and estrangement, for instance. But it is also possible for couples and families who have been in chaos to become more secure and problem-solve, by airing their differences, and renegotiating how to relate more harmoniously.

CHAPTER TEN

Conclusion: therapy as secure process

One aim of this work has been to reinvigorate psychodynamic practice and tradition with contemporary findings on attachment, to make a focus on the basics of good practice. The focus on the frame is a way of providing safety and clarity for both participants in psychotherapy, after the efforts of Donald Winnicott (1971) and Robert Langs (1998), and coincides with the fact that therapy is not always helpful (Crawford et al., 2016). The connection between these themes is to recognise that understanding attachment and the secure process concerns how to create a secure frame (Gutheil & Gabbard, 1998). The common theme shared by these perspectives is to create an agreed starting point for a relationship that is asymmetric. Therapy is one-sided because it is clients who self-disclose and feel vulnerable, and the meetings are built around their clinical needs, and not those of their workers. In order to support a necessary level for trust in fallible workers, the literature on managing the frame notes that making a connection with clients is important. The therapeutic relationship is one of vulnerability, resistance to self-disclosure, and unmet need meeting with persons who do not self-disclose, are invulnerable, and comparatively, have their needs met. There is a hierarchy of enlightenment in these relationships, which are themselves unlike any other

232   ON ATTACHMENT

relationship because of the asymmetry of self-disclosure and roles for the optimum provision of care. However, the idea that the secure process is another aspect of the secure frame creates the basics of good practice in all forms of psychotherapy and mental health care, and includes promoting how high quality services are delivered in clinics and larger organisation.

This last chapter emphasises grounding psychotherapy and mental health care in attachment theory. Psychodynamic therapy since Freud has been about paying attention to emotions and to the conscious meaningful senses that are made by unconscious processes. The Bowlby-Ainsworth view of attachment shows how the intimate life makes sense. It is easy to recognise childhood attachment and that means that more complex versions of child patterns can be the recognised and understood by the wider audience of users of attachment theory, through concepts referring to collectively understood senses. Emotional intelligence for therapeutic practice is manifest in the creation of sessions with secure process, and this can be achieved with the majority of the public, given sufficient time. When there is clarity about the phenomena of the secure base, as subjective confidence and the feeling of being safe and trusting, as a safe haven for return, and of the other phenomenon, then it is possible to understand their equivalents in adulthood, such as seeking the help of a mental health professional. Security concerns the felt sense that attachment figures are available and that their wisdom remains available, even though they are physically absent. Earned security can occur for adults who have had poor parenting. Attachment theory functions in such a way that once the range of adult processes are understood then it is possible to influence therapeutic relationships to be secure, and help clients make their lives more secure. One practical consequence of understanding attachment is that awareness is harnessed and adequately interpreted to create a positive lifestyle where care and attention goes to the needs of others and self.

However, the initial development of problems, usually in childhood or adolescence, and the perpetuation of problems in the present day are *not* the same. Working towards lessening attachment problems concerns undoing the maintenance of the current state of affairs, where the social learning of inaccurate understanding, reified objects, inaccurate beliefs, and habits of being aware need to be purposefully replaced with a more accurate understanding, followed by self-managed self-care. New accurate understanding can lead to self-care. Changes can happen informally in the person's life or through therapy whereby one takes responsibility for one's own actions, emotions, and distress, and, if suitable, there is problem solving to create a new lifestyle. Because social learning is a significant causal and maintaining influence in psychological problems, social triggers or stressors are frequently a psychosocial partial cause of a first occurrence of a psychological problem. The meanings of several objects in their contexts constitute the ongoing perpetuation of problems. There is the ongoing phenomenon of the maintenance and persistence of the neurotic aspect of personality and of psychological problems that accrue through the inter-relationship between personal choice, the current social situation, and biological traits. When it comes to therapy practice, in the light of the lack of certainty about what is truly causative of the ills of any specific individual, it is true to say that people are unique individuals comprised of biopsychosocial forces of multifactorial inter-actions as maintaining factors. In a wholistic language, individuals are a system of parts within their social system, which has different sorts of parts. Accordingly, it is best practice to tailor formulations and interventions to individuals and use research findings about what might work with judicious care. Therefore, with that in mind, the following are some key theoretical points that describe persons in their attachment world.

Whatever the brand name of relating and caring being practised, being secure means being emotionally available, responsive, and providing a professional relationship that does not follow the same rules as those of friendship, which is more egalitarian. To generate secure processes with the general public, it is best not to answer personal questions under any circumstances, and be able to limit any forthcoming curiosity and disappointment by explaining why this is the case. It also means making sessions focus on clients' needs, rather than avoiding things that therapists may find difficult to discuss because of the emotions that the topics bring; for example, hearing about the death of babies and the intimate details of what it feels like to be tortured are disturbing. However, it is unprofessional to reject clients with these experiences just because they are difficult to hear. If therapists refuse to feel intense distress then such clients cannot be treated in the first place, and in order to practice with people with such experiences, therapists would need to expand their capacity to tolerate distress.

Being a temporary secure attachment figure means making oneself approachable by having mini-reviews at the end of each session and

234   ON ATTACHMENT

longer reviews of the progress made every few sessions. This creates a direct means of making the received quality of the meetings important and open for discussion. Clients often have the tendency not to discuss what they rightly or wrongly interpret to be the limits of their therapist's ability to care. However, to improve the received quality of care, it can be necessary to elicit unspoken material that clients anticipate might jeopardise their care, and allay their anxieties. Because clients may have come from families full of violence, or never talked about how they felt, their understanding of how to become aware and reflect psychologically, may not include the sense of permission to talk about what the distress is about. Therapists provide secure caring responses that add value to the meetings in ways that are more than just being interested and agreeable. Such responses in the moment, enable clients to participate and be committed to working on reducing their distress and beginning acceptance and change. The discussions then have the ability to change the reified meanings and mental processes discussed, through helping clients see themselves and their objects in a new light. When it is unclear *how* to resolve their meanings, and mere discussion and emotional expression in the relationship make no difference, then clients may cease to value the sessions. Furthermore, if discussion does not provide change nor alter what clients understand and how they feel, there is no benefit to attendance, as nothing significantly changes, and it feels awful to talk when no gains are made.

Attachment processes are one way to understand emotions, the meanings of experiences, and other here-and-now objects of awareness. When a secure process is produced it is a safe holding space. During the first six meetings in particular and in any session where distressing material is discussed, time should be made to debrief at the end of a session as a matter of course. There is an important minimal structure to the first six sessions, that is, to check with clients when they enter and leave the room, to make sure that they can voice any concerns about their distress, or comment in an open way about what has happened in the meeting. People may have begun a train of thought that takes them to self-harm and suicide where their alienation from others and themselves increases without a sense of connection to their helper or to crisis services. Thus, checking with clients about how they are at the end of sessions lessens the possibility that clients are distressed in ways that are invisible even to the most experience practitioner, because their manner of meeting with a stranger is such that they repress their nonverbal expression, and are unable to speak about what they feel and ask for help.

From the perspective of attachment security, there are a number of fundamental awarenesses and egoic actions. The relationship is a whole out of which there arise the following distinctions. First, for clients, there is an attunement to self that varies in how they feel themselves to be and understand themselves, before beginning to act. There is the most basic emotional and sensual experience of bodiliness in the current relationship or social context. It is the full self-awareness of one's self-presence, at the level of permitting oneself to be aware emotionally, that co-exists with speech, before beginning to interpret and contextualise accurately what experiences and motivations mean. Following the awareness of sensations and interpretation, there is possibility of accurate beliefs and self-correction. Psychological causes are felt motivations that need interpreting adequately according to the influence of the past and present. For those who have received responsive caring and have gained the possibility of accurate understanding, the increasing toleration of distress and ambivalence are one sign of accurate understanding in action. For those who have had trauma and abuse, these experiences of past contexts superimpose their meanings on the here and now. In the latter case, a momentary blip of anxiety becomes evidence, for instance, of a long-experienced reified felt sense of "I am no good". Alternatively, some catastrophic interpretation of the experience is made that has little or nothing to do with the here-and-now context. Usually, the meanings attributed to the experiences come from a different time and context altogether, and are usually anxious, negative, and fixed. The primary attitude towards the therapist is care-seeking, but that may be influenced by insecure tendencies about negative responses to what is being discussed. Pro-secure verbal acts are required that begin to regulate clients' emotions and work towards learning about self-soothing and making changes. When therapists soothe clients, they also soothe themselves.

Therapists may not always be accurate in their empathising of clients, but the reasons for this are usually having their attention wander off because they are not fully engaged on what is being said to them. Another potential problem is not managing the high expectations of clients, concerning what is going to be delivered by the meetings. It is a part of the assessment process and the first few sessions, to discuss and agree the methods to be used, and regulate downwards over-optimistic

236   ON ATTACHMENT

expectations. The strategy for therapists is to aim for win-win outcomes and remain in-role as a secure care-giver. The best policy is to pre-empt forthcoming problems that can be expected during the first few meetings. For instance, if clients complain that people "keep letting them down" then it must be discussed how to proceed if they feel their therapist is doing the same. This means agreeing with clients what to do if the problems they experience in relationships might spill into the therapeutic one. Such a manoeuvre is achieved by asking clients to discuss their doubts, fears, worries, and things that they do not understand or like about the therapy with their therapists. Ideally, all complaints that clients might have about the meetings need to be brought out for discussion with their therapist. Often assumptions are based on what clients believe should be happening, which, if not elicited, might motivate them to cease attending. By discussing what is happening and how it feels to get help, and how clients expect it should be happening, it becomes possible to reduce ineffective communication where the negative impressions of clients promote a series of events that lead to tension and dissatisfaction in the relationship, and the degree of security is lessened rather than strengthened.

Problems ensue in situations where an insecure process has begun if, for any reason, therapists feel self-conscious and anxious, and these feelings promote failure to understand what clients are explaining, which should be dealt with by staying empathic, and not blocking awareness and responsiveness. The possibility of two-way connection is not closed down, even if clients put some topics off limits. If therapists try to push clients to do something highly specific, it is usually a telltale sign that the attitude of co-working and sharing responsibility has ceased. If that is the case, it is best to set aside one's own impressions and focus on what clients are trying to discuss. Similarly, just by hearing about the broad sweep of a person's life, it is possible to empathise and begin to feel strong emotion in response to what clients say, and infer intellectually about how they see themselves, and what they believe they are capable of doing. Clients have difficulty self-disclosing generally yet they have a need to trust their worker in order to speak the truth. But if therapists feel genuinely confident in being able to help in some way, and share any misgivings about clients' expectations, it is congruent to express these thoughts and feelings to promote security. The therapy's outcome needs to be something that is good enough and works for clients' attachment needs. This discussion will make the meetings, and what clients expect to get out of them, and the focus of them, transparent and shared. The alternative is two people pulling in different directions and having their own unspoken agendas of where they would like to take the meetings, and such a lack of agreement is disruptive.

In order to understand meaning as a social phenomenon, the following conditions of possibility are mentioned. Personality theory describes aspects of a multi-factorial biopsychosocial whole. Human nature is biopsychosocial and contains complex inter-actions between three types of cause: (i) inherited biological characteristics exist in a complex interaction with early and later adult life experience, plus (ii) there are personal choice and habituated mental processes, and (iii) the influence of others and culture. It is impossible to ignore the full range of influences and there is often genuine uncertainty about what causes are operating. For many clients though, there is neither sufficient understanding nor corrective action to reduce distress and imbalance. Clients are distressed and have their own explanatory ideas as to the cause of their suffering. Therapists bring with them the sum total of their clinical experience plus their theoretical stance for understanding the various stages of practice, and how to treat specific personality and psychological syndromes. One sticking point for therapy is that clients who cannot believe that things can be different may not permit the healing process to begin without some extra discussion and explanation to help them trust the process, and be open to believing that they can be helped. Lack of self-belief about the ability to change needs to be elicited and presented as another aspect of the problem on which they can engage. The following three points are central:

- Persons in a secure process are often confident in gaining support from others. They know that distress is changeable and can turn into positive senses again. They are open to evidence, tolerate ambiguity and are more likely to have accurate conceptualisations about relationships, emotions, the intentions of others and their abilities, leading to collaborative negotiation and problem-solving with others.
- Persons who are habitually secure assume that expressing one's distress to others who are trusted will elicit their positive response. What this promotes is the general ability to provide a sufficiently detailed coherent and readily understandable account of any psychological context or process. The manner of speaking, even if anxious and depressed or otherwise distressed, is liable to be a clear description of

238   ON ATTACHMENT

thoughts, behaviours, and feelings that are well verbalised story-telling, where what motivates the choices of the players in the story is narrated and is made explicit.

- On both sides of a secure process, it feels easy to be truthful and congruent about problems and gain the support of others. Not only is a secure process more relaxed and feels connected, but it promotes further exploration and dealing with unsafe matters in the wider world, through more assertiveness and action.

The secure process exists because the acquired IWMs influence current and future anticipations about how caring will occur: it is expected that a felt-warmth in psychological contact will be experienced. Self and other are expected to be mutually autonomous and supportive of each other most of the time, now and in the future. It follows that secure habituation is learning to depend on each other in ways that are healthy, productive, and mature. It is good to give and receive attention. People in a secure process easily initiate co-operation in a relaxed and optimistic way, even to the extent of winning the other over, and mending ruptures and tensions in the relationship. People in a secure process are comfortable when getting close and find the process of connection comparatively easy. One major benefit of a secure process between client and therapist is that it becomes possible to discuss both persons' thoughts and feelings about the meetings. This aids the process of trust that requires clients to feel more trusting and relaxed when they self-disclose. The benefit for therapists of secure process is that they feel more relaxed and able to help. Therapists are more disposed to help when they are not criticised unreasonably by anxious and protesting clients, and such anxieties can be comparatively easily brought out and laid to rest. It is galling when working hard to help people when they criticise and berate their worker, and that type of hostility, even if well-founded, can give rise to the false impression that clients cannot be helped by what is being offered. So even if the first two sessions have been anxiety-laden, and the meetings have been more insecure than secure, by the third meeting, approximately, what should be evident is a relaxation in clients and therapists that promotes an increased ability to discuss the quality of the meetings so far in a productive way. Secure co-regulation phenomena show as mutual relaxation and openness in the meetings, promoting a shared sense of safety because both parties feel sufficiently comfortable with each other. The meetings become a

CONCLUSION   239

safe place for reflection to be expressed on the felt quality of what it is like to attend, and this makes explicit the felt value of attending. Therapists can, for instance, aid this process by explicitly stating what they are trying to do. This includes discussing treatment rationales and putting options forward to help clients actively participate in their own care. And indeed, if they object or do not understand what they are being asked to do, then these objections need to be brought out prior to starting agreed, collaborative work.

There is a tension between engaging people whilst paying attention to the current attachment dynamic and understanding how clients are present. Vice versa, if therapists glance at their watch that could be enough for some people to think that their worker is tired of them and wants them to go. In some cases, letters and explicit verbal statements are not read or heard as they were intended, for a variety of reasons, including the meaningful motivation that clients wanted something else to happen altogether, so did not understand what had been explicitly put to them.

Clients can learn to care for themselves and work through what is happening for them. The best policy is to create a type of teamwork, with a division of labour whereby clients are actively involved in their own care and therapists progressively lead less, across the course of the meetings. When it comes to practice in the light of attachment, one learning point is to be collaborative and employ co-thinking between therapist and client. While collaboration is no guarantee of agreement, it is a means of being responsive by encouraging clients to take a new perspective. In this way, therapy gives clients tools for self-care and for thinking through their situations prior to action. Therapists can provide care in a spontaneous and intuitive way alongside the use of research findings. However, it is only the other person who can confirm or disconfirm how accurately empathic we have been.

This introductory work on the developmental psychology view of attachment has surveyed the central issues. It remains to be seen how research and theory will respond as the art of practising with secure attachment develops.

REFERENCES

Ainsworth, M. D. S. (1969). Object relations, dependency, and attachment: A theoretical review of the infant–mother relationship. *Child Development*, *40*: 969–1025.

Ainsworth, M. D. S., & Bowlby, J. (1991). An ethological approach to personality development. *American Psychologist*, *46*: 333–341.

Ainsworth, M. D. S., & Wittig, B. A. (1969). Attachment and exploratory behavior of one-year-olds in a strange situation. In: B. M. Foss (Ed.) *Determinants of Infant Behavior, Vol. 4.* (pp. 113–136). London: Methuen.

Ainsworth, M. D. S., Blehar, B. C., Waters, E., & Wall, S. (1978). *Patterns of Attachment: A Psychological Study of the Strange Situation.* Hillsdale: Lawrence Erlbaum.

Akhtar, S. (1994). Object constancy and adult psychopathology. *International Journal of Psycho-Analysis*, *75*: 441–455.

Alexander, F. (1963). The dynamics of psychotherapy in the light of learning theory. *American Journal of Psychiatry*, *120*: 440–448.

Alexander, F., & French, T. M. (1946). *Psychoanalytic Therapy.* New York: Ronald.

Alisic, E., Jongmans, M. J., van Wesel, F., & Kleber, R. J. (2011). Building child trauma theory from longitudinal studies: A meta-analysis. *Clinical Psychology Review*, *31*: 736–747.

242 REFERENCES

Allgulander, C., Nowak J., & Rice, J. P. (2007). Psychopathology and treatment of 30,344 twins in Sweden II. Heritability estimates of psychiatric diagnosis and treatment in 12,884 twin pairs. *Acta Psychiatrica Scandinavica, 83*: 12–15.

Ammaniti, M., van IJzendoorn, M. H., Speranza, A. M., & Tambelli, R. (2000). Internal working models of attachment during late childhood and early adolescence: An exploration of stability and change. *Attachment and Human Development, 2*: 328–346.

Bakermans-Kranenburg, M. J., & van IJzendoorn, M. H. (2009). The first 10,000 Adult Attachment Interviews: Distributions of adult attachment representations in clinical and non-clinical groups. *Attachment and Human Development, 11*: 223–263.

Bateson, G. (1972). *Steps to an Ecology of Mind: A Revolutionary Approach to Man's Understanding of Himself*. New York: Ballantine.

Baumeister, R. F., Campbell, J. D., Krueger, J. I., & Vohs, K. D. (2003). Does high self-esteem cause better performance, interpersonal success, happiness, or healthier lifestyles? *Psychological Science in the Public Interest, 4*: 1–44.

Baumeister, R. F., Dale, K., & Sommer, K. L. (1998). Freudian defense mechanisms and empirical findings in modern social psychology: Reaction formation, projection, displacement, undoing, isolation, sublimation, and denial. *Journal of Personality, 66*: 1081–1124.

Baumeister, R. F., Vohs, K. D., DeWall, C. N., & Zang, L. (2007). How emotion shapes behavior: Feedback, anticipation, and reflection, rather than direct causation. *Personality and Social Psychology Review, 11*: 167–203.

Beck, A. T., Rush, A. J., Shaw, B. F., & Emery, G. (1979). *Cognitive Therapy of Depression*. New York: Guilford Press.

Beckwith, L., Cohen, S. E., & Hamilton, C. E. (1999). Maternal sensitivity during infancy and subsequent life events relate to attachment representation at early adulthood. *Developmental Psychology, 35*: 693–700.

Belsky, J. (1997). Theory testing, effect-size evaluation, and differential susceptibility to rearing influence: The case of mothering and attachment. *Child Development, 68*: 598–600.

Belsky, J., & Fearon, R. M. P. (2008). Precursors to attachment security. In: J. Cassidy & P. R. Shaver (Eds.), *Handbook of Attachment: Theory, Research, and Clinical Applications (second edition)* (pp. 295–316). New York: Guilford.

Belsky, J., Campbell, S. B., Cohn, J. F., & Moore, G. (1996). Instability of infant–parent attachment security. *Developmental Psychology, 32*: 921–924.

Bernet, R. (1996). The unconscious between representation and drive: Freud, Husserl, and Schopenhauer. In: J. J. Drummond & J. G. Hart (Eds.), *The Truthful and the Good: Essays in Honor of Robert Sokolowski* (pp. 81–95). Dordrecht: Kluwer.

REFERENCES   243

Bernet, R. (2003). Unconscious consciousness in Husserl and Freud. In: D. Welton (Ed.), *The New Husserl: A Critical Reader* (pp. 199–219). (Trans. C. Jupp & P. Crowe). Bloomington: Indiana Press.

Blankstein, K. R., Flett, G. L., & Johnston, M. E. (1992). Depression, problem-solving ability, and problem-solving appraisals. *Journal of Clinical Psychology, 48*: 749–759.

Boon, S., Steele, K., & van der Hart, O. (2011). *Coping With Trauma-related Dissociation: Skills Training for Patients and Therapists.* New York: Norton.

Boston Change Process Study Group (2010). *Change in Psychotherapy: A Unifying Paradigm.* New York: Norton.

Bowlby, J. (1944). Forty-four juvenile thieves: Their characters and home life. *International Journal of Psycho-Analysis, 25*: 19–52.

Bowlby, J. (1958). The nature of the child's tie to his mother. *International Journal of Psycho-Analysis, 39*: 350–373.

Bowlby, J. (1969). *Attachment and Loss: Vol. 1, Attachment.* New York: Basic Books.

Bowlby, J. (1973). *Attachment and Loss: Vol. 2, Separation.* New York: Basic Books.

Bowlby, J. (1977). The making and breaking of affectional bonds II. Some principles of psychotherapy. *British Journal of Psychiatry, 130*: 412–431.

Bowlby, J. (1980). *Attachment and Loss: Vol. 3, Loss: Sadness and Depression.* New York: Basic Books.

Bowlby, J. (1988). *A Secure Base: Clinical Applications of Attachment Theory.* Hove: Brunner-Routledge.

Boysen, G. A., & VanBergen, A. (2013). A review of published research on adult dissociative identity disorder. *Journal of Nervous Disease, 201*: 5–11.

Bradford-Brown, B., Mounts, N., Lamborn, S. D., & Steinberg, L. (1993). Parenting practices and peer group affiliation in adolescence. *Child Development, 64*: 467–482.

Brennan, K. A., Clark, C. L., & Shaver, P. R. (1998). Self-report measurement of adult attachment: An integrative overview. In: J. A. Simpson & W. S. Rholes (Eds.), *Attachment Theory and Close Relationships* (pp. 46–76). New York: Guilford.

Breuer, J., & Freud, S. (1895d). *Studies on Hysteria (1893–1895). S. E., 2.* London: Hogarth.

British Psychological Society. (2011). *Good Practice Guidelines on the Use of Psychological Formulation.* Leicester: Division of Clinical Psychology.

Cannon, W. B. (1932). *The Wisdom of the Body.* London: Kegan Paul, Trench, Trubner.

Carlson, E. A. (1998). A prospective longitudinal study of attachment disorganization/disorientation. *Child Development, 69*: 1107–1128.

Cassidy, J. (1994). Emotion regulation: Influences of attachment relationships. *Monographs of the Society for Research in Child Development, 59*: 228–249.

244 REFERENCES

Cassidy, J., & Berlin, L. J. (1994). The insecure/ambivalent pattern of attachment: Theory and research. *Child Development, 65*: 971–981.

Cassidy, J., & Kobak, R. R. (1988). Avoidance and its relationship with others defensive processes. In: J. Belsky & T. Nezworski (Eds.), *Clinical Implications of Attachment* (pp. 300–323). Hillsdale: Erlbaum.

Cassidy, J., & Shaver, P. R. (Eds.) (1999). *Handbook of Attachment: Theory, Research, and Clinical Applications.* New York: Guilford.

Cassidy, J., & Shaver, P. R. (Eds.) (2008). *Handbook of Attachment: Theory, Research, and Clinical Applications (second edition).* New York: Guilford.

Colin, V. L. (1996). *Human Attachment.* New York: McGraw-Hill.

Cortina, M., & Liotti, G. (2007). New approaches to understanding unconscious processes: Implicit and explicit memory systems. *International Forum of Psychoanalysis, 16*: 204–212.

Craik, K. J. W. (1943). *The Nature of Explanation.* Cambridge: Cambridge University Press.

Crawford, M. J., Thana, L., Farquharson, L., Palmer, L., Hancock, E., Bassett, P., Clarke, J., & Parry, G. D. (2016). Patient experience of negative effects of psychological treatment: Results of a national survey. *The British Journal of Psychiatry, 208*: 260–265.

Crittenden, P. M. (1994). Peering into the black box: An exploratory treatise on the development of self in young children. In: D. Cicchetti & S. L. Toth (Eds.), *Rochester Symposium on Developmental Psychopathology: Vol. 5, Disorders and Dysfunctions of the Self* (pp. 79–148). Rochester: University of Rochester Press.

Crowell, J. A., & Owens, G. (1996). Current relationship interview and scoring system. Unpublished manuscript, State University of New York at Stony Brook.

Crowell, J. A., & Treboux, D. (1995). A review of adult attachment measures: Implications for theory and research. *Social Development, 4*: 294–327.

Crowell, J.A. & Waters, E. (1994). Bowlby's theory grown up: The role of attachment in adult love relationships. *Psychological Inquiry, 5*: 31–34.

Crowell, J. A., & Waters, E. (2005). Attachment representations, secure-base behavior, and the evolution of adult relationships: The Stony Brook adult relationships project. In: K. E. Grossmann, K. Grossmann & E. Waters (Eds.), *Attachment from Infancy to Adulthood: The Major Longitudinal Studies* (pp. 223–244). New York: Guilford Press.

Crowell, J. A., Pan, H., Gao, Y., Treboux, D., & Waters, E. (1998). Scales for scoring secure base use and support from couple problem-solving interactions. Unpublished manuscript, State University of New York at Stony Brook.

Crowell, J. A., Treboux, J. A, Gao, Y., Fyffe, C., Pan, H., & Waters, E. (2002). Assessing secure base behavior in adulthood: Development of a measure, links to adult attachment representations, and relations to couples' communication and reports of relationships. *Developmental Psychology, 38:* 679–693.

Crowell, J. A., Treboux, D., & Waters, E. (2002). Stability of attachment representations: The transition to marriage. *Developmental Psychology, 38:* 467–479.

Dalgleish, T., & Watts, F. N. (1990). Biases of attention and meaning in disorders of anxiety and depression. *Clinical Psychology Review, 10:* 589–604.

Davila, J., Burge, D., & Hammen, C. (1997). Why does attachment style change? *Journal of Personality and Social Psychology, 73:* 826–838.

De Haas, M. A., Bakermans-Kranenburg, M. J., & van IJzendoorn, M. H. (1994). The Adult Attachment Interview for attachment style, temperament, and memories of parental behavior. *The Journal of Genetic Psychology, 155:* 471–486.

Degnan, A., Seymour-Hyde, A., Harris, A., & Berry, K. (2014). The role of therapist attachment in alliance and outcome: A systematic literature review. *Clinical Psychology and Psychotherapy.* doi: 10.1002/cpp.1937

Department of Health (2001). *12 Key Points on Consent: The Law in England.* London: Department of Health.

Delius, A., Bovenschen, I. & Spangler, G. (2008). The inner working model as a "theory of attachment": Development during the preschool years. *Attachment and Human Development, 4:* 395–414.

DeWolff, M. & van IJzendoorn, M. (1997). Sensitivity and attachment: A meta-analysis on parental antecedents of infant attachment. *Child Development, 68:* 571–591.

Diamond, D., Blatt, S. J., Stayner, D. A., & Kaslow, N. (1993). Differentiation-relatedness scale of self and object representations. Unpublished research manual. New Haven: Yale University.

Dillon, J., Johnstone, L., & Longden, E. (2012). Trauma, dissociation, attachment and neuroscience: A new paradigm for understanding severe mental distress. *The Journal of Critical Psychology, Counselling and Psychotherapy, 12:* 145–155.

Dilthey, W. (H. P. Rickman, Ed.) (1976). *W. Dilthey: Selected Writings.* Cambridge: Cambridge University Press.

Dixon, W. A., Heppner, P. P., Burnett, J. W., Anderson W. P., & Wood, P. K. (1993). Distinguishing among antecedents, concomitants, and consequences of problem-solving appraisals and depressive symptoms. *Journal of Counseling Psychology, 40:* 357–364.

Ellenberger, H. F. (1970). *The Discovery of the Unconscious: The History and Evolution of Dynamic Psychiatry.* New York: Basic Books.

Fairbairn, W. R. D. (1952). *Psychoanalytic Studies of the Personality.* London: RKP.

246 REFERENCES

Fearon, P., Shmueli-Goetz, Y., Viding, E., Fonagy, P., and Plomin, R. (2014). Genetic and environmental influences on adolescent attachment. *The Journal of Child Psychology and Psychiatry, 55*: 1033–1041.

Fearon, R. M. P., van IJzendoorn, M. H., Fonagy, P., Bakermans-Kranenburg, M. J., Schuengel, C., & Bokhorst, C. L. (2006). In search of shared and nonshared environmental factors in security of attachment: A behaviour-genetic study of the association between sensitivity and attachment security. *Developmental Psychology, 2*: 1026–1040.

Fenichel, O. (1945). *The Psychoanalytic Theory of Neurosis.* New York: Norton.

Festinger, L. (1985). *A Theory of Cognitive Dissonance.* Stanford: Stanford University Press.

Fonagy, P., & Target, M. (1994). Efficacy of psychoanalysis for children with emotional disorders. *Journal of the American Academy of Child and Adolescent Psychiatry, 33*: 361–371.

Fonagy, P., Moran, G., Steele, M., & Higgitt, A. (1991). The capacity for understanding mental states: The reflective self in parent and child and its significance for security of attachment. *Infant Mental Health Journal, 13*: 200–217.

Fox, N. A., Kimmerly, N. L., & Schafer, W. D. (1991). Attachment to mother/attachment to father: A meta-analysis. *Child Development, 62*: 210–225.

Fraley, R. C. & Brumbaugh, C. C. (2007). Adult attachment and preemptive defences: Converging evidence on the role of defensive exclusion at the level of encoding. *Journal of Personality, 75*: 1033–1050.

Fraley, R. C., Waller, N. G., & Brennan, K. A. (2000). An item response theory analysis of self-report measures of adult attachment. *Journal of Personality and Social Psychology, 78*: 350–365.

French, T. M. (1933). Interrelations between psychoanalysis and the experimental work of Pavlov. *American Journal of Psychiatry, 89*: 1165–1203.

Freud, S. (1891b). *On Aphasia: A Critical Study.* (Trans. E. Stengel). London: Imago.

Freud, S. (1894a). The neuro-psychoses of defence. *S. E., 3*: 41–68. London: Hogarth.

Freud, S. (1896b). Further remarks on the neuro-psychoses of defence. *S. E., 3*: 157–186. London: Hogarth.

Freud, S. (1900a). *The Interpretation of Dreams. S. E., 5*: 339–625. London: Hogarth.

Freud, S. (1904a). Freud's psycho-analytic procedure. *S. E., 7*: 247–254. London: Hogarth.

Freud, S. (1905d). *Three Essays on the Theory of Sexuality. S. E., 7*: 123–246. London: Hogarth.

Freud, S. (1905e). Fragment of an analysis of a case of hysteria. *S. E., 7*: 3–122. London: Hogarth.

REFERENCES 247

Freud, S. (1910d). The future prospects of psycho-analytic therapy. *S. E. 11*: 139–152. London: Hogarth.

Freud, S. (1911b). Formulations on the two principles of mental functioning. *S. E., 12*: 215–226. London: Hogarth.

Freud, S. (1911e). The handling of dream-analysis in psycho-analysis *S. E., 12*: 89–96. London: Hogarth.

Freud, S. (1912b). The dynamics of transference. *S. E., 12*: 97–108. London: Hogarth.

Freud, S. (1912e). Recommendations to physicians practising psychoanalysis. *S. E., 12*: 109–120. London: Hogarth.

Freud, S. (1913c). On beginning the treatment (further recommendations on the technique of psycho-analysis). *S. E., 12*: 121–144. London: Hogarth.

Freud, S. (1913i). The disposition to obsessional neurosis. *S. E., 12*: 311–326. London: Hogarth.

Freud, S. (1914g). Remembering, repeating and working-through (further recommendations on the technique of psycho-analysis, II). *S. E., 12*: 147–156. London: Hogarth.

Freud, S. (1915a). Observations on transference-love (further recommendations on the technique of psycho-analysis, III). *S. E., 12*: 157–171. London: Hogarth.

Freud, S. (1915c). Instincts and their vicissitudes. *S. E., 14*: 109–140. London: Hogarth.

Freud, S. (1915d). Repression. *S. E., 14*: 141–158. London: Hogarth.

Freud, S. (1915e). The unconscious. *S. E., 14*: 159–216. London: Hogarth.

Freud, S. (1916). *Introductory Lectures on Psychoanalysis. S. E., 15*: London: Hogarth.

Freud, S. (1919a). Lines of advance in psycho-analytic therapy. *S. E., 17*: 157–168. London: Hogarth.

Freud, S. (1920g). Beyond the pleasure principle. *S. E., 18*: 3–64. London: Hogarth.

Freud, S. (1923b). The ego and the id. *S. E., 19*: 1–66. London: Hogarth.

Freud, S. (1925d). An autobiographical study. *S. E., 20*: 3–74. London: Hogarth.

Freud, S. (1925h). Negation. *S. E., 19*: 235–240. London: Hogarth.

Freud, S. (1926d). Inhibitions, symptoms and anxiety. *S. E., 20*: 87–175. London: Hogarth.

Freud, S. (1933a). *New Introductory Lectures on Psycho-Analysis. S. E., 22*. London: Hogarth.

Freud, S. (1937c). Analysis terminable and interminable. *S. E., 23*: 209–254. London: Hogarth.

Freud, S. (1940a). An outline of psycho-analysis. *S. E., 23*: 139–207. London: Hogarth.

248 REFERENCES

Freud, S. (1940b). Some elementary lessons in psycho-analysis. *S. E., 23*: 279–286. London: Hogarth.

Freud, S. (1940e). Splitting of the ego in the process of defence. *S. E., 23*: 271–278. London: Hogarth.

Freud, S. (1950a). Project for a scientific psychology. *S. E., 1*: 281–293. London: Hogarth.

Garland, A., & Scott, J. (2008). Chronic depression. In: M. A. Whisman (Ed.), *Adapting Cognitive Therapy for Depression: Managing Complexity and Comorbidity* (pp. 88–109). New York: Guilford.

Garland, A., Harrington, J. House, R., & Scott, J. (2000). A pilot study of the relationship between problem-solving skills and outcomes in major depressive disorder. *British Journal of Medical Psychology, 73*: 303–309.

George, C., Kaplan, N., & Main, M. (1996). Adult Attachment Interview Protocol (3rd ed.). Unpublished manuscript, University of California at Berkeley.

Gilbert, P. (2010). *The Compassionate Mind: A New Approach to Life's Challenges*. London: Constable.

Gillath, O., Giesbrecht, B., & Shaver, P. R. (2009). Attachment, attention, and cognitive control: Attachment style and performance on general attention tasks. *Journal of Experimental Social Psychology, 42*: 647–654.

Goldsmith, H. H., & Alansky, J. A. (1987). Maternal and infant temperament predictors of attachment: A meta-analytic review. *Journal of Consulting and Clinical Psychology, 55*: 805–816.

Goleman, D. (1995). *Emotional Intelligence and Working with Emotional Intelligence*. London: Bloomsbury.

Greenberg, M. T., Kusche, C. A., & Speltz, M. (1991). Emotional regulation, self-control and psychopathology: The role of relationships in early childhood. In: D. Cichetti & S. Toth, (Eds.), *Rochester Symposium on Developmental Psychopathology, Vol. 2* (pp. 21–56), New York: Cambridge University Press.

Gregory, R. L. (1998). *Eye and the Brain: The Psychology of Seeing (fifth edition)*. Oxford: Oxford University Press.

Gross, J. J. (1998). Antecedent- and response-focused emotion regulation: Divergent consequences for experience, expression, and physiology. *Journal of Personality and Social Psychology, 74*: 224–237.

Grossmann, K. E., Grossmann, K., & Waters, E. (Eds.) (2005). *Attachment From Infancy to Adulthood: The Major Longitudinal Studies*. New York: Guilford Press.

Gutheil, T. G., & Gabbard, G. O. (1998). Misuses and misunderstandings of boundary theory in clinical and regulatory settings. *The American Journal of Psychiatry, 155*: 409–414.

Hammersley, P., Read, J., Woodall, S., & Dillon, J. (2008). Childhood trauma and psychosis: The genie is out of the bottle. *The Journal of Psychological Trauma, 6*: 7–20.

Harris, J. R. (2007). *No Two Alike: Human Nature and Human Individuality*. New York: Norton.

Harris, J. R. (2009). *The Nurture Assumption: Why Children Turn Out The Way They Do (2nd ed)*. New York: Free Press.

Haydon, K. C., Collins, W. A., Salvatore, J. E., Simpson, J. A., & Roisman, G. I. (2012). Shared and distinctive origins and correlates of adult attachment representations: The developmental organisation of romantic functioning. *Child Development, 83*: 1689–1702.

Haydon, K. C., Roisman, G. I., Owen, M. T., Booth-LaForce, C., & Cox, M. J. (2014). Shared and distinctive antecedents of Adult Attachment Interview state-of-mind and inferred experience dimensions. *Monographs of the Society for Research in Child Development, 79*: 108–125.

Hazan, C., & Shaver, P. R. (1987). Romantic love conceptualized as an attachment process. *Journal of Personality and Social Psychology, 52*: 511–524.

Heard, D. H., & Lake, B. (1986). The attachment dynamic in adult life. *British Journal of Psychiatry, 149*: 430–438.

Heard, D. H., & Lake, B. (1997). *The Challenge of Attachment for Caregiving*. London: Routledge.

Heard, D. H., Lake, B., & McCluskey, U. (2009). *Attachment Therapy with Adolescents and Adults: Theory and Practice Post Bowlby*. London: Karnac.

Hesse, E. (1996). Discourse, memory, and the Adult Attachment Interview: A note with emphasis on the emerging cannot classify category. *Infant Mental Health Journal, 17*: 4–11.

Hesse, E. (2008). The Adult Attachment Interview: protocol, method of analysis, and empirical studies. In: J. Cassidy & P. R. Shaver (Eds.), *Handbook of Attachment: Theory, Research, and Clinical Applications (second edition)* (pp. 552–598). New York: Guilford.

Hesse, E., & Main, M. (2006). Frightened, threatening, and dissociative parental behaviour in low-risk samples: Description, discussion, and interpretations. *Development and Psychopathology, 18*: 309–343.

Heyes, C. M. (2010a). Where do mirror neurons come from? *Neuroscience and Biobehavioural Reviews, 34*: 575–583.

Heyes, C. M. (2010b). Mesmerising mirror neurons. *NeuroImage, 51*: 789–791.

Hilgard, E. R. (1974). Toward a neo-dissociation theory: Multiple cognitive controls in human functioning. *Perspectives in Biology and Medicine, 17*: 301–316.

Hocking, W. E. (1926). *Man and the State*. New Haven: Yale University Press.

Husserl, E. (1977). *Cartesian Meditations: An Introduction to Phenomenology*. (Trans. D. Cairns). The Hague: Martinus Nijhoff.

Husserl, E. (1989). *Ideas Pertaining to a Pure Phenomenology and to a Phenomenological Philosophy: Second Book*. (Trans. R. Rojcewicz & A. Schuwer). Dordrecht: Kluwer Academic.

250 REFERENCES

Insel, I. R., & Young, L. J. (2001). The neurology of attachment. *Nature Reviews Neuroscience, 2*: 129–136.

Janet, P. (1903). *Les Obsessions et la Psychasthénie*. Paris: Alcan.

Johnson, J. G., Cohen, P., Kasen, S., & Brook, J. S. (2006). Dissociative disorders among adults in the community, impaired functioning, and axis I and II comorbidity. *Journal of the Psychiatric Research, 40*: 131–140.

Kabat-Zinn, J. (1994). *Wherever You Go, There You Are: Mindfulness Meditation for Everyday Life*. London: Piatkus.

Kern, I., & Marbach, E. (2001). Understanding the representational mind: A pre-requisite for intersubjectivity proper. *Journal of Consciousness Studies, 8*: 69–82.

Klinnert, M. D., Emde, R. N., Butterfield, P., & Campos, J. J. (1986). Social referencing: The infant's use of emotional signals from a friendly adult with mother present. *Developmental Psychology, 22*: 427–432.

Klohnen, E. C., & Bera, S. (1998). Behavioural and experiential patterns of avoidantly and securely attached women across adulthood: A 31-year longitudinal perspective. *Journal of Personality and Social Psychology, 74*: 211–223.

Kobak, R. R., Cole, H. E., Ferenz-Gillies, R., Fleming, W. S., & Gamble, W. (1993). Attachment and emotion regulation during mother-teen problem solving: A control theory analysis. *Child Development, 64*: 231–245.

Kruger, J., & Dunning, D. (1999). Unskilled and unaware of it: How difficulties in recognizing one's own incompetence lead to inflated self-assessments. *Journal of Personality and Social Psychology, 77*: 1121–1134.

Kuo, J. R., & Linehan, M. M. (2009). Disentangling emotion processes in borderline personality disorder: Physiological and self-reported assessment of biological vulnerability, baseline intensity, and reactivity to emotionally evocative stimuli. *Journal of Abnormal Psychology, 118*: 531–544.

Lane, L. W., Groisman, M., & Ferreira, V. S. (2006). Don't talk about pink elephants!: Speakers' control over leaking private information during language production. *Psychological Science, 17*: 273–277.

Langs, R. (1998). *Ground Rules in Psychotherapy and Counselling*. London: Karnac.

Levenson, R. W., & Ruef, A. M. (1992). Empathy: A physiological substrate. *Journal of Personality and Social Psychology, 63*: 234–246.

Linehan, M. M. (1993). *Cognitive-Behavioral Treatment of Borderline Personality Disorder*. New York: Guilford Press.

Lohser, B., & Newton, P. M. (1996). *Unorthodox Freud: The View from the Couch*. New York: Guilford Press.

Maes, M., Schotte, C., Maes, L., & Cosyns, P. (1990). Clinical subtypes of unipolar depression II: Quantitative and qualitative clinical differences between the vital and nonvital depression groups. *Psychiatry Research, 34*: 43–57.

REFERENCES   251

Magai, C., Hunziker, J., Mesias, W., & Culver, L. C. (2000). Adult attachment styles and emotional biases. *International Journal of Behavioural Development*, 24: 301–309.

Maier, M. A., Bernier, A., Pekrun, R., Zimmermann, P., Strasser, K., & Grossmann, K. E. (2005). Attachment state of mind and perceptual processing of emotional stimuli. *Attachment and Human Development*, 7: 67–81.

Main, M. (1991). Metacognitive knowledge, metacognitive monitoring, and singular (coherent) vs. multiple (incoherent) model of attachment: Findings and directions for future research. In: C. M. Parkes, J. Stevenson-Hinde & P. Marris (Eds), *Attachment Across the Life Cycle* (pp. 127–159). London: Routledge.

Main, M., & Cassidy, J. (1988). Categories of response to reunion with the parent at age six: Predictable from infant attachment classifications and stable over a one-month period. *Developmental Psychology*, 24: 415–426.

Main, M., & Hesse, E. (1990). Parents' unresolved traumatic experiences are related to infant disorganized attachment status: Is frightened and/or frightening parental behaviour the linking mechanism? In: M. T. Greenberg, D. Cicchetti & M. Cummings (Eds.), *Attachment in the Preschool Years: Theory, Research, and Intervention* (pp. 161–182). Chicago: University of Chicago Press.

Main, M., & Solomon, J. (1986). Discovery of an insecure disorganised/disoriented attachment pattern. In: T. B. Brazelton & M. W. Yogman (Eds.), *Affective Development in Infancy* (pp. 52–124). Westport: Ablex.

Main, M., & Solomon, J. (1990). Procedures for identifying infants as disorganized/disorientated during the Ainsworth Strange Situation. In: M. T. Greenberg, D. Cicchetti & M. Cummings (Eds.), *Attachment in the Preschool Years: Theory, Research, and Intervention* (pp. 121–160). Chicago: University of Chicago Press.

Main, M., Goldwyn, R., & Hesse, E. (2003). Adult Attachment Interview scoring and classification system version 7.2. Unpublished manuscript. University of California: Berkeley.

Main, M., Kaplan, N., & Cassidy, J. (1985). Security in infancy, childhood, and adulthood: A move to the level of representation. *Monographs of the Society for Research in Child Development*, 50: 66–104.

Martell, C. R., Addis, M. E., & Jacobson, N. S. (2001). *Depression in Context: Strategies for Guided Action*. New York: W. W. Norton.

Marty, P. (1991). *Mentalisation et Psychosomatique*. Paris: Payot.

Marvin, R., Cooper, G., Hoffman, K., & Powell, B. (2002). The Circle of Security project: Attachment-based intervention with caregiver-pre-school child dyads. *Attachment and Human Development*, 4: 107–124.

Marx, E. M., & Schulze, C. C. (1991). Interpersonal problem-solving in depressed students. *Journal of Clinical Psychology*, 47: 361–367.

McCluskey, U. (2005). *To Be Met as a Person: The Dynamics of Attachment in Professional Encounters*. London: Karnac.

McCrae, R. R., & Costa, P. T. (2003). *Personality in Adulthood: A Five-Factor Theory Perspective*. New York: Guilford.

Mercer, J. (2006). *Understanding Attachment: Parenting, Child Care, and Emotional Development*. Westport: Praeger.

Mercer, J. (2011). Attachment theory and its vicissitudes: Toward an updated theory. *Theory and Psychology, 21*: 25–45.

Meredith, P. J., Strong, J., & Feeney, J. A. (2006). The relationship of adult attachment to emotion, catastrophising, control, threshold and tolerance, in experimentally-induced pain. *Pain, 120*: 44–52.

Moore, R. M., & Garland, A. (2003). *Cognitive Therapy for Chronic and Persistent Depression*. Chichester: Wiley.

Moss, E., Parent, S., Gosselin, C., Rousseau, D., & St-Laurent, D. (1996). Attachment and teacher-reported problems during the preschool and early school-age period. *Development and Psychopathology, 8*: 511–525.

Open Science Collaboration (2015). Estimating the reproducibility of psychological science. *Science, 349*: 6251. doi 10.1126/science.aac4716

Osman, M. (2004). An evaluation of dual-process theories of reasoning. *Psychosomatic Bulletin and Review, 11*: 988–1010.

Owen, I. R. (1998). Reference, temporality and the defences. *Existential Analysis, 9*: 84–97.

Owen, I. R. (2006a). Attachment and intersubjectivity. *Existential Analysis, 17*: 14–38.

Owen, I. R. (2006b). *Psychotherapy and Phenomenology: On Freud, Husserl and Heidegger*. Lincoln: iUniverse.

Owen, I. R. (2007). Understanding the ubiquity of the intentionality of consciousness in commonsense and psychotherapy. *Indo-Pacific Journal of Phenomenology*, 7.1. http://www.ipjp.org/index.php?option=com_jdownloads&view=download&id=107:ianowen7e1&catid=318

Owen, I. R. (2009). *Talk, Action and Belief: How Intentionality Combines Attachment-oriented Psychodynamic Therapy and Cognitive Behavioural Therapy*. Lincoln: iUniverse.

Owen, I. R. (2015). *Phenomenology in Action in Psychotherapy: On Pure Psychology and its Applications in Psychotherapy and Mental Health Care*. Cham: Springer.

Owens, G., Crowell, J. A., Pan, H., Treboux, D., O'Connor, E., & Waters, E. (2008). The prototype hypothesis and the origins of attachment working models: Adult relationships with parents and romantic partners. *Monographs of the Society for Research in Child Development, 60*: 216–233.

Pallini, S., & Barcaccia, B. (2014). A meeting of minds: John Bowlby encounters Jean Piaget. *Review of General Psychology, 18*: 287–292.

REFERENCES   253

PDM Task Force (2006). *Psychodynamic Diagnostic Manual*. Silver Spring: Alliance of Psychoanalytic Organizations.

Pearson, J. L., Cohn, D. A., Cowan, P. A., & Cowan, C. P. (1994). Earned- and continuous-security in adult attachment: Relation to depressive symptomatology and parenting style. *Development and Psychopathology*, 6: 359–373.

Perner, J. (1991). *Understanding the Representational Mind*. Massachusetts: MIT Press.

Perner, J., Ruffman, T., & Leekam, S. R. (1994). Theory of mind is contagious: You catch it from your sibs. *Child Development, 65*: 1228–1238.

Pfohl, B. (1999). Axis I and axis II: Comorbidity or confusion? In: C. R. Cloninger (Ed.), *Personality and Psychopathology* (pp. 83–98). Arlington: American Psychiatric Publishing.

Phelps, J. L., Belsky, J., & Crnic, K. (1998). Earned security, daily stress, and parenting: A comparison of five alternative models. *Development and Psychopathology, 10*: 21–38.

Popper, K. R. (1959). *The Logic of Scientific Discovery (3rd ed.)*. London: Hutchinson.

Prior, V., & Glaser, D. (2006). *Understanding Attachment and Attachment Disorders: Theory, Evidence and Practice*. London: Jessica Kingsley.

Pylyshyn, Z. W. (1978). When is attribution of beliefs justified? *Behavioral and Brain Sciences, 1*: 592–593.

Racker, H. (1958). Counterresistance and its interpretation. *Journal of the American Psychoanalytic Association, 6*: 215–221.

Reich, W. (1950). *Character analysis (3rd ed.)*. (Trans. V. R. Carfagno). London: Vision.

Reik, T. (1952). *Listening with the Third Ear: The Inner Experience of a Psychoanalyst*. New York: Farrar, Straus & Giroux.

Richardson, S. (2008). The hungry self: Working with attachment trauma and dissociation in survivors of childhood abuse. In: S. Benamer & K. White, (Eds.), *Trauma and Attachment: The John Bowlby Memorial Conference Monograph 2006* (pp. 65–72). London: Karnac.

Rogers, C. (1986). Reflection of feelings. *Person-Centred Review, 1*: 375–377.

Rose-Krasnor, L., Rubin, K. H., Booth, C. L., & Coplan, R. (1996). The relation of maternal directiveness and child attachment security to social competence in preschoolers. *International Journal of Behavioral Development, 19*: 309–325.

Rutter, M. (1997). Clinical implications of attachment concepts: Retrospect and prospect. In: L. Atkinson & K. J. Zucker (Eds.), *Attachment and Psychopathology* (pp. 17–46). New York: Guilford.

254 REFERENCES

Rutter, M. (2006). *Attachment from Infancy to Adulthood: The Major Longitudinal Studies*, edited by Klaus E. Grossmann, Karin Grossmann, & Everett Waters. The Guildford Press, London, 2005. *Journal of Child Psychology and Psychiatry*, 47: 974–977.

Rutter, M., Kreppner, J., & Sonuga-Barke, K. (2009). Emmanuel Miller lecture: Attachment insecurity, disinhibited attachment, and attachment disorders: Where do research findings leave the concepts? *The Journal of Child Psychology and Psychiatry*, 50: 529–543.

Schachter, D. L., Dobbins, I. G., & Schnyer, D. M. (2004). Specificity of priming: A cognitive neuroscience perspective. *Nature Reviews Neuroscience*, 5: 853–862.

Shea, M. T., & Yen, S. (2003). Stability as a distinction between axis I and axis II disorders. *Journal of Personality Disorders*, 17: 373–386.

Shevlin, M., Dorahy, M., & Adamson, G. (2007). Trauma and psychosis: An analysis of the National Comorbidity Survey. *American Journal of Psychiatry*, 164: 166–169.

Shoda, Y., Mischel, W., & Peake, P. K. (1990). Predicting adolescent cognitive and self-regulatory competencies from preschool delay of gratification. *Developmental Psychology*, 26: 978–986.

Solnit, A. J. (1982). Developmental perspectives on self and object constancy. *The Psychoanalytic Study of the Child*, 37: 201–218.

Spangler, G., & Zimmermann, P. (2014). Emotional and adrenocortical regulation in early adolescence: Prediction by attachment security and disorganisation in infancy. *International Journal of Behavioral Development*, 38: 1–13.

Spasojevic, J., & Alloy, L. B. (2002). Who becomes a depressive ruminator? Developmental antecedents of ruminative response style. *Journal of Cognitive Psychotherapy*, 16: 405–419.

Sprock, J., Braff, J. L., Saccuzzo, D. P., & Atkinson, J. H. (1983). The relationship of depression and thought disorder in pain patients. *British Journal of Medical Psychology*, 56: 351–360.

Sroufe, L. A. (1985). Attachment classification from the perspective of infant-caregiver relationships and infant temperament. *Child Development*, 56: 1–14.

Sroufe, L. A., & Waters, E. (1977). Attachment as an organizational construct. *Child Development*, 48: 1184–1199.

Steele, H., Steele, M., & Croft, C. (2008). Early attachment predicts emotion recognition at 6 and 11 years old. *Attachment and Human Development*, 10: 379–393.

Stevenson-Hinde, J. (1994). An ethological perspective. *Psychological Inquiry: An International Journal of Peer Commentary and Review*, 5: 62–65.

Thompson, R. A. (2000). The legacy of early attachments. *Child Development*, 71: 145–152.

Thompson, R. A. (2009). Doing what *doesn't* come naturally. *Zero to Three, November*, 33–39.

Treboux, D., Crowell, J. A., & Waters, E. (2004). When "new" meets "old": Configurations of adult attachment representations and their implications for marital functioning. *Developmental Psychology, 40*: 295–314.

Tyson, P. (1996). Object relations, affect management, and psychic structure formation: The concept of object constancy. *Psychoanalytic Study Child, 51*: 172–189.

van IJzendoorn, M. H., & Bakermans-Kranenburg, M. J. (2014). Confined quest for continuity: The categorical versus continuous nature of attachment. *Monographs of the Society for Research in Child Development, 79*: 157–167.

van Putten, A. F. P. (2009). *The Sustainability of Western Society: On the Reliability of Policy and Finances*. Eindhoven: Hollandpromote.

Verhage, M. L., Schuengel, C., Madigan, S., Fearon, R. M. P., Oosterman, M., Cassibba, R., Bakermans-Kranenburg, M. J., & van IJzendoorn, M. H. (2016). Narrowing the transmission gap: A synthesis of three decades of research on intergenerational transmission of attachment. *Psychological Bulletin, 142*: 337–366.

Verschueren, K., Marcoen, A., & Schoefs, V. (1996). The internal working models of the self, attachment, and competence in five-year-olds. *Child Development, 67*: 2493–2511.

Wakefield, J. C. (1990). Why instinctual impulses can't be unconscious: An exploration of Freud's cognitivism. *Psychoanalysis and Contemporary Thought, 13*: 265–288.

Wakefield, J. C. (1992). Freud and the intentionality of affect. *Psychoanalytic Psychology, 9*: 1–23.

Walker, S. F. (1984). *Learning Theory and Behaviour Modification*. London: Methuen.

Waters, E. (1978). The reliability and stability of individual differences in infant–mother attachment. *Child Development, 49*: 483–494.

Waters, E., & Beauchaine, T. P. (2003). Are there really patterns of attachment? Comment on Fraley and Spieker (2003). *Developmental Psychology, 39*: 417–422.

Waters, E., & Cummings, E. M. (2000). A secure base from which to explore close relationships. *Child Development, 71*: 164–172.

Waters, E., Crowell, J., Elliott, M., Corcoran, D., & Treboux, D. (2002). Bowlby's secure base theory and the social/personality psychology of attachment styles: Work(s) in progress, a commentary on Shaver and Mikulincer's *Attachment-related Psychodynamics. Attachment and Human Development, 4*: 230–242.

Waters, E., Hamilton, C. E., & Weinfeld, N. S. (2000). The stability of attachment security from infancy to adolescence and early adulthood: General introduction. *Child Development, 71*: 678–683.

256 REFERENCES

Waters, E., Merrick, S., Treboux, D., Crowell, J., & Albersheim, L. (2000). Attachment security in infancy and early adulthood: A twenty-year longitudinal study. *Child Development*, 71: 684–689.

Waters, H. S., Rodrigues, L. M., & Ridgeway, D. (1998). Cognitive underpinnings of narrative attachment assessment. *Journal of Experimental Child Psychology*, 71: 211–234.

Waters, H. S., & Rodrigues, L. M. (2001). Narrative assessment of adult attachment representations: The scoring of secure base script content. Unpublished manuscript. State University of New York at Stony Brook.

Waters, E., & Valenzuela, M. (1999). Explaining disorganized attachment: Clues from research on mild-to-moderately undernourished children in Chile, In: J. Solomon & C. George (Eds.), *Attachment Disorganization* (pp. 265–287). New York: Guilford Press.

Waters, E., Weinfield, N. S., & Hamilton, C. E. (2000). The stability of attachment security from infancy to adolescence and early adulthood: General Discussion. *Child Development*, 71: 703–706.

Waters, H. S., & Waters, E. (2006). The attachment working models concept: Among other things, we build script-like representations of secure base experiences. *Attachment and Human Development*, 8: 185–197.

Weinfield, N. S., Sroufe, L. A., Egeland, B., & Carlson, E. A. (2008). The nature of individual differences in infant-caregiver attachment: Conceptual and empirical aspects of security. In: J. Cassidy & P. R. Shaver (Eds.), *Handbook of Attachment: Theory, Research, and Clinical Applications, Second Edition* (pp. 78–101). New York: Guilford.

Weiss, E. (1950). *Principles of Psychodynamics*. New York: Grune Stratton.

Weiss, R. S. (1991). The attachment bond in childhood and adulthood. In: C. M. Parkes, J. Stevenson-Hinde & P. Marris (Eds.) *Attachment Across the Life Cycle* (pp. 66–76). London: Routledge.

Wenzlaff, R. M., & Wegner, D. (2000). Thought suppression. *Annual Reviews: Psychology*, 51: 59–91.

Wilson, T. (2002). *Strangers to Ourselves: Discovering the Adaptive Unconscious*. Cambridge: Harvard University Press.

Winnicott, D. W. (1971). *Playing and Reality*. Harmondsworth: Penguin.

Wyss, D. (1966). *Depth Psychology: A Critical History, Development, Problems, Crises*. (Trans. G. Onn). London: Allen & Unwin.

INDEX

Adamson, G., 57
Addis, M. E., 146
Adult Attachment Interview (AAI), xv, 7–8, 35, 46–51, 54–56, 154
Ainsworth, M. D. S., xv, 12–13, 50
Akhtar, S., 45
Alansky, J. A., 6
Albersheim, L., 10
Alexander, F., 4, 241
Alisic, E., 43
Allgulander, C., 63
Alloy, L. B., 146
Ammaniti, M., 9
Anderson, W. P., 146
anxious attachment pattern, 20, 39, 41, 53
anxious attachment process, 53, 61, 188, 218
association, social learning, meaning, 68, 71, 84
attachment, 5–10, 20–24, 39–44, 105

attachment as a biologically inherited drive, 22, 27, 33, 39, 42–43, 84, 88, 111, 118, 137, 173
Atkinson, J. H., 146
avoidant attachment pattern, 20, 41, 43
avoidant attachment process, 54, 61, 192, 220
awareness, 6, 9, 14, 70, 72, 82, 94–95, 112, 116–119, 132, 137, 147, 157, 169–172, 224, 232–236

Bakermans-Kranenburg, M. J., xiv, 7–9, 64
balance as metaphor for coping with distress, 84, 112–115, 131–136
Barcaccia, B., 86
Bassett, P., 231
Bateson, G., 21
Baumeister, R. F., 30, 70, 75

258 INDEX

Beauchaine, T. P., 8
Beck, A. T., 183
Beckwith, L., 30
belief, 7–8, 17, 23, 28
Belsky, J., 25, 30, 38, 121
Bera, S., 17
Berlin, L. J., 40
Bernet, R., 72
Bernier, A., 50
Berry, K., 227
Blankstein, K. R., 146
Blatt, S. J., 50
Blehar, B. C., 13
body, physical body as the biological
        object of the natural
        sciences, (see also living or
        sensuous body), 21–22, 45,
        63–64, 166, 203
Bokhorst, C. L., 64
Boon, S., 216
Booth, C. L., 38
Booth-LaForce, C., 49
Boston Change Process Study Group,
        169
Bovenschen, I., 13
Bowlby, J., 9–11, 18, 154
Boysen, G. A., 57
Bradford-Brown, B., 28
Braff, J. L., 146
Brennan, K. A., 7
Breuer, J., 4
British Psychological Society, 14
Brook, J. S., 56
Brumbaugh, C. C., 75
Burge, D., 154
Burnett, J. W., 146
Butterfield, P., 33

Campbell, J. D., 30
Campbell, S. B., 30
Campos, J. J., 33
Cannon, W. B., 21

Carlson, E. A., 40, 44
Cassibba, R., xiv
Cassidy, J., 6, 16, 37, 40, 42
cathexis, emotional tie or bond, 38
causation, naturalistic cause by
        natural being, physical
        cause, 4, 46, 48, 100–101, 104
Clark, C. L., 7
Clarke, J., 231
Cohen, P., 56
Cohen, S. E., 30
Cohn, D. A., 121
Cohn, J. F., 30
Cole, H. E., 10
Colin, V. L., 15
Collins, W. A., 47
complexity of therapy cases, 209
conceptual intentionality or
        reference, conceptualisation,
        conceptual interpretation,
        speech, discourse, narrative,
        72, 81
consciousness and its unconscious
        primary processes, 8, 19, 72,
        167, 173
control theory, AKA cybernetics,
        systems theory, xiv, 14,
        21–23, 56, 97, 111–112, 131,
        139, 142–143, 131
Cooper, G., 26
coping with distress, 115, 121
Coplan, R., 38
Corcoran, D., 12
Cortina, M., 144
Costa, P. T., 134
Cosyns, P., 146
Cowan, C. P., 121
Cowan, P. A., 121
Cox, M. J., 49
Craik, K. J. W., 103
Crawford, M. J., 231
Crittenden, P. M., 13

INDEX   259

Crnic, K., 121
Croft, C., 38
Crowell, J. A., 9–10, 12, 47–48
Culver, L. C., 49
Cummings, E. M., 12

Dale, K., 70
Dalgleish, T., 146
Davila, J., 154
defence, reducing threat and
        incurring distress, 41, 45, 56,
        67–77, 84–86, 101, 115, 117,
        121–123, 125, 127, 142, 190,
        192, 209
defensive exclusion, 70, 73–75, 78, 82,
        86, 112
    and inter-temporal choice, 79,
        97, 115
Degnan, A., 227
De Haas, M. A., 7
Delius, A., 13
Department of Health, 187
depression, 146–148
development, 26–32
DeWall, C. N., 75
DeWolff, M., 6, 75
Diamond, D., 50
Dillon, J., 56
Dilthey, W., 164
disorganised attachment pattern, 43–45
disorganised attachment process, 56,
        62, 196, 223
dissociation, dissociative disorder
        not otherwise specified
        (DDNOS) and dissociative
        identity disorder (DID), 57,
        74, 107, 223, 228
distress, imbalance, 98
Dixon, W. A., 146
Dobbins, I. G., 160
Dorahy, M., 57
Dunning, D., 85

dynamic, psychodynamic,
        vicissitudes, xiii, 9, 11, 21–22,
        35, 41, 65, 67–83, 139, 141

economic, concerning cathexis and
        emotional investment and
        dis-investment in others, 160
Egeland, B., 40
ego, The I, das Ich, me or self, 96,
        114–115
    splitting of the ego, 74
egoic, I-acts of choice, action,
        deliberation, decision-
        making, 84, 167
Ellenberger, H. F., 68
Elliott, M., 12
Emde, R. N., 33
Emery, G., 183
emotional investment, 17, 38, 43, 59,
        219 see also cathexis
emotions, emotions as products of
        the unconscious, regulation
        and dysregulation, 78,
        119–120, 126, 131–132
empathy, accurate empathy, of the
        sense of another person and
        their perspective on cultural
        objects, inaccurate empathy,
        116, 128, 139
empirical psychology, 45–46
Experiences in Close Relationships
        (ECR), 6–7
    ECR-R, 7

Fairbairn, W. R. D., 86
Farquharson, L., 231
Fearon, R. M. P., xiv, 25, 63–64
feedback, positive/negative, 142–143
Feeney, J. A., 12
Fenichel, O., 76
Ferenz-Gillies, R., 10
Ferreira, V. S., 167

260 INDEX

Festinger, L., 107
Fleming, W. S., 10
Flett, G. L., 146
Fonagy, P., 12, 63–64
formulation of repeating mental
    processes, 20, 126, 179, 184,
    196, 214
Fox, N. A., 49
Fraley, R. C., 7
French, T. M., 4, 241
Freud, S., 4, 74, 70, 72, 79, 81, 103,
    154, 158–160, 164–165, 167,
    173, 181
Fyffe, C., 47

Gabbard, G. O., 231
Gamble, W., 10
Gao, Y., 47
Garland, A., 145
George, C., xv
gestalt, meaning, nonverbal sense, 9,
    12, 19, 21, 36, 38, 51–52, 59,
    63, 65, 71–72, 141–142, 144,
    146, 164–165, 167, 169, 174,
    180, 210, 235
Giesbrecht, B., 172
Gilbert, P., 119
Gillath, O., 172
Glaser, D., 15
Goldsmith, H. H., 6
Goldwyn, R., xv
Goleman, D., 119
Gosselin, C., 42
Greenberg, M. T., 42
Gregory, R. L., 83
Groisman, M., 167
Gross, J. J., 112
Grossmann, K., 48
Grossmann, K. E., 48, 50
Gutheil, T. G., 231

Hamilton, C. E., 10, 30
Hammen, C., 154

Hammersley, P., 56
Hancock, E., 231
Harrington, J., 145
Harris, A., 227
Harris, J. R., 28
Haydon, K. C., 47, 49
Hazan, C., 7
Heard, D. H., 174
Heppner, P. P., 146
Hesse, E., xv, 44
Heyes, C. M., 101
Higgitt, A., 12
Hilgard, E. R., 74
Hocking, W. E., 179
Hoffman, K., 26
House, R., 145
Hunziker, J., 49
Husserl, E., 20, 105

I, Ich, ego, I-acts, egoic, 143
identity of an object or process,
    formulation, 171
individual differences, 36
Insel, I. R., 10
intentionality, modes of awareness
    in the five senses of
    consciousness and its
    subliminal awareness, 160
interpretation of meaning in
    concepts, interpretation of
    nonverbal meaning or sense,
    3–4, 6, 37, 50, 58, 65, 67, 79,
    99, 125, 137, 140, 160,
    162–165, 169, 173, 196,
    199, 216
intersubjectivity, 20, 23, 25, 27, 64,
    101, 116, 158, 173
introjection, introjection of social
    context and relationships,
    mapping of the world in
    memory, emotion and belief,
    85–86, 224
intuition, 80, 168–176, 183, 199, 217

INDEX   261

Jacobson, N. S., 146
Janet, P., 127
Johnson, J. G., 56
Johnston, M. E., 146
Johnstone, L., 56
Jongmans, M. J., 43

Kabat-Zinn, J., 119
Kaplan, N., xv, 37
Kasen, S., 56
Kaslow, N., 50
Kern, I., 96
Kimmerly, N. L., 49
Kleber, R. J., 43
Klinnert, M. D., 33
Klohnen, E. C., 17
Kobak, R. R., 10
Kreppner, J., 47
Krueger, J. I., 30
Kruger, J., 85
Kuo, J. R., 123
Kusche, C. A., 42

Lake, B., 174
Lamborn, S. D., 28
Lane, L. W., 167
Langs, R., 231
Leekam, S. R., 28
Levenson, R. W., 79
Linehan, M. M., 122–123
Liotti, G., 144
living sense of the sensuous body, 197
Lohser, B., 159
Longden, E., 56

Madigan, S., xiv
Maes, L., 146
Maes, M., 146
Magai, C., 49
Maier, M. A., 50
Main, M., xv, 16, 37, 44, 95
Marbach, E., 96

Marcoen, A., 38
Martell, C. R., 146
Marty, P., 76
Marvin, R., 26
Marx, E. M., 146
McCluskey, U., 174–175
McCrae, R. R., 134
measures, 46–47
memory, representations in memory, 72
mentalization, map of world of other persons, 93, 95, 157
Mercer, J., 15
Meredith, P. J., 12
Merrick, S., 10
Mesias, W., 49
meta-representation of intentional forms and relations to manifolds of senses about objects, 93–96
    and relations between map and territory, 94
Mischel, W., 80
Moore, G., 30
Moore, R. M., 145
Moran, G., 12
Moss, E., 42
motive, motivational sequence, script or psychological cause, 61, 84, 101–102, 118, 173
Mounts, N., 28

neurological processes, biochemical substrate, neuroscience, neurology, 82
Newton, P. M., 159
Nowak, J., 63

object of attention or reflection, manifold of senses, understood as repeating shapes, patterns, sequences between meanings, 170

262 INDEX

O'Connor, E., 47
Oosterman, M., xiv
Open Science Collaboration, 45
Osman, M., 144
Owen, I. R., 20, 50, 70, 59, 115, 160
Owen, M. T., 49
Owens, G., 47

Pallini, S., 86
Palmer, L., 231
Pan, H., 47
Parent, S., 42
Parry, G. D., 231
PDM Task Force, 76
Peake, P. K., 80
Pearson, J. L., 121
Pekrun, R., 50
Perner, J., 28, 94
personality style, 134
Pfohl, B., 212
Phelps, J. L., 121
pleasure, 70, 79, 97–99, 135, 148, 201
Plomin, R., 63
Popper, K. R., xii
possibility, 4, 11–12, 26, 69, 129, 135,
        141, 173, 175, 223
post traumatic stress disorder
        (PTSD), 75, 86, 135, 168, 223
Powell, B., 26
pre-reflexive, prior to awareness and
        reflection, 14, 19, 44, 102,
        106, 116, 128, 134, 136–137,
        144, 169, 171
Prior, V., 15
psycho-analysis, 168, 172–173
psychodynamic, motivation, 68–69,
        72
psychosis, hallucination,
        psychoticism, 57, 65, 76, 81–
        82, 86–87, 98, 111, 115, 123,
        125, 134–135, 168, 173, 197,
        199, 209, 213, 216, 225

Pylyshyn, Z. W., 94

Racker, H., 163
Read, J., 56
Reich, W., 164
Reik, T., 228
representation, 8, 17, 19, 67–68, 71–
        72, 76, 88, 93–102, 105–106,
        115–116, 119, 133, 137, 165,
        167–168, 181, 184, 227
repression, 26, 41–43, 54–55, 57, 62,
        70–72, 74–77, 84, 106–107,
        162, 167–169, 193
resistance, xiii, 39–40, 59, 62, 113, 157,
        159–163, 169, 175, 186, 191,
        215, 218, 231
Rice, J. P., 63
Richardson, S., 24
Ridgeway, D., 137
Rodrigues, L. M., 47, 137
Rogers, C., 176
Roisman, G. I., 47, 49
Rose-Krasnor, L., 38
Rousseau, D., 42
Rubin, K. H., 38
Ruef, A. M., 79
Ruffman, T., 28
Rush, A. J., 183
Rutter, M., 16, 25, 47

Saccuzzo, D. P., 146
Salvatore, J. E., 47
Schachter, D. L., 160
Schafer, W. D., 49
Schnyer, D. M., 160
Schoefs, V., 38
Schotte, C., 146
Schuengel, C., xiv, 64
Schulze, C. C., 146
science, 180
Scott, J., 145
script, motional sequence, 14–15

secondary process, egoic deliberation, conceptualisation, 173
secure attachment pattern, 37–39
secure attachment process, 52, 59, 132, 137
and secure frame, 204, 231–239
sensation, carrier of nonverbal sense or meaning, 85, 108
Seymour-Hyde, A., 227
Shaver, P. R., 6–7, 172
Shaw, B. F., 183
Shea, M. T., 212
Shevlin, M., 57
Shmueli-Goetz, Y., 63
Shoda, Y., 80
Simpson, J. A., 47
Solnit, A. J., 45
Solomon, J., 44
Sommer, K. L., 70
Sonuga-Barke, K., 47
Spangler, G., 38
Spasojevic, J., 146
Speltz, M., 42
Speranza, A. M., 9
Sprock, J., 146
Sroufe, L. A., 10, 37, 40
SSP *see* Strange Situation Procedure
Stayner, D. A., 50
Steele, H., 38
Steele, K., 38, 216
Steele, M., 12
Steinberg, L., 28
Stevenson-Hinde, J., 15
St-Laurent, D., 42
Strange Situation Procedure (SSP), xv, 7–8, 12–15, 20, 35, 37, 39–40, 42, 44, 46–48, 50–51, 154
Strasser, K., 50
Strong, J., 12

Tambelli, R., 9
Target, M., 12

Thana, L., 231
therapy practice, 118, 162, 226, 233
Thompson, R. A., 9, 13
transference, mis-empathy, inaccurate empathy, 154, 177, 215
Treboux, D., 9–10, 12, 47–48
Treboux, J. A., 47
Tyson, P., 45

unconscious involuntary, automatic, primary processes, non-egoic processes, 72, 141, 143, 173
unconscious processes, pre-reflexive primary processes, passive consciousness, non-egoic passive synthesis, anonymously functioning consciousness, adaptive unconscious, unconscious processes, 144, 154
unconscious processes, AKA implicit intentionality or mental processes, tacit, unconscious, preconscious or pre-reflexive
unconscious processes interpreted as inner working model of attachment figure (IWM), self-other connection, influence of attachment map in relation to a current attachment figure, xiii, 8, 14, 16–20, 24, 33, 36, 48–49, 67, 69, 83, 86, 94, 102–108, 111, 116, 158, 174–175, 204, 238
unity of consciousness, 84
unmet need, 23, 40–41

Valenzuela, M., 44
van der Hart, O., 216

INDEX

van IJzendoorn, M. H., xiv, 6–9, 64
van Putten, A. F. P., 21
van Wesel, F., 43
VanBergen, A., 57
Verhage, M. L., xiv
Verschueren, K., 38
Viding, E., 63
Vohs, K. D., 30, 75

Wakefield, J. C., 181
Walker, S. F., 70
Wall, S., 13
Waller, N. G., 7
Waters, E., 8–10, 12, 14, 44, 48, 137
Waters, H. S., 14
Watts, F. N., 146
Wegner, D., 26

Weinfield, N. S., 9–10, 40
Weiss, E., 21
Weiss, R. S., 18
Wenzlaff, R. M., 26
Wilson, T., 144
Winnicott, D. W., 231
Wittig, B. A., xv
Wood, P. K., 146
Woodall, S., 56
Wyss, D., 84

Yen, S., 212
Young, L. J., 10

Zang, L., 75
Zimmermann, P., 38, 50